Survival

GLOBAL POLITICS AND STRATEGY

Volume 56 Number 5 | October–November 2014

'ISIS's seizure of Mosul in June and its swift advance across a wide swathe of Iraqi territory was not caused by a century-old legacy of Anglo-French colonialism. It was the direct result of the contemporary flaws within the political system set up after the regime change of 2003.'

Toby Dodge, Can Iraq Be Saved?, p. 16.

'What would a chess player do if an opponent simply stood up and left the table? Would it make sense to continue on with the same amount of effort, concentrating instead on the capabilities of his or her own pieces? This is essentially what the US has done since the collapse of the Soviet Union.'

Christopher J. Fettweis, Threatlessness and US Grand Strategy, pp. 51–2.

'Whether Piketty's rates are appropriate depends on what he is aiming to accomplish. Behind a serious wealth tax should be a coherent vision of a good society accepted by public opinion, fostered by tax policy and protected by constitutional balances.'

David P. Calleo, Wealth and the Good Society, p. 174.

Survival
GLOBAL POLITICS AND STRATEGY
Volume 56 Number 5 | October–November 2014

Contents

Cover: AP Photo/militant website

On the cover
Fighters from the Islamic State of Iraq and al-Sham travel through Anbar Province, Iraq, 7 January 2014.

On the web
Visit http://www.iiss.org/publications/survival for brief notices on new books on the Middle East; Politics and International Relations; South Asia; and War, Conflict and the Military.

Palliser Prize
The deadline for the £2,500 Palliser Essay Prize is 15 October 2014. See http://bit.ly/ZBzIFf for details.

Review Essays

Closing Argument

Survival

GLOBAL POLITICS AND STRATEGY

The International Institute for Strategic Studies
2121 K Street, NW | Suite 801 | Washington DC 20037 | USA
Tel +1 202 659 1490 Fax +1 202 659 1499 E-mail survival@iiss.org Web www.iiss.org

Arundel House | 13–15 Arundel Street | Temple Place | London | WC2R 3DX | UK
Tel +44 (0)20 7379 7676 Fax +44 (0)20 7836 3108 E-mail iiss@iiss.org

14th Floor, GBCorp Tower | Bahrain Financial Harbour | Manama | Kingdom of Bahrain
Tel +973 1718 1155 Fax +973 1710 0155 E-mail iiss-middleeast@iiss.org

9 Raffles Place | #51-01 Republic Plaza | Singapore 048619
Tel +65 6499 0055 Fax +65 6499 0059 E-mail iiss-asia@iiss.org

Survival Online www.tandfonline.com/survival and www.iiss.org/publications/survival

Aims and Scope *Survival* is one of the world's leading forums for analysis and debate of international and strategic affairs. Shaped by its editors to be both timely and forward thinking, the journal encourages writers to challenge conventional wisdom and bring fresh, often controversial, perspectives to bear on the strategic issues of the moment. With a diverse range of authors, *Survival* aims to be scholarly in depth while vivid, well written and policy relevant in approach. Through commentary, analytical articles, case studies, forums, review essays, reviews and letters to the editor, the journal promotes lively, critical debate on issues of international politics and strategy.

Published for the IISS by
Routledge Journals, an imprint of Taylor & Francis, an Informa business.

About the IISS The IISS, a registered charity with offices in Washington, London, Manama and Singapore, is the world's leading authority on political–military conflict. It is the primary independent source of accurate, objective information on international strategic issues. Publications include *The Military Balance*, an annual reference work on each nation's defence capabilities; *Strategic Survey*, an annual review of world affairs; *Survival*, a bi-monthly journal on international affairs; *Strategic Comments*, an online analysis of topical issues in international affairs; and the *Adelphi* series of books on issues of international security.

SUBMISSIONS

To submit an article, authors are advised to follow these guidelines:

- *Survival* articles are around 4,000–10,000 words long including endnotes. A word count should be included with a draft. Length is a consideration in the review process and shorter articles have an advantage.
- All text, including endnotes, should be double-spaced with wide margins.
- Any tables or artwork should be supplied in separate files, ideally not embedded in the document or linked to text around it.
- All *Survival* articles are expected to include endnote references. These should be complete and include first and last names of authors, titles of articles (even from newspapers), place of publication, publisher, exact publication dates, volume and issue number (if from a journal) and page numbers. Web sources should include complete URLs and DOIs if available.
- A summary of up to 150 words should be included with the article. The summary should state the main argument clearly and concisely, not simply say what the article is about.
- A short author's biography of one or two lines should also be included. This information will appear at the foot of the first page of the article.
- *Survival* has a strict policy of listing multiple authors in alphabetical order.

Submissions should be made by email, in Microsoft Word format, to the Assistant Editor, Chris Raggett, survival@iiss.org. Alternatively, hard copies may be sent to *Survival*, IISS–US, 2121 K Street NW, Suite 801, Washington, DC 20037, USA. Please direct any queries to Chris Raggett.

The editorial review process can take up to three months. *Survival*'s acceptance rate for unsolicited manuscripts is less than 20%. *Survival* does not normally provide referees' comments in the event of rejection. Authors are permitted to submit simultaneously elsewhere so long as this is consistent with the policy of the other publication and the Editors of *Survival* are informed of the dual submission.

Readers are encouraged to comment on articles from the previous issue. Letters should be concise, no longer than 750 words and relate directly to the argument or points made in the original article.

ADVERTISING AND PERMISSIONS

For advertising rates and schedules

USA/Canada: The Advertising Manager, Taylor & Francis Inc., 325 Chestnut Street, 8th Floor, Philadelphia, PA 19106, USA Tel +1 (800) 354 1420 Fax +1 (215) 625 2940

UK/Europe/Rest of World: The Advertising Manager, Routledge Journals, Taylor & Francis, 4 Park Square, Milton Park, Abingdon, Oxfordshire OX14 4RN, UK Tel +44 (0) 207 017 6000 Fax +44 (0) 207 017 6336.

SUBSCRIPTIONS

Survival is published bi-monthly in February, April, June, August, October and December by Routledge Journals, an imprint of Taylor & Francis, an Informa Business.

Annual Subscription 2014

Institution	$706	£403	€593
Individual	$194	£115	€157
Online only	$619	£353	€519

Taylor & Francis has a flexible approach to subscriptions, enabling us to match individual libraries' requirements. This journal is available via a traditional institutional subscription (either print with online access, or online only at a discount) or as part of the Strategic, Defence & Security Studies Collection or Conflict, Security & Strategic Studies Library. For more information on our sales packages please visit http://www.tandfonline.com/page/librarians.

All current institutional subscriptions include online access for any number of concurrent users across a local area network to the currently available backfile and articles posted online ahead of publication.

Subscriptions purchased at the personal rate are strictly for personal, non-commercial use only. The reselling of personal subscriptions is prohibited. Personal subscriptions must be purchased with a personal cheque or credit card. Proof of personal status may be requested.

Dollar rates apply to all subscribers outside Europe. Euro rates apply to all subscribers in Europe, except the UK and the Republic of Ireland where the pound sterling rate applies. If you are unsure which rate applies to you please contact Customer Services in the UK. All subscriptions are payable in advance and all rates include postage. Journals are sent by air to the USA, Canada, Mexico, India, Japan and Australasia. Subscriptions are entered on an annual basis, i.e. January to December. Payment may be made by sterling cheque, dollar cheque, euro cheque, international money order, National Giro or credit cards (Amex, Visa and Mastercard).

Survival (USPS 013095) is published bi-monthly (in Feb, Apr, Jun, Aug, Oct and Dec) by Routledge Journals, Taylor & Francis, 4 Park Square, Milton Park, Abingdon, OX14 4RN, United Kingdom.

The US annual subscription price is $676. Airfreight and mailing in the USA by agent named Air Business Ltd, c/o Worldnet Shipping Inc., 156-15, 146th Avenue, 2nd Floor, Jamaica, NY 11434, USA. Periodicals postage paid at Jamaica NY 11431.

US Postmaster: Send address changes to Survival, C/O Air Business Ltd / 156-15 146th Avenue, Jamaica, New York, NY11434.

Subscription records are maintained at Taylor & Francis Group, 4 Park Square, Milton Park, Abingdon, OX14 4RN, United Kingdom.

ORDERING INFORMATION

Please contact your local Customer Service Department to take out a subscription to the Journal: **USA, Canada:** Taylor & Francis, Inc., 325 Chestnut Street, 8th Floor, Philadelphia, PA 19106, USA. Tel: +1 800 354 1420; Fax: +1 215 625 2940. **UK/Europe/Rest of World:** T&F Customer Services, Informa UK Ltd, Sheepen Place, Colchester, Essex, CO3 3LP, United Kingdom. Tel: +44 (0) 20 7017 5544; Fax: +44 (0) 20 7017 5198; Email: subscriptions@tandf.co.uk.

Back issues: Taylor & Francis retains a three-year back issue stock of journals. Older volumes are held by our official stockists: Periodicals Service Company, 11 Main Street, Germantown, NY 12526, USA to whom all orders and enquiries should be addressed. *Tel* +1 518 537 4700 *Fax* +1 518 537 5899 *e-mail* psc@periodicals.com *web* http://www.periodicals.com/tandf.html.

The issue date is August–September 2014.

The print edition of this journal is printed on ANSI conforming acid free paper.

Can Iraq Be Saved?

Toby Dodge

Policymakers, journalists and pundits have struggled to understand the seizure of Mosul by the Islamic State of Iraq and al-Sham (ISIS) on 10 June 2014, the group's drive south towards Baghdad and the collapse of the Iraqi army in the face of its advance. The way in which this fast-moving crisis is perceived will determine the response of leaders in Iraq, the wider Middle East and across the international system. It will not only shape the initial military response to ISIS but, much more importantly, the formulation of longer-term policies that aim to tackle the underlying causes of the group's rise and its seizure of territory in both Iraq and Syria.

A common, if surprising, explanation of ISIS's stunning military success involves reaching back to the Sykes–Picot agreement, a secret bargain negotiated by British diplomat Mark Sykes and his French counterpart François Georges-Picot in May 1916. Across the Arab Middle East, the story of the agreement has become a narrative depicting the perfidious influence of British and French colonial power during and after the First World War. Within the Arab political discourse, 'Sykes–Picot' refers to both the conquest of the Middle East by Britain during the war and the covert attempts to retain control over Arab lands in the aftermath of the conflict through the division of the region into separate states. Soon after seizing Mosul, ISIS posted photographs of its fighters demolishing barriers marking the dividing line between Syria and Iraq. Their declaration that they were 'smashing the

Toby Dodge is Professor of International Relations at the London School of Economics and Political Science, and Consulting Senior Fellow for the Middle East at the IISS.

Survival | vol. 56 no. 5 | October–November 2014 | pp. 7–20 DOI 10.1080/00396338.2014.962795

Sykes–Picot border' was made in an attempt to rally wider Arab support for their movement by claiming that they were overturning a historic injustice.[1]

Given the infamy of the Sykes–Picot agreement, it was no surprise that Lebanese Druze politician Walid Jumblatt declared its demise in June, going so far as to present Hassan Nasrallah, his colleague and the leader of Hizbullah, with a book that explained the genesis of the deal.[2] But it is alarming that both academics and senior statesmen have also used the Sykes–Picot narrative in their accounts of the crisis in Syria and Iraq.[3] The portrayal of the agreement as a catalyst for a century of Middle Eastern history is empirically and analytically unsustainable. It extrapolates from a brief moment in time, employing a snapshot that does not represent the wider socio-political dynamics that unfolded across the region during and after the First World War. This misuse of history may well lead to weak policy prescriptions.

As outlined in the book that Jumblatt gave to Nasrallah, Sykes and Georges-Picot did indeed reach a secret agreement that would allow the French and the British to divide the Middle East into separate areas of influence in the aftermath of the war.[4] This was at the high point of Anglo-French imperial ambition, and of their optimism about how the conflict would end. However, the confidence that underpinned the deal was questioned at the time, with the head of British military intelligence likening its creators to 'hunters who divided up the skin of the bear before they had killed it'.[5]

The suppositions on which the agreement rested quickly came under siege from events both on the ground and within the international system. The British government radically changed its policy towards the Middle East twice, first in 1917 and again in 1918.[6] Faced with the Russian Revolution and America's entry into the war, Sykes himself declared that 'imperialism, annexation, military triumph, prestige, White man's burdens, have been expunged from the popular political vocabulary, consequently Protectorates, spheres of interest or influence, annexations, bases, etc. have to be consigned to the Diplomatic lumber-room.'[7]

The post-war settlements that created the majority of states in the Middle East had little connection with the Sykes–Picot agreement. Instead, they were hammered out at a series of multilateral peace conferences and meetings produced by a region and an international order that had been transformed by the war. This shift resulted from an upsurge in Arab nationalism, the emergence of a coherent Turkish state from the wreckage of the Ottoman Empire, the US entry into the conflict, the Russian Revolution and the subsequent dramatic reduction in French and British state power.

The misleading use of the Sykes–Picot agreement to explain the rise of ISIS highlights the inherent dangers of employing historical analogies in analyses of contemporary events.[8] The use of the Sykes–Picot narrative may lend commentators a veneer of historical learning, but it also encourages them to see the current crisis in a specific and inaccurate way. Such attempts to understand the politics of the modern Middle East naturally lead to a static view of the societies in the region over the last century. Firstly, they condemn the states that came into being after the First World War as false creations, produced by exogenous machinations that were bound to fail. The policy prescriptions that originate from such an approach are clear: these false states have gained no loyalty from their populations and are thus the source of the problem; they should be replaced with smaller, more coherent units that can gain the allegiance of their citizens. Even a cursory examination of a world map should problematise such an argument. Most of the states that form the international system resulted from imperial conquest and a subsequent struggle for self-determination. Against this background, the post-colonial origins of a state do not in any way nullify its ability to function once the metropole has been driven out.

The Sykes–Picot narrative is damaging

The second analytical outcome of the Sykes–Picot narrative is, if anything, even more damaging. In negating the validity, legitimacy and influence of Middle Eastern states, it seeks an alternative organising dynamic or principle, primarily the religious identity of the populations that reside in these states. By identifying faith as the key factor in the Middle East, an unchanging 'essence' that traces back centuries, proponents of the Sykes–Picot narrative are guilty of 'primordialisation'. This analysis refuses to register the almost continual transformation that the region has undergone since 1916, and leads to the claim that sub-state communities there are for the most part geographically homogenous, mutually hostile and trapped in artificial, minority-dominated states. It also promotes the view that the civil wars in Iraq and Syria have been unavoidable tragedies stemming from a regional politics that has always been animated by deeply held communal antipathies.[9] The narrative therefore allows religion rather than the state to become the focus of analysis and hence policy formation. Today's Middle East can then be compared to the '30 years' religious war of 17th-century Europe', and the current crisis explained by 'rivalries among tribes and religious sects'.[10]

A sustained and detailed examination of Middle Eastern states, specifically Iraq and Syria, shows that their evolution has been much more complex than the Sykes–Picot narrative would suggest, and that societal attitudes towards the state have developed through several stages. Political identities in the region have been transformed; religion is certainly a major theme, but it has merged with a vibrant nationalism that is tied to, and delineated by, the geographical boundaries of states.

The Iraqi state after regime change

When the Sykes–Picot narrative is applied to Iraq, it leads to a very rigid analysis of the country's problems and hence to a set of misguided policy prescriptions for their resolution. Instead of blaming the exogenous creation of the state and the dominance of pre-state religious identities, such prescriptions should focus on the ways in which Iraq has been weakened since the regime change of 2003, and on methods for reforming the Iraqi state that could sustain the country in the future.

A comparative study of modern states suggests that their sustainability rests not on their indigenous or exogenous creation, but on their ability to fulfil three functions. The first of these concerns the state's capacity to wield coercion and control the activities of its subjects. Externally, this involves a state's power to defend its own borders, deploying its armed forces to deter other states from encroaching on, or seizing, its territory. In the post-1945 world, in which the United Nations and international law guarantee de jure, if not de facto, recognition of already demarcated borders, it has become more important for a state to use coercion to control its population, and to maintain a monopoly on the collective employment of violence within its own territory.

The second pillar of a state's sustainability is its infrastructural power, which is determined by the delivery of government services and rule-making authority through a set of institutions that radiate out from the capital to the population as a whole.[11] Measuring coercive and institutional capacity is fairly straightforward, as this is reflected in the degree to which the country experiences violence that is not instigated by the state, and the government's ability to provide the population with services such as law enforcement, electricity and running water.

However, it is harder to gauge the final pillar of a state's sustainability: its ideological power, or ability to be perceived as legitimate by the population. To some extent, such legitimacy can also be linked to the capacity to deliver services. As citizens' day-to-day lives become more dependent on state institutions, they come to see its presence within society as necessary. One aspect of this process involves enrolling students in state schools, where they may be subjected to government propaganda. Another is the prevalence of television sets, which can be used as a medium for promoting state legitimacy.[12]

This legitimacy is closely linked to the state's ability to harness, sustain or create a unitary nationalism within its own borders, one that ties the population together and to the ruling elite. In ways that are comparable to the use of schools and television, a state's existence can be naturalised or 'flagged' in the everyday lives of citizens through its institutional presence or references to it in the media.[13] Finally, stressing the ideological power at the centre of both state legitimacy and nationalism focuses attention on the state's role in producing and manipulating 'a set of foundational myths that define and institutionalize a particular nationalist imaginary'.[14]

Baghdad's failure to repel the advance of ISIS is best understood by examining the ways in which the governments that have ruled Iraq since 2003 have systematically undermined each pillar of the state's sustainability.

The crisis of the Iraqi state was obviously caused, in the first instance, by the collapse of the Iraqi military. The Second Division of the Iraqi army was the first to capitulate during the ISIS offensive in Mosul. The First Division had already lost two brigades as it attempted to counter the group's pre-Mosul offensive in Fallujah and Ramadi in December 2013. It subsequently lost two more brigades in June and July. Two of the Third Division's battalions fled the ISIS advance; half of the Fourth Division disappeared, and is believed to have been massacred by the group.[15]

The reasons for the speedy collapse of the Iraqi army go to the heart of the problems faced by the state as a whole. Firstly, the armed forces have been impaired by widespread corruption in Iraq. Junior officers complain that defence officials demand bribes of $3,000 for a place at the Officer Training Academy, and the price of promotion to general is as high as $30,000. Repaying the costs of gaining promotion leads to the existence of 'ghost payrolls' – which supply the names of fictitious soldiers to the Ministry of Defence and have defrauded it of an estimated 25% of its annual wage budget – and the embezzlement of funds earmarked for soldiers' food and fuel.[16] Reports suggest that soldiers in Mosul had to buy their own supplies from local markets and cook the food themselves.[17] This level of corruption would have been obvious to front-line soldiers, undermining their ability to fight effectively while sapping their morale and willingness to defend the state.

The coherence of the Iraqi army was broken

Beyond corruption, the coherence of the Iraqi army was broken by the direct interference of Nuri al-Maliki during his tenure as prime minister. After his appointment in 2006, Maliki worked successfully to coup-proof the military, tying senior commanders and paramilitary units to him personally and thereby subverting the formal chain of command. The new Iraqi military was built with such haste that the institutionalisation of its political oversight has been fragile. With his own political vulnerability in mind, Maliki exploited this and used the Office of the Prime Minister to cement his grip on the army, special forces and the intelligence services.

Maliki secured control of the Iraqi security forces by creating two extra-constitutional organisations. The first, the Office of the Commander in Chief, was originally envisaged by US advisers as a coordinating forum that the prime minister would chair. But Maliki, quickly realising its potential importance, increased its staff, influence and reach. He moved the organisation into the Office of the Prime Minister and appointed a close ally to run it.[18] The Office of the Commander in Chief then began to directly issue orders to battalion leaders, thus circumventing and, in effect, destroying the army's chain of command.[19] The office was also directly involved in the appointment and promotion of senior army staff.[20]

The second extra-constitutional innovation Maliki deployed to control the security forces entailed the proliferation of Provincial Command Centres. After the adoption of the Baghdad Security Plan in February 2007, the Baghdad Operations Command was created to coordinate all Iraqi forces in the city, including both the police and the military.[21] Provincial Command Centres were then set up in unstable areas across south and central Iraq. The facilities brought together the command and control of the police and the army under one general in each province. These generals were chosen and directed from a Baghdad office under Maliki's control. Thus, the Provincial Command Centres bypassed the Ministry of Defence's command and control of the army, and gave Maliki the power to appoint and direct the most important leaders in strategically sensitive areas of the country. Unsurprisingly, the generals appointed to run the centres were politically or personally aligned with the prime minister.

The politicisation of the higher reaches of the armed forces had negative effects that were clearly visible during the collapse of the Second Division in Mosul. On 7 June 2014, Lieutenant-General Ali Ghaidan and Lieutenant-General Abboud Qanbar flew into the city to personally oversee the fight against ISIS.[22] As the commander of Iraqi ground forces and the commander of joint operations respectively, they had benefited from their close relationship with Maliki. However, as ISIS advanced on the main army base in Mosul, Ghaidan and Qanbar quickly left the city, fleeing to Irbil and then flying back to Baghdad. Reports that they had made their escape disguised as civilians began to circulate soon after, further undermining the rank and file's commitment to defending the city.

The seizure of Mosul by ISIS exposed the fact that the Iraqi army had been weakened. Meanwhile, the other two pillars of state sustainability have also been continually undermined over the last six years, if not more. The damage that corruption has inflicted on Iraqi institutions has been partly due to the *muhasasa* system, which has required that the governments of national unity formed in 2005, 2006 and 2010 fulfil sectarian quotas. Cabinet posts, along with the positions of prime minister and president, are allocated in line with a sectarian formula that also takes into account the number of seats that each party wins in elections. The payrolls and budgets of ministries have become the private fiefdoms of the parties to which they are awarded, fostering personal and political corruption, as well as an incoherent approach to governance.

Transparency International's Corruption Perceptions Index 2013, a survey of 177 countries and territories, ranked Iraq in 171st place.[23] The World Bank produced comparable figures for its Worldwide Governance Indicators, allocating Iraq just five points out of a maximum of 100 due to the failings of the country's anti-corruption institutions.[24] Graft of this level directly hinders the state's reconstruction efforts and capacity to deliver services. Judge Rahim al-Ugaili, the most senior government figure responsible for tackling corruption during 2008–11, identified Baghdad's contracting process as 'the father of all corruption issues in Iraq'.[25] Contracts have often been awarded to companies run by, or very close to, senior Iraqi politicians. These firms are typically given large cash payments up front, and complaints about their work are ignored due to the protection they receive from patrons in government.

The result of this corruption is abysmal government services, despite the fact that Iraq is an oil-rich country. In 2011 the UN estimated that only 26% of the population was covered by the public-sewerage network. This left 83% of the country's wastewater untreated. Although two-thirds of Iraqi households rely on the public water supply for their drinking water, surveys conducted in 2012 suggested that as much as 25% of them received only two hours of water per day. Overall, UN figures suggest that 7.6 million people, or around one-quarter of the population, lack access to safe drinking water.[26]

Electricity has become the main touchstone for Iraqis who seek to judge the capacity of their state and its cause. In August 2011, with temperatures reaching 50°C, Minister of Electricity Ra'ad Shalal al-Ani was forced to resign when it emerged that he had signed contracts for developing Iraq's electricity industry worth $1.7 billion with two suspect companies from Canada and Germany.[27] Nationwide surveys carried out by the Iraqi Knowledge Network in the same year found that the average household received just 7.6 hours of electricity from the national grid each day, with 79% of those surveyed rating electricity delivery as 'bad' or 'very bad'.[28]

The weakness of power infrastructure has meant that the state has had a minimal institutional presence within Iraqi society, a situation that is widely blamed on corruption. This has led to deep alienation from the state and the widespread perception that it is being run in accordance with the narrow interests of a kleptocracy.

The final pillar of state sustainability, its ideological power, is also absent in Iraq. Opinion polls taken in the years following the regime change of 2003 showed that the Iraqi population had a strong commitment to a unified state and was bound to it by a vibrant nationalism. Surveys carried out in February and May 2004 revealed support for a strong, centralised state with Baghdad as its capital. The Iraqi Centre for Research and Strategic Studies found that 64.7% of Iraqis favoured 'a politically centralised, unitary state as opposed to a federation', with 67% saying that they wanted both fiscal and administrative centralisation.

The conflict was framed in sectarian terms

Oxford Research International polls carried out in February, March and June of that year had broadly similar results. In response to the question 'which structure should Iraq have in the future?', 79% of respondents chose 'one unified Iraq with a central government in Baghdad'. Although responses differed according to the ethnic and regional backgrounds of those surveyed, only 12% of Kurds and 3.8% of all Iraqis called for the country to be broken up into separate states.[29]

But, after the Governing Council was created in 2003, Iraqi politics was organised around the *muhasasa* system and most parties began to strengthen the support they received by appealing to religious and ethnic identities within their constituencies. As Iraq descended into civil war, the rhetoric used to justify the rise in civilian deaths, population transfers and mass-casualty attacks was infused with sectarian language.[30] By 2006, the conflict was framed in aggressively divisive sectarian terms. This language is still used, to varying degrees, by the majority of Iraq's ruling elite. As a result, the population has been politically mobilised, and Iraqi governments chosen and the civil war understood, using ideologies that deliberately undermine unitary nationalism in favour of sub-state identities. This is not a return to the supposedly dominant religious allegiances that, according to those who favour the Sykes–Picot narrative, have always animated Iraqi politics. Instead, it is the deliberate development or reinvention of sectarian identities by a ruling elite that judges this the best method for rallying an alienated electorate.

Against this background, ISIS's seizure of Mosul in June and its swift advance across a wide swathe of Iraqi territory was not caused by a century-old legacy of Anglo-French colonialism. It was the direct result of the contemporary flaws within the political system set up after the regime change of 2003.

Reforming the Iraqi state

The first step in dealing with ISIS will clearly have to involve its military defeat. Nevertheless, the long-term stabilisation of Iraq will require the resolution of the political problems that created the space in which the group has thrived. Although its forerunner, al-Qaeda in Iraq, was defeated militarily by the application of US-led counter-insurgency tactics from 2007 onwards, the 'surge' did not tackle the underlying political dynamics that caused the Iraqi civil war, allowing ISIS to rebuild, expand its area of operations and go on to become more powerful than its predecessor.

The replacement of Maliki with new prime minister Haider al-Abadi has the potential to spur much-needed reform of the Iraqi state. However, Abadi will be required to do much more than create another government of national unity that includes a greater number of Sunni politicians. He will need to break with the approach to governing Iraq that has prevailed since 2006, if not earlier, and his first task will be to repair the damage that Maliki inflicted on the state during his eight years in office. This will certainly involve removing the 'Maliki politburo', his set of powerful advisers, and the *Malikiyoun*, his followers who have been placed in influential positions throughout Iraqi institutions.[31]

But to blame the rise of ISIS solely on mistakes made during Maliki's tenure would be to severely underestimate the size of the problem that Iraq faces. The corruption eroding the Iraqi state from within is an integral part of a *muhasasa* system that has, in effect, privatised the Iraqi state. The system has allowed the Iraqi political elite to strip state assets for personal gain and to fund the parties they represent. It has also led to a violent and divisive language becoming the main currency of Iraqi politics. The growth of both sectarianism and corruption are the responsibility of this elite, which has maintained its power since 2003. In order to neutralise the threat from ISIS, stabilise Iraq and create a sustainable future for the country, Abadi will not only have to reform the state but persuade the elite to change. This will require them to work towards unifying a society that they played a central role in dividing, and to exchange their corrupt, secretive approach to governance for a style of leadership that is open and accountable. As a central member of that group, Abadi must recognise the difficulty of the task that he has taken on, and the obstacles that stand in his way.

Notes

1 Sammy Ketz, 'Despite Jihadist Drive, Mideast Colonial Borders Seen Intact', Agence France-Presse, 26 June 2014, http://news.yahoo.com/despite-jihadist-drive-mideast-colonial-borders-seen-intact-102035587.html.

2 See 'Jumblatt Presents Nasrallah with Sykes–Picot Book', *Daily Star*, 29 July 2014, http://www.dailystar.com.lb/News/Lebanon-News/2014/Jul-29/265418-jumblatt-presents-nasrallah-with-sykes-picot-book.ashx#axzz3CQXUhjyG; and Robert Fisk, 'The Old Partition of the Middle East is Dead. I Dread to Think What Will Follow', *Independent*, 13 June 2014, http://www.independent.co.uk/news/world/middle-east/robert-fisk-the-old-partition-of-the-middle-east-is-dead-i-dread-to-think-what-will-follow-9536467.html.

3 See, for example, Vali R. Nasr, 'A Crisis a Century in the Making', *New York Times*, 10 August 2014, http://www.nytimes.com/2014/08/11/opinion/a-crisis-a-century-in-the-making.html?smid=tw-share; and Paddy Ashdown, 'Western Intervention Over Isis Won't Prevent the Break-up of Iraq', *Guardian*, 14 August, 2014, http://www.theguardian.com/commentisfree/2014/aug/14/western-intervention-isis-iraq-muslim.

4 James Barr, *A Line in the Sand: Britain, France and the Struggle that Shaped the Middle East* (London: Simon & Schuster, 2012), Kindle edition.

5 *Ibid.*

6 See Toby Dodge, *Inventing Iraq: The Failure of Nation Building and a History Denied* (New York and London: Columbia University Press and C. Hurst & Co., 2003), pp. 5–41.

7 Quoted in Dodge, *Inventing Iraq*, p. 13.

8 See, for example, Yuen Foong Khong, *Analogies at War: Korea, Munich, Dien Bien Phu and the Vietnam Decisions of 1965* (Princeton, NJ: Princeton University Press, 1992).

9 For a short account of this argument, see Leslie H. Gelb, 'The Three-State Solution', *New York Times*, 25 November 2003, http://www.nytimes.com/2003/11/25/opinion/the-three-state-solution.html; and 'Divide Iraq into Three States', *International Herald Tribune*, 26 November 2004. Peter Galbraith develops the argument at greater length in 'How to Get Out of Iraq', *New York Review of Books*, 13 May 2004; and *The End of Iraq: How American Incompetence Created a War Without End*, (New York: Simon & Schuster, 2006). For the policy prescriptions that arise from this approach, see Joseph R. Biden, Jr and Leslie H. Gelb, 'Unity Through Autonomy in Iraq', *New York Times*, 1 May 2006, http://www.nytimes.com/2006/05/01/opinion/01biden.html.

10 Ashdown, 'Western Intervention Over Isis Won't Prevent the Break-up of Iraq'; and Nasr, 'A Crisis a Century in the Making'.

11 Michael Mann, 'The Autonomous Power of the State: Its Origins, Mechanisms and Results', in *States, War and Capitalism: Studies in Political Sociology* (Oxford: Blackwell, 1988).

12 Malik Mufti, *Sovereign Creations: Pan-Arabism and Political Order in Syria and Iraq* (Ithaca, NY: Cornell University Press, 1996), p. 14.

13 Michael Billig, *Banal Nationalism* (Los Angeles, CA: Sage, 1995), pp. 93–127; Christopher Phillips, *Everyday Arab Identity: The Daily Reproduction of the Arab World* (Abingdon: Routledge, 2013), p. 4.

14 Eric Davis, *Memories of State: Politics, History and Collective Identity in Modern Iraq* (Berkeley, CA: University of California Press, 2005), p. 2.

15 See Mitchell Prothero,'Iraqi Army Remains on Defensive as Extent of June Debacle Becomes Clearer', *McClatchy*, 14 July 2014, http://www.mcclatchydc.com/2014/07/14/233295/iraqi-army-remains-on-defensive.html?sp=/99/100/&ihp=1.

16 Alexandra Zavis, 'Iraqi Troops Not Ready to Go It Alone', *Los Angeles Times*, 1 September 2008, http://articles.latimes.com/2008/sep/01/world/fg-army1; Ernesto Londoño, 'Lower Oil Prices Put Iraq's Security Forces in Bind at Crucial Time', *Washington Post*, 20 May 2009, http://www.washingtonpost.com/wp-dyn/content/article/2009/05/19/AR2009051903259.html; Nir Rosen, 'Iraq's Fragile Peace Rests on Its Own Forces', *National*, 9 September 2010, http://thenational.ae/apps/pbcs.dll/article?AID=/20100910/REVIEW/709099998/1008.

17 Yasir Abbas and Dan Trombly, 'Inside the Collapse of the Iraqi Army's 2nd Division', 1 July, 2014, http://warontherocks.com/2014/07/inside-the-collapse-of-the-iraqi-armys-2nd-division/.

18 Barak A. Salmoni, 'Responsible Partnership: The Iraqi National Security Sector after 2011',

Washington Institute for Near East Policy, May 2011, p. 14.

19 Linda Robinson, *Tell Me How This Ends: General David Petraeus and the Search for a Way Out of Iraq* (New York: Public Affairs, 2008), p. 157.

20 Anthony H. Cordesman, Adam Mausner and Lena Derby, *Iraq and the United States: Creating a Strategic Partnership* (Washington DC: Centre for Strategic & International Studies, 2010), p. 268.

21 International Crisis Group, 'Loose Ends: Iraq's Security Forces Between U.S. Drawdown and Withdrawal', p. 7, http://www.crisisgroup.org/~/media/Files/Middle%20East%20North%20Africa/Iraq%20Syria%20Lebanon/Iraq/99%20Loose%20Ends%20-%20Iraqs%20Security%20Forces%20between%20US%20Drawdown%20and%20Withdrawal.pdf.

22 'Ali Ghaidan and Abboud Qanbar Arrive to Nineveh', *Shafaq News*, 7 June 2014, http://english.shafaaq.com/index.php/security/10061-ali-ghaidan-and-abboud-qanbar-arrive-to-nineveh.

23 Transparency International, 'Corruption Perceptions Index 2013', http://cpi.transparency.org/.

24 Special Inspector General for Iraq Reconstruction, 'Quarterly Report and Semiannual Report to the United States Congress', 30 January 2012, p. 9.

25 Special Inspector General for Iraq Reconstruction, 'Quarterly Report and Semiannual Report to the United States Congress', 30 July 2011, p. 8.

26 Special Inspector General for Iraq Reconstruction, 'Quarterly Report and Semiannual Report to the United States Congress', 30 January 2011, p. 98; 30 April 2011, p. 119; and 30 January 2012, p. 76.

27 Ben Lando and staff, 'Power Deals Could Lead to Minister's Ouster', *Iraq Oil Report*, 7 August 2011, http://www.iraqoilreport.com/energy/electricity/power-deals-could-lead-to-ministers-ouster-6047/.

28 Iraq Knowledge Network, 'Essential Services Fact Sheet', December 2011, http://www.jauiraq.org/documents/1583/ServicesFactsheet-English.pdf.

29 See Toby Dodge, *Iraq's Future: The Aftermath of Regime Change*, Adelphi 372 (Abingdon: Routledge for the IISS, 2005), p. 55.

30 Nir Rosen, 'Anatomy of a Civil War: Iraq's Descent into Chaos', *Boston Review*, 8 November 2006, http://bostonreview.net/BR31.6/rosen.php.

31 For an excellent explanation of this, see Joel Rayburn, *Iraq After America: Strongmen, Sectarians, Resistance* (Stanford, CA: Stanford University Press, 2014), pp. 49–58.

The Unintended Consequences of European Sanctions on Russia

Erik Jones and Andrew Whitworth

On 30 July 2014, the European Union published its 'third-stage' sanctions on Russia in response to Russian policy towards Ukraine.[1] These measures, which came into effect the following day, target whole sectors of the economy rather than individuals and companies, as in the previous two stages. Specifically, they take aim at oil exploration, military assistance, sensitive advanced technology and state-owned banks.

The sanctions are all forward-looking rather than reactive. Existing agreements may be honoured, yet future deals will not be made. Moreover, their intended consequences are readily apparent. European policymakers have taken advantage of Russia's economic dependence on the EU to squeeze Russian economic activity and to lower long-term growth prospects. This effect is both direct and indirect. The restrictions on the future sales of military hardware and investment goods will directly affect Russia's military and production capacities; the indirect effects are largely financial.

From 1 August, Europeans are not allowed to facilitate or purchase new equity or bonds with a maturity greater than 90 days issued by financial institutions owned or controlled by Russian public authorities.[2] This prohibition does not completely exclude Russia from European capital markets. Russian banks still have access to syndicated loans and short-term credit facilities. Nevertheless, the sanctions do restrict the supply of foreign-currency-denominated credit to Russia, so should increase upward pres-

Erik Jones is Director of European and Eurasian Studies at the Johns Hopkins School of Advanced International Studies (SAIS) and a Contributing Editor of *Survival*. **Andrew Whitworth** is a PhD student in the European and Eurasian Studies programme at SAIS.

Survival | vol. 56 no. 5 | October–November 2014 | pp. 21–30 DOI 10.1080/00396338.2014.962797

sure on interest rates and downward pressure on the exchange rate. Both factors will raise the cost of capital and lower the amount of borrowing for investment. These effects will increase gradually, so long as Russian banks and firms face the need to refinance existing foreign-currency obligations, yet cannot gain access to alternative markets. The pressure will drop only once the Russian government changes its position on Ukraine and European policymakers reopen the financial taps. That is how the sanctions work as a diplomatic lever.

The unintended consequences are less obvious than the intended ones. European policymakers have accepted that the sanctions will impose costs on Western financial firms that have to forgo the revenues they would otherwise have earned by facilitating Russian access to European capital markets and investing in Russian bank equity or debt obligations. They have also accepted that European banks and non-financial firms that do business with Russia will suffer from the slowdown in Russian economic activity as a kind of knock-on effect. But it is unclear whether European policymakers have recognised the impact that the sanctions will have as a demonstration effect. If economic interdependence with Europe and the United States comes to be seen as a diplomatic vulnerability, governments in Russia and countries that might one day face sanctions have an interest in looking for alternate arrangements that are less easily exploited.

A contest of wills

The argument that EU sanctions against Russia have unintended consequences is neither critical nor surprising. The design of the sanctions reflects political as well as diplomatic requirements. In addition to limiting Russia's ability to destabilise European security, the targeted sectors – meaning trade as well as finance – were selected to spread the cost across EU member states as evenly as possible. This was done to foster a sense of fairness within the EU, but also to make sure that multiple EU countries would have a material interest at stake. Otherwise, divisions between post-communist Europe and Western Europe, and between countries dependent upon Russia for natural gas and those with easier access to other energy resources, would continue to complicate efforts to forge a common policy.

The political complexity and large economic interests at stake explain why European policymakers have been slower to agree on sanctions than Barack Obama's administration in the US and some more hawkish voices in the EU would have liked. That said, the implications of Europe's deliberative process are not wholly negative. By proceeding cautiously and ratcheting up sanctions gradually, European policymakers created opportunities for Russia to de-escalate the situation (which Moscow did not take), while at the same time building consensus within and between member states and European economic sectors. The tragic downing of Malaysia Airlines flight MH17 provided the final catalyst for action, but the build-up was important. Moreover, European consensus has been necessary for the effectiveness of the policy. Despite much rhetoric to the contrary, sanctions are slow-moving economic weapons and their success relies on the ability to maintain support over a long period and at potentially escalating costs.

The EU's gamble is that solidarity among the member states will overpower Russian President Vladimir Putin's desire to intervene in Ukraine.[3] One month into the sanctions, that bet is still hard to call. European economic performance is faltering, and economic conflict with Russia is only adding to the drag. When the sanctions were first announced, Nomura estimated that the impact would shave 0.3 percentage points off European output growth in 2014.[4] After Russia responded by banning imports of European agricultural products and threatening to close its airspace to commercial traffic, the situation only got worse.[5] Of course, the impact on Russia is greater, and the Russian economy was already suffering. Even before the third-stage sanctions were imposed, the IMF cut its forecast for Russian growth in 2014 to 0.2%, down from the 1.3% estimated in April of last year.[6] Nevertheless, Putin's policy towards Ukraine appears popular in Russia, and his public-approval rating shot up to 87%.[7] Even if that number proves ephemeral or inaccurate, it is unlikely that the Putin regime will automatically alter its stance in response to greater domestic opposition.[8] Hence the decisive factor in the contest of wills will be solidarity among EU member states – and, by implication, between Europe and the US.[9]

The initial impact of the sanctions on the EU has been felt more in terms of trade than finance. Countries that export large quantities of goods to Russia, such as Germany and the easternmost EU member states, were among the first to complain.[10] The banks that finance these exports, such as Rabobank in the Netherlands, have also expressed concern.[11] Russia's retaliatory ban on European food exports only made matters worse.[12] Meanwhile, other parts of the financial community have been more sanguine. The European banks that are active across Eastern Europe and Russia – such as Erste Bank, Raiffeisen Bank, UniCredit, SEB, Société Générale, Commerzbank and Deutsche Bank – have downplayed the significance of the sanctions. UniCredit Chief Executive Federico Ghizzoni said the effect on his business would be 'marginal', and Raiffeisen Chief Executive Karl Sevelda estimated that any impact on his organisation would be 'very low'.[13]

These banks have invested heavily in establishing a presence in the region, confirmed their commitment in the succession of Vienna processes during the recent economic and financial crisis, and are unlikely to scare investors now by emphasising the risks of their exposure. They will have to prepare for potential losses nonetheless. Moreover, the pressure on large banking groups exposed to Central and Eastern Europe comes at the same time as the European Central Bank is undertaking its 'comprehensive assessment' of systemically important European banks' balance sheets. In other words, these banks are already deleveraging in order to build up and protect their capital buffers. Hence the sanctions will encourage the banks to redouble their efforts in order to subtract even more liquidity from European markets. In turn, this will further weaken the macroeconomic performance of Central and Eastern European member states.

The different channels of influence on EU economic performance will increase both the depth and the breadth of the impact of sanctions over time. Thus, while some experts expressed concern that financial firms in London would bear the initial brunt of sanctions, the long-term and more significant damage to the European economy will be felt in countries such as Austria, Germany, Hungary, Slovenia, Bulgaria, Romania, Poland and the Baltic states.[14]

Moscow's response

Russia is not a passive actor in this situation.. Its response is two-fold: protective and aggressive. On the protective side, the Central Bank of Russia is attempting to fill the gap left by Western credit institutions by offering to support Russian banks as they lend to the Russian real economy. However, the bank is constrained in this by the fact that its foreign-currency reserves are limited, even if still large, and by its fear of inflation.[15] This fear is exacerbated by the aggressive side of Russia's response: bans on foodstuffs from the EU and other sanctioning nations. This will lead to an increase in the cost of living for Russian citizens, in the short-run at least. Initial reports suggest that this is a price that Russians are willing to pay in support of Putin; the question is whether they will remain so sanguine if Russia is unable to boost domestic production or find alternative suppliers abroad.[16] Again, it is also worth considering how much the Putin regime will respond to any growing discontent.

The problem for the Russian authorities is less a matter of public opinion than the fact that they cannot tackle all challenges at once. The ban on European food exports is one illustration of this; the Central Bank of Russia's decision to raise its policy rates by 50 basis points (or half of 1%) on 25 July is another. In the short term, this policy helps to stave off inflation and shore up the rouble in foreign-exchange markets. In the longer term, however, it adds upward pressure on the cost of capital for Russian banks and firms. In this way, Russian policy inadvertently makes the sanctions more effective.

The only lasting solution for Moscow is to limit Russian vulnerability to European pressure. Autarky is not the answer; more selective engagement with the outside world is more likely. Since Russia's vulnerability stems from economic interdependence, the country's authorities will learn that they need to engage with partners who have less interest in exploiting their economic relationship. In simple terms, this means that they will try to find permanent alternatives to European foodstuffs, and will devote at least as much effort to this goal as the European authorities will to persuading other food exporters not to profit from European exclusion from Russian markets. It also means that Russian banks and firms will look to draw capital from other markets.[17]

A change in Russian trade patterns is possible, but Europe's geographical proximity to Russia gives it a large and permanent advantage. And distance matters: even the countries that suffered most under Soviet rule have been willing to exploit their proximity to Russia for commercial gain. Hence the simple illustration of Russian efforts to limit vulnerability is unlikely to be the most enduring or meaningful.

International economic institutions are another matter. The question is how much European sanctions will encourage Russia (and other governments wary of their vulnerability to Western pressure) to build their own market institutions beyond European influence. Such activities are already well under way, and can be seen both in long-standing projects such as the Chiang Mai Initiative (which does not include Russia) and in more recent proposals such as the New Development Bank (which does). Western leaders have urged that these initiatives complement rather than compete with established organisations such as the IMF and the World Bank. But their arguments ignore the fact that finding an arrangement less subject to American and European manipulation is precisely the point.

Moreover, the trend is to look ever more deeply into market infrastructures. This is an old trend that dates back to US restrictions on dollar clearing for energy exporters. It gained deeper significance when the EU voted in March 2012 to exclude Iran from the SWIFT financial-communication network. SWIFT executives warned at the time that such actions jeopardised the trust required to maintain truly global institutions.[18] SWIFT's continued predominance should not lead to the conclusion that their concern was misplaced. On the contrary, there was much speculation during the early months of the Ukraine crisis that Russia could also be denied access to the SWIFT network.[19] European leaders stepped back from that 'nuclear option', yet it remains a potent threat. Small wonder, therefore, that Russia is now considering building its own alternative.[20]

* * *

European leaders are right to oppose Russia's policy in Ukraine for a large number of reasons that go beyond the scope of this argument. The cost of the

EU sanctions for Europe may nevertheless prove great. By exercising their financial leverage, European leaders have created an incentive for Russia to seek new institutions around which to structure its economic interdependence with other parts of the globe. They have also created similar incentives for other countries that might be subject to such action in the future. The unintended consequence will be to exacerbate the divisions in global financial-market infrastructures, which are responsible not only for balance-of-payments assistance and development aid, but also post-trading activity and communication. This is likely to be more lasting than any deviation in trading relations because financial transactions are more easily affected by operating standards than by geographical distance. The result will be less efficient and less effective global financial markets.

Should the US and Europe succeed in their efforts to change Russian policy in Ukraine, this will be cause for celebration. The challenge would then be to reassure Russia and other countries that their participation in a global economy structured around American- and European-dominated financial institutions did not carry with it an unacceptable, implicit threat.

Acknowledgements

The authors would like to thank Samuel Charap for his comments on an earlier draft of the article.

Notes

1 European Council, 'Council Regulation (EU) No 833/2014 of 31 July 2014 Concerning Restrictive Measures in View of Russia's Actions Destabilising the Situation in Ukraine', 31 July 2014, http://eur-lex.europa.eu/legal-content/EN/TXT/PDF/?uri=CELEX:32014R0833&from=EN.

2 The five institutions targeted in Annex III of the European Council regulation are Sberbank, VTB Bank, Gazprombank, Vnesheconombank and Rosselkhozbank.

3 Rajan Menon, 'A Game of Russian Roulette? The West's Dangerous Sanctions Play against Russia', *National Interest*, 14 August 2014, http://nationalinterest.org/feature/game-russian-roulette-the-wests-dangerous-sanctions-play-11075.

4 Jacques Cailloux et al., 'Euro Area to Feel Impact from Russian Economic Crisis', Nomura, 29 July 2014.

5 Christian Oliver, Iain Mount and Kerin Hope, 'Europe's Peach Growers Feel Pain of Russian Sanctions',

Financial Times, 13 August 2014, http://www.ft.com/cms/s/2/ecbf2fe8-222e-11e4-9d4a-00144feabdc0.html#axzz3BbuZuePy.

6 IMF, 'World Economic Outlook Update', 24 July 2014, http://www.imf.org/external/pubs/ft/weo/2014/update/02/pdf/0714.pdf.

7 'Putin's Approval Rating Soars to 87%, Poll Says', *Moscow Times*, 6 August 2014, http://www.themoscowtimes.com/article/504691.html.

8 Menon, 'A Game of Russian Roulette?'.

9 The point here is not to deny the relevance of diplomacy. Sanctions are an instrument of diplomacy to force reluctant actors to engage in negotiations. That said, Putin is unlikely to come to negotiate in a meaningful way until he can no longer exploit divisions among Europeans and so prevent them from taking decisive action.

10 Jeevan Vasagar, 'Russia Sanctions Take Toll on Germany', *Financial Times*, 25 August 2014, http://www.ft.com/intl/cms/s/0/46cc2e0c-2c6e-11e4-ada0-00144feabdc0.html#axzz3BbuZuePy.

11 Avantika Chilkoti and James Shotter, 'Rabobank and Raiffeisen Warn on Impact of Russian Sanctions', *Financial Times*, 21 August 2014, http://www.ft.com/intl/cms/s/0/6bc09436-2909-11e4-9d5d-00144feabdc0.html#axzz3BOTF9BP8.

12 Alexander Panin, 'Putin's Food Ban Splits EU on Wisdom of Russia Sanctions', *Moscow Times*, 17 August 2014, http://www.themoscowtimes.com/business/article/putin-s-food-ban-splits-eu-on-wisdom-of-russia-sanctions/505218.html.

13 Chad Bray, 'European Banks Expect Only "Limited" Impact from Sanctions on Russia', *New York Times*, 21 August 2014, http://dealbook.nytimes.com/2014/08/21/european-banks-expect-limited-impact-from-sanctions-on-russia/.

14 See Bruno Waterfield, 'City of London to Bear the Brunt of EU Sanctions on Russia', *Telegraph*, 24 July 2014, http://www.telegraph.co.uk/news/worldnews/europe/eu/10987685/City-of-London-to-bear-the-brunt-of-EU-sanctions-on-Russia.html.

15 The Central Bank of Russia had $418 billion in foreign-exchange reserves on 1 July 2014. That is a lot of money. But it is worth remembering that Russia burned through more than $220bn in such reserves trying to stem the decline of the rouble between August 2008 and March 2009. Moreover, the external indebtedness of the Russian private sector has increased in the meantime – from around $500bn in June 2008 to roughly $650bn in June 2014.

16 Courtney Weaver, 'Finding the Right Stomach for Sanctions', *Financial Times*, 26 August 2014, http://www.ft.com/intl/cms/s/2/2bc50e5e-2d0d-11e4-911b-00144feabdc0.html#axzz3BfuFhl5g.

17 Russia's efforts to rely on Chinese capital markets to replace what the country would have raised in Europe have so far proved unsuccessful. See Silvia Merler, 'Fact: Dim Sum Bonds are Not Coming to Rescue Russia's Banks', Bruegel, 28 August 2014, http://www.bruegel.org/nc/blog/detail/article/1421-fact-dim-sum-bonds-are-

not-coming-to-rescue-russias-banks/.

18 Susan V. Scott and Markos Zachariadis, *The Society for Worldwide Interbank Financial Telecommunication (SWIFT): Cooperative Governance for Network Innovation, Standards, and Community (Global Institutions)* (Abingdon: Routledge, 2014), pp. 133–7.

19 Gideon Rachman, 'The Swift Way to Get Putin to Scale Back His Ambitions', *Financial Times*, 12 May 2014, http://www.ft.com/intl/cms/s/0/d6ded902-d9be-11e3-920f-00144feabdc0.html#axzz3BfuFhl5g.

20 'Russia Looks for Alternatives to SWIFT to Curtail Sanctions Risk', *Moscow Times*, 21 August 2014, http://www.themoscowtimes.com/business/article/russia-looks-for-alternatives-to-swift-to-curtail-sanctions-risk/505617.html.

The Survival Strategies of Small Nations

James E. Goodby

Milan Kundera, the Czech writer, once suggested that a key difference between big nations and small nations is that the latter cannot take their own survival for granted. 'The small nation', he wrote,

> is one whose very existence may be put in question at any moment; a small nation can disappear and it knows it. A French, a Russian, and an English man is not used to asking questions about the very survival of his nation. His anthems speak only of grandeur and eternity. The Polish anthem, however, starts with the verse: 'Poland has not yet perished…'.[1]

Similarly, Lee Kuan Yew, the founding father of the very small nation of Singapore, once said:

> To understand Singapore … you've got to start off with an improbable story: It should not exist. What you see today – the superstructure of a modern city … could easily disintegrate.[2]

Not all small nations take quite such an extreme a view of their place in the world, but most of them have had historical experiences that justify

James E. Goodby is currently Annenberg Distinguished Visiting Fellow at Stanford University's Hoover Institution, where he works with former US Secretary of State George Shultz. He is a former career diplomat who has served as the chief US representative in several negotiations on international security, as well as the ambassador to Finland. He is a member of the American Academy of Diplomacy. This essay is based on a lecture that he has delivered to students of foreign relations in Washington DC.

Survival | vol. 56 no. 5 | October–November 2014 | pp. 31–39 DOI 10.1080/00396338.2014.962796

this kind of existential fear. After all, the vulnerabilities of small nations have been demonstrated countless times throughout history. Thucydides famously recorded the fate of the island of Melos in his history of the Peloponnesian War between Athens and Sparta in the fifth century BCE. A passage in this history, usually called the 'Melian Dialogue', describes how the leaders of Athens decided that Melos, which was aligned with Sparta, should be absorbed into their empire. Accordingly, they demanded that Melos capitulate, under threat of all-out war. In response to this coercive diplomacy, the Melians asked if the Athenians would accept a guarantee of a neutral and friendly Melos. The Athenians rejected the offer, citing public opinion: 'our people would regard that as a sign of weakness in us'. Next, the Melians suggested that the weak don't always lose against the strong: 'in war, fortune sometimes makes the odds more level than could be expected from the difference in numbers of the two sides'. This recourse to the possibilities of asymmetric warfare failed to move the Athenians, so the Melians cited extended deterrence: 'as for what we lack in power, we trust that it will be made up for by our alliance with the Spartans, who are bound … to come to our help.' The Athenians dismissed this possibility by arguing that the Spartans would not endanger their own country for Melos: 'if one follows one's self-interest one wants to be safe … The Spartans are not, as a rule, very venturesome.'

A negotiated settlement having failed to materialise, the Melians stubbornly defended themselves against the siege of the Athenians for a long time, but were finally undone through treachery from within. As was usual in those days, all military-aged men were slaughtered, while the women and children were sold into slavery. And so it has been for small nations ever since. As Thucydides wrote, 'the strong do what they have the power to do and the weak accept what they have to accept.'[3]

An attempt to change this story's usual ending was made after the First World War when, under the leadership of Woodrow Wilson, the idea of 'self-determination' led to independence for peoples in Eastern Europe who had been part of the Austro-Hungarian and Ottoman empires. But it was business as usual when, in 1940, Stalin's foreign minister, V.M. Molotov, declared that 'the time of small nations has passed'.[4] The remark was made during a conversation with the foreign minister of Lithuania, not long after the Soviet Union and Germany's Third Reich had carved up the map of Europe between them.

The Finnish model

And yet, despite their obvious disadvantages, numerous small nations have managed to preserve their identities for thousands of years. Those that have done so appear to share certain key characteristics, the first of which is a propensity towards strong self-identification as a distinctive people with a unique language and culture. This identity has often proved more enduring than any given political superstructure under which the people might find themselves. Empires wax and wane; identity as one people persists. 'Wir sind ein Volk,' as the Germans chanted while toppling the Berlin Wall. Moreover, some empires have found that accommodating subject peoples can be easier than trying to liquidate their languages and cultures, something that small countries have been able to take advantage of by accentuating their special characteristics. This was the pattern under the Ottoman Empire. In contrast, the Empire of Japan sought to suppress the use of the Korean language during its 35-year occupation of Korea, with the result that Koreans continue to harbour resentment towards Japan, nearly 70 years after Japanese rule ended.

Another hallmark of resilient small nations is a strong preference for self-rule over rule by 'the other'. Governance by an imperial power might be tolerated for a time where it is an improvement over what went before, but ultimately it is resented, and overthrown. In addition, political leaders in small countries know that drawing on tradition and indigenous culture helps them gain legitimacy in the eyes of their people. Thus, there are powerful incentives for the political classes to preserve the nation's special identity. Finally, those small nations that have been the most successful as neighbours of large and powerful nations have prized education, which enhances self-awareness and encourages self-government.

Finland perfectly illustrates the power of these principles. Although the country is not perceived as particularly nationalistic, national identity is important to the Finns, especially when it is threatened. Culture, including design, music and architecture, is a vital, living part of the Finnish sense of self. The country enjoys ethnic cohesiveness (only recently achieved in historical terms, through an emphasis on the Finnish language and culture), a sense of pride in the Finnish identity, skilled statecraft, economic prowess, and an almost Confucian devotion to education.

During my long association with the Finns (including a term as US ambassador to Finland in 1980–81), I have noticed some features of Finnish culture that I believe derive from the country's status as a small, vulnerable nation on the border of what Finns called their 'big neighbour'. One is a stubborn defence of national positions. Another is a willingness to be accommodating on small things. Put these two admirable traits together and you get what foreign critics have shortsightedly called 'Finlandisation'. The term was meant to imply subservience to the Soviet Union, but the opposite was true. There was a degree of self-censorship in Finland during the Cold War, designed to avoid provoking Moscow. This could be criticised, and many Finns did complain, but at the same time, Finland's private sector was steadily building the infrastructure and practices of a capitalist, free-market economy.

I presented my credentials to the president of Finland in spring 1980, only a few months after the Soviet invasion of Afghanistan. At that time, speculation was rife in Washington that the invasion marked a new chapter in Soviet history: Moscow was expanding its empire beyond the lands that it had occupied at the end of the Second World War. Having gained confidence from its nuclear weapons, the narrative went, Moscow now felt free to use military force to obtain whatever it believed would meet its geopolitical needs. Many expected that Finland, a former part of the Russian Empire, would be next, despite its being at the opposite end of the Asian continent from Afghanistan. Tellingly, this belief was taken seriously only in Washington. In Finland, it was not even discussed. As in other small nations, the Finns were proud of their special qualities as a nation and derived confidence from that. Milan Kundera has written about this phenomenon in small nations generally, at one point quoting Franz Kafka to the effect that this is 'nothing less than a life-or-death decree'.[5] This kind of confidence is often overlooked by big countries, which tend to be self-absorbed in their own way.

How did this Finnish sense of self influence its negotiating behaviour during the Cold War? The long-time Finnish president, Urho Kekkonen, worked hard to gain the trust of his Soviet counterparts. They rewarded him by tacitly supporting his election campaigns. But one of his slogans was 'the closer we are to the East, the closer we can be to the West'. Strict neutrality was his policy. (This was much appreciated in Washington when Helsinki, unlike Stockholm, refrained from criticising the United States during the Vietnam War.) Behind the scenes, I heard from Soviet diplomats that the Finns were adamant in defending their basic interests in their relations with Moscow. 'Mutta', meaning 'but', was the word they heard most often from the Finns, they said. Among other things, in the midst of the Cold War, Finland succeeded in getting a Soviet naval base removed from Finnish territory, a remnant of the country's 'defeat' in the Second World War that still rankled.

Interpreting small-nation behaviour

Can the Finnish experience help us to interpret the behaviour of other small nations? I think so. Take, for example, North Korea. At first glance, it would appear that Finland and Korea, at opposite ends of Eurasia, have almost nothing in common, yet both are small countries on the periphery of larger ones, and both have long nurtured a strong determination to survive. At this, Korea, like Finland, has been very successful, surviving as a nation for thousands of years despite being, as the Koreans themselves put it, 'a shrimp among whales'. In his 2007 book, *Korea at the Crossroads*, author Bae Kichan points out that Korea's geographic location straddling 'the border between continental and maritime powers', particularly China and, later, Japan and the United States, meant the country became 'a field of battle whenever these powers clashed'.[6] Despite this, Korean culture, language and identity have endured, although the Korean peninsula is currently divided between north and south.

The fact that Korea is today divided has implications for both sides of the border, but analysts tend to focus on North Korea, seeking to identify those characteristics that explain its mystifying behaviour. According to US scholar Scott Snyder, for example, some of this behaviour stems from characteristics that North Korea shares with South Korea, particularly its Confucian-based thinking and its experience of the Japanese colonial period. At the same time, he emphasises the importance of several factors that are specific to North Korea, including the country's partisan guerrilla tradition carried over from the Second World War; the imposition of a socialist system following the war; the development of the *Juche* (self-reliance) ideology; and the cult of Kim Il-sung and his descendants.[7] Another observer of Korean affairs, Selig Harrison, has argued that the near total destruction of North Korea following three years of US bombardment during the Korean War helped create the narrative of a North Korea that survived the worst that the United States could throw at it. Harrison suggests that this narrative must have some effect on North Korea's sense of being exceptional.[8]

The kind of mutual incomprehension that often exists between large and small states is probably at its most extreme in the case of North Korea and the United States, where the countries' respective types of what Kundera called 'provincialism' exaggerate the differences that would exist under the best of circumstances.[9] One the one hand, North Korea, a small nation acutely aware that it could disappear overnight, exaggerates its national traits in order to justify its existence, and therefore acts in a highly paranoid, nationalistic way, exhibiting extreme levels of stubbornness and self-reliance. On the other hand, the United States, a big nation, remains principally absorbed in its own affairs, very conscious of its own values and interests but only dimly aware of the internal workings of Korea as a whole, not to mention the special circumstances of North Korea. As a result, misunderstandings are inevitable. Bae Kichan, for example, points out that 'although Korea has maintained an identity independent from that of China for thousands of years and has historical memories of resistance to China, the United States believes that Korea is likely to be absorbed into China's sphere of influence out of inertia and that it needs Japan to offset China's pull'.[10] His own view, as a Korean who has held senior posts with the South Korean government, is that the Korean peninsula, if it could only be reunified, has the makings of a 'larger Switzerland', 'a shining city on a hill'.[11]

Asymmetry in international relations

Former Soviet Foreign Minister Andrei Gromyko was reported to spend part of every week staring at a map of the world.[12] This is not a bad idea. If we look at a map of the contemporary world, we see that small nations are plentiful. With some notable exceptions, like Pakistan, they are doing rather well. They are not vassal states. They have a large amount of freedom of action. So what's going on here? Why aren't there fewer small states?

Any consideration of these questions by Americans – assuming they can throw off the burden of their own 'provincialism' as citizens of a great power and accurately construe the thinking of people in smaller countries – seems to present two further problems. The first is how to deal with asymmetries that weak nations exploit to their advantage. The second concerns the erosion of deterrence or coercion as a tool of US foreign policy. Former US Secretary of State George Shultz sometimes speaks of the 'age of asymmetry' because he sees asymmetric methods being used with increasing frequency to attack Americans and their friends.[13] He's thinking of Hamas and Hizbullah and al-Qaeda, but also of the ability of relatively weak nations such as Iran and North Korea to defy American power with impunity. Meanwhile, deterrence of every kind (not just nuclear) appears to be declining in importance. Simply put, there are fewer cases of threats to US interests that are responsive to threat-based policies, which is what deterrence is.

Emanuel Adler, a scholar at the University of Toronto, has written about the 'lose–lose' situation that confronts would-be deterrers in asymmetric confrontations.[14] The first loss comes when a threatened country rebuffs coercive diplomacy. The second comes when an asymmetric conflict begins. Things don't always unfold this way, of course, but the position of small nations in disputes with large ones seems to have become more favourable than was the case in centuries past. Andrew Mack, an Australian scholar, pointed this out some years ago, and the trend has only strengthened since then.[15]

The conclusion of the Melian Dialogue (the strong decide; the weak accept) is no longer reflective of what is happening in the world. Small countries are often getting their way when faced with a hostile big power. Sometimes, mutual accommodation is the clear answer. Sometimes, the game simply is not worth the candle for a big country ensnared in a war with a small one. Despite the lessons of history, small nations have survived and in many cases prospered, even as big nations have suffered through hard times.

Meanwhile, the advent of globalisation has made fragmentation as strong a feature of the international scene as integration. The rise of independence movements in places like Scotland and Catalonia appears to stem from the belief that national governments cannot manage all of the transnational issues with which they are now confronted, and that salvation lies in closer-to-home solutions. This view may not be right, but it nevertheless appears to be spurring a desire for smaller polities. Molotov, it seems, was wrong: the era of small nations is not over; in fact, it may just be beginning.

Notes

1 Milan Kundera, 'The Tragedy of Central Europe', *New York Review of Books*, vol. 31, no. 7, 26 April 1984, p. 8. This quotation resonated with Max Jakobson, the late Finnish statesman, who referred to it in his own writings. See, for example, *Finland Survived: An Account of the Finnish–Soviet Winter War, 1939–1940* (Helsinki: Otava Publishing, 1984) and *Finland in the New Europe* (Santa Barbara, CA: Praeger, 1998).

2 As quoted in Seth Mydans and Wayne Arnold, 'Modern Singapore's Creator is Alert to Perils', *New York Times*, 2 September 2007, http://www.nytimes.com/2007/09/02/world/asia/02singapore.html?pagewanted=all&_r=0.

3 See Thucydides (Rex Warner, trans.), *The Peloponnesian War*, Book 5, Chapter 7, 'Sixteenth Year of the War. The Melian Debate' (New York: The Penguin Classics, 1954), pp. 358–66.

4 As quoted in Jakobson, *Finland in the New Europe*, p. 4.

5 Milan Kundera, *The Curtain* (New York: Harper Perennial, 2005), pp. 37–45.

6 Bae Kichan, *Korea at the Crossroads* (Seoul: Happy Reading Books, 2007), p. 438.

7 See Scott Snyder, *Negotiating on the Edge: North Korean Negotiating Behavior* (Washington DC: United States Institute of Peace Press, 1999), especially Chapter One, 'The North Korean Context: Factors Shaping North Korean World Views'.

8 Selig S. Harrison, *Korean Endgame* (Princeton, NJ: Princeton University Press, 2002), pp. 8–9.

9 Kundera, *The Curtain*, pp. 37–43. In a more political analysis in his essay 'Czech Destiny' (*Listy*, no. 7–8, 1968, pp. 1,5, translated by Tim West and available at http://www.academia.edu/2503513/Czech_Destiny_Milan_Kundera_), Kundera describes the 'mentality of great powers and the

mentality of small nations'. A great power, he argues, 'tends to see in its grandness a preordained calling to save the world' and is 'politically extroverted … yet culturally highly egocentric'.

10 Bae Kichan, *Korea at the Crossroads*, p. 430.

11 *Ibid.*, pp. 440–3. Bae Kichan's precise words are as follows: 'We must turn Korea into a city shining on the hill'. I use the more familiar American version of the same thought.

12 See Zbigniew Brzezinski, *Game Plan, How to Conduct the U.S.–Soviet Contest* (Boston, MA: The Atlantic Monthly Press, 1986), p. 3: 'several times a week [Gromyko] made it a special point to retire from his busy office to a small and private study where he could meditate in solitude … [and] where a comfortable armchair faced a large wall map of the world. "For an hour or so" Gromyko said, "I do nothing but sit here, looking at that map and reflecting..."'.

13 See, for example, George P. Shultz, *Issues on My Mind: Strategies for the Future* (Stanford, CA: Hoover Institution Press, 2013), pp. 73–6.

14 Emanuel Adler, 'Complex Deterrence in the Asymmetric Warfare Era', in T.V. Paul, Patrick M. Morgan and James J. Wirtz (eds), *Complex Deterrence: Strategy in the Global Age* (Chicago, IL: University of Chicago Press, 2009), pp.85–108.

15 Andrew Mack, 'Why Big Nations Lose Small Wars: The Politics of Asymmetric Conflict', *World Politics*, vol. 27, no. 2, January 1975, pp. 175–200.

Noteworthy

11

Percentage of Ukrainians who had 'unfavourable' opinions of Russia in 2011

60

Percentage in 2014[1]

Interesting times

'We always have a mix of complicated interests. That's not unusual. What's unusual is there's this outbreak of violence and instability everywhere.'

Gary Samore, a former national-security aide in the Obama administration.[2]

Fury and dilemma

'We will drown all of you in blood.'

From a video released by the Islamic State of Iraq and al-Sham in response to US air-strikes against its forces in Iraq.[3]

'I was impressed in my conversation with him about his vision for an inclusive government. But they've got to get this done because the wolf is at the door.'

US President Barack Obama on a conversation with Iraqi Prime Minister Haidar al-Abadi in which he urged Abadi to take action against militant groups in Iraq.[4]

'Syria is prepared to cooperate and coordinate regionally and internationally to fight terrorism.'

Syrian Foreign Minister Walid al-Moallem on 25 August 2014.[5]

'It is inconceivable to me that the United States would coordinate with the Syrian government in any way. How can we see over the mountain of bodies that they have created?'

Steven Simon, senior fellow at the Middle East Institute and a former White House adviser to Obama on the Middle East.[6]

Attitude adjustment

'It's definitely a civilian aircraft.'

From an intercepted conversation purported to have taken place between pro-Russian militants in Ukraine, during which they confirmed that they had mistakenly shot down Malaysia Airlines flight MH17.[7]

'If president Putin does not change his approach on Ukraine, then Europe and the West must fundamentally change our approach to Russia.'

British Prime Minister David Cameron in a Sunday Times *editorial published on 20 July 2014.*[8]

'The events of the last months have pushed us into a real war, albeit an undeclared one. Over the last six months, a new Ukrainian army has been born in heavy and exhausting fighting.'

Ukrainian President Petro Poroshenko speaks at a ceremony on 24 August 2014, the anniversary of Ukraine's independence from the Soviet Union.[9]

Survival | vol. 56 no. 5 | October–November 2014 | pp. 40–42 DOI 10.1080/00396338.2014.962798

Tunnel vision

'We will not finish the operation without neutralising the tunnels, which have the sole purpose of destroying our citizens, killing our children.'

Israeli Prime Minister Benjamin Netanyahu on Operation Protective Edge, *launched against Gaza on 8 July 2014.*[10]

'People can't believe this is happening – that a medical hospital was shelled without the briefest warning. It was already full with patients.'

Fikr Shalltoot, director of programmes at Medical Aid for Palestinians, on an Israeli attack that damaged the al-Asqa Martyrs Hospital in Gaza.[11]

'As I've said many times, Israel has a right to defend itself against rocket and tunnel attacks from Hamas. And as a result of its operations, Israel has already done significant damage to Hamas's terrorist infrastructure in Gaza. I've also said, however, that we have serious concerns about the rising number of Palestinian civilian deaths and the loss of Israeli lives. And that is why it now has to be our focus and the focus of the international community to bring about a cease-fire that ends the fighting and that can stop the deaths of innocent civilians, both in Gaza and in Israel.'

US President Barack Obama, in a press statement delivered at the White House on 21 July 2014.[12]

'Obama, leave us alone. Let us take care of ourselves and [you] take care of Syria.'

Tweet by Israeli Housing Minister Uri Ariel on 28 July 2014.[13]

2,127

Number of Ebola cases in Guinea, Liberia, Nigeria and Sierra Leone as of 13 August 2014

1,145

Number of deaths from Ebola as of 13 August 2014[14]

Legacy of absence

'Both Sierra Leone and Liberia were at war 10 years ago and all the infrastructure was destroyed. It's the worst place on earth to have these epidemics.'

Brice de la Vigne, operations director of Médecins Sans Frontières, on the Ebola outbreak in West Africa.[15]

Ordnungspolitik

'The only problem that some countries have is that they have to stick to the rules.'

German Finance Minister Wolfgang Schäuble responds to criticism of the eurozone's fiscal rules.[16]

'We have to prioritise growth. We shouldn't focus solely on the deficit … You have Nobel economists – Joseph Stiglitz and Paul Krugman – as well as [former German chancellor] Gerhard Schröder, all of them are arguing that it's impossible to reduce the deficit without growth.'

Former French economy minister Arnaud Montebourg criticises EU economic policy, following his sudden departure from government in August.[17]

Sources

1 Pew Research Center, 'Russia's Global Image Negative amid Crisis in Ukraine', Spring 2014, http://www.pewglobal.org/2014/07/09/russias-global-image-negative-amid-crisis-in-ukraine/.

2 David Remnick, 'Aflame', *New Yorker*, 4 August 2014, http://www.newyorker.com/magazine/2014/08/04/aflame-2.

3 Mirren Gidda, 'ISIS to U.S.: "We Will Drown All of You in Blood"', *Time*, 19 August 2014, http://www.worldaffairsjournal.org/content/isis-us-%E2%80%98we-will-drown-all-you-blood%E2%80%99.

4 Barack Obama, 'Statement by the President', Washington DC, 18 August 2014, http://www.whitehouse.gov/the-press-office/2014/08/18/statement-president.

5 Ben Hubbard, 'Syria Declares Its Readiness in Backing Efforts to Fight Jihadists', *New York Times*, 25 August 2014, http://www.nytimes.com/2014/08/26/world/middleeast/syria-declares-its-readiness-in-backing-efforts-to-fight-jihadists.html?ref=world.

6 *Ibid.*

7 Shaun Walker, Harriet Salem and Alec Luhn, 'Missile Destroys Malaysia Airlines Plane over Ukraine, Killing 298 People', *Guardian*, 18 July 2014, http://www.theguardian.com/world/2014/jul/17/malaysia-airlines-plane-missile-attack-ukraine.

8 David Cameron, 'This Is an Outrage Made in Moscow…', *Sunday Times*, 20 July 2014, http://www.thesundaytimes.co.uk/sto/news/world_news/Ukraine/article1436658.ece.

9 Andrew Higgins, 'Ukraine Leader, Set to Meet Putin for Talks, Warns of Long Struggle', *New York Times*, 24 August 2014, http://www.nytimes.com/2014/08/25/world/europe/ukraine-russia.html.

10 'Israel Intensifies Gaza Attacks after Netanyahu Warning', BBC, 29 July 2014, http://www.bbc.co.uk/news/world-middle-east-28539528.

11 Peter Beaumont, Harriet Sherwood and Matthew Weaver, 'Gaza Crisis: Palestinian Death Toll Climbs Past 500 as Hospital is Hit', *Guardian*, 21 July 2014, http://www.theguardian.com/world/2014/jul/21/gaza-crisis-obama-ceasefire-fighting-goes-on.

12 Barack Obama, 'Statement by the President on the Situation in Ukraine and Gaza', Washington DC, 21 July 2014, http://www.whitehouse.gov/the-press-office/2014/07/21/statement-president-situation-ukraine-and-gaza.

13 John Cassidy, 'Israel Goes it Alone', *New Yorker*, 29 July 2014, http://www.newyorker.com/news/john-cassidy/israel-goes-alone-2.

14 World Health Organization, 'Ebola Virus Disease Update – West Africa', 15 August 2014, http://www.who.int/csr/don/2014_08_15_ebola/en/.

15 Lisa O'Carroll, 'World Leaders "Failing to Help" Over Ebola Outbreak in Africa', *Guardian*, 19 August 2014, http://www.theguardian.com/society/2014/aug/19/western-leaders-ebola-outbreak-africa-medecins-sans-frontieres.

16 Claire Jones, Peter Spiegel and Robin Harding, 'Draghi Softens Tone on Austerity', *Financial Times*, 22 August 2014, http://www.ft.com/cms/s/0/d438a334-2a15-11e4-a068-00144feabdc0.html?siteedition=uk#axzz3BavmaQDj.

17 David Jolly, 'Ex-Minister Fires Back After Ouster in France', *New York Times*, 27 August 2014, http://www.nytimes.com/2014/08/28/business/international/ex-minister-fires-back-after-ouster-in-france.html.

Threatlessness and US Grand Strategy

Christopher J. Fettweis

As the Soviet Union was in the process of collapsing, Georgi Arbatov sent a letter to the *New York Times* that contained a warning for the United States. Arbatov, who was one of the Kremlin's leading 'Amerikanists', wrote that the Soviets were unleashing a 'secret weapon', one 'that will work almost regardless of the American response'. It was not the stuff of Cold War nightmares, some sort of last-minute *deus ex machina* from the Academy of Sciences that would rescue the Soviet Union from oblivion. No, in this instance, the weapon was psychological and unequivocal: the Kremlin was about to deprive America of the Enemy.[1]

In the 25 years since Arbatov issued his warning, the effects of the removal of the last great threat to the US have become rather clear. Although some of the specific predictions that he made have not come to pass – NATO avoided disintegration, for instance, and no significant wedges have been driven between the US and its allies – it is true that strategic thinking in the US has suffered without an enemy on which to focus. The West has no great threats to worry about today, and precious few smaller ones either; although those who get their information from the breathless media might not realise it, America is a fundamentally safe country. Pessimists may be able to point to a variety of minor and hypothetical future problems, but none are terribly worrisome, especially when compared to those challenges faced by other countries in earlier, less stable eras.

Christopher J. Fettweis is Associate Professor in the Department of Political Science, Tulane University, and the author of *The Pathologies of Power: Fear, Honor, Glory and Hubris in U.S. Foreign Policy* (Cambridge University Press, 2013).

Survival | vol. 56 no. 5 | October–November 2014 | pp. 43–68 DOI 10.1080/00396338.2014.962793

It is not only the media that have been unable to put the current era into proper perspective, however. The US strategic community has struggled for 25 years even to understand this new period, much less chart a logical course forward. Two decades without danger have had a significant, and mostly deleterious, impact on the American approach to grand strategy.

A good deal has been written on the American tendency to exaggerate threats, both during the Cold War and since it ended.[2] Far less space has been dedicated to analysing the effect that 'threatlessness' has had on the way the US thinks about the world, and about how its leaders and strategists have dealt with the secret weapon unleashed by Arbatov and his colleagues. Among other things, the reduction of danger in the wake of the Soviet collapse has been met with denial in the US, where new dangers, either minor or wholly imagined, have risen to take its place. In addition, strategy has been redefined and force-planning constructs altered to reflect a turn inward, where threats can still be imagined, rather than outward, where they no longer exist. A variety of concepts that were important means to Cold War ends – influence, access and credibility, among others – have been elevated to become ends in themselves. And, finally, in the absence of national-security imperatives, domestic and fiscal factors have come to dominate decision-making.

Overall, although the implosion of the Soviet Union and the general decline in global violence were certainly welcome phenomena, US strategists have not been able to make timely, productive adjustments to their analytical frameworks. As a result, the country has ambled along, rudderless, committing blunders large and small along the way. Until its strategic community comes to recognise the nature of the system in which it operates, such blunders will continue, and true victory in the Cold War will remain elusive, just as Arbatov predicted.

Denial and the rise of new terrors

The US strategic community's initial reaction to the collapse of the Soviet Union, like the first stage of grief, was denial. As if to refute Arbatov, the conventional wisdom became that the US never lost its enemies; more were always right around the corner, just waiting to be discovered. What had been second- and third-order threats – proliferation, terrorism, rogue states, failed states, 'super-empowered individuals', economic crises or merely chaos itself – quickly rose to primary status, as if levels of danger were a mathematical constant.[3] Since those minor threats were more numerous than the singular Soviet Union, the world seemed to have become a more dangerous place. 'Yes, we have slain a large dragon', James Woolsey said during confirmation hearings prior to his appointment as director of Central Intelligence, 'but we live now in a jungle filled with a bewildering variety of poisonous snakes. And in many ways, the dragon was easier to keep track of.'[4] Secretary of State Madeleine Albright lamented that 'we must plot our defense not against a single powerful threat, as during the Cold War, but against a viper's nest of perils.'[5] A very senior military officer preferred this formulation a decade later: during the Cold War, the US was locked in a room with a cobra, but afterward it had to deal with a limitless number of bees.[6] Creators of such metaphors tended to overlook the fact that there had always been smaller threats in the world, only no one paid them much attention in the presence of a greater danger. Terrorism and the other threats of the twenty-first century were not new, but the amount of time US leaders had to devote to worrying about them grew substantially once the Soviets were gone. Background problems were moved to the foreground, elevated to replace what had been a much larger threat emanating from Moscow.[7]

Empirical realities of the post-Cold War system tell a different story. As most scholars of international politics are now, or should be, aware, global conflict levels have dropped precipitously since the collapse of the Soviet empire. Great powers have not fought one another for at least six decades, depending on definitions used, which is the longest such stretch in history. Smaller powers resort to violence much less frequently as well, and levels of internal conflict (civil wars, ethnic conflict, massacres of civilians, coups, and so on) are at historic lows.[8] The various 'new' threats of the current age are neither terribly new nor particularly threatening. Terrorism remains a problem, but it is a relatively minor one. Even the Islamic State of Iraq and al-Sham (ISIS), though a brutal and frightening group, is at the time of writing nothing more than a potential threat to the West. While some of its members apparently hold Western passports, it is important to remember that the predecessor to ISIS, al-Qaeda in Iraq, was never able to carry out attacks outside the Middle East. Indeed, there have been no al-Qaeda attacks anywhere in the Western world since 2005. The several thousand militants of ISIS certainly need to be monitored, but they hardly pose an existential threat to the US or its allies. Proliferation is not gaining momentum; in fact, for most classes of weapons (including nuclear, chemical and biological arms), its pace has slowed significantly since the Cold War.[9] Neither are there more failed states, and the threat posed by them remains minimal.[10] Perhaps most significantly, the conquest of states by their neighbours is all but dead: the number of UN members that have disappeared against their will is precisely zero (South Vietnam held only observer status in 1975). Some have disappeared due to implosion or voluntary division, but none have been absorbed following aggression. Vladimir Putin's conquest of Crimea was a notably rare exception to the otherwise sacrosanct borders of the twenty-first century.[11] The states of the twenty-first century are essentially safe, and the strongest is the safest. Future historians will look back on this era as either a golden age of peace and security, or perhaps the beginning of a sustained period of relative peace.[12]

This diminution in global violence is occasionally acknowledged in the community of strategists, but it is rarely taken seriously. A much more common reaction comes from senior strategist Colin Gray, who dismisses the new trends out of hand. For decades, Gray has argued that nothing of fundamental importance to international politics ever changes, that there is nothing new under the sun, and that history shows how bad times inevitably follow good. As the 1990s came to a close, Gray argued that 'all truly transformational theory about international politics is, and has to be, a snare and a delusion … humankind faces a bloody future, just as it has recorded a bloody past'.[13] 'The cold war is over, but does it really matter?', he wrote in 1993.[14] New wars, big and small, loom on the horizon, even if it may be hard for the average person to see them, or even imagine what they might be.

While grieving people eventually move past denial, many US strategists appear stuck in that initial phase. One of the very few works to address the implications of essential threatlessness (or at least the absence of an enemy) on strategy denies that relative safety tends to accompany the collapse of rivals. In her book, *Power in Uncertain Times*, Emily Goldman argues that 'relative to the Cold War context', the US now confronts 'a *greater number* of threats, *greater diversity* in the types of security actors that can threaten our interests, and a *more interdependent* world in which rapidly emerging technologies quickly diffuse and are exploited by others in unanticipated ways'.[15] A Soviet-free world is not necessarily a more secure world, in other words. Goldman then goes on to identify a series of precedents for the strategic situation in which the US finds itself. Her examples, which include Russia and Britain between the Crimean War and First World War, as well as the US and Britain between the world wars, are not well chosen. The states in her case studies all faced real threats, or at least rival great powers willing to pursue their interests by force. The inclusion of the interwar period is particularly bizarre, since the latter half of that epoch was dominated by an expansionist empire in the Pacific and a rising, revisionist power in Europe. These periods were hardly analogous to the post-Cold War US, which has little to learn from them. While the past may contain some examples of societies that could operate in virtually threat-free environments due to geographic isolation, it is hard to think of a great power in more recent times that had to make strategy without danger. Widespread denial has guaranteed that few have spent much time considering the ways in which greatly reduced levels of threat affect foreign policy or grand strategy.

The vague and the meaningless: complexity, uncertainty and 'unknown unknowns'

The list of tangible threats in the post-Cold War system may seem insufficient to justify consistently high levels of spending. Fortunately for those who fear major cuts to the budget, there is no limit to the dangers posed by intangible, vague, unknowable dangers that fecund Pentagon imaginations can devise. If there is one unifying theme across two decades of US strategic thinking, it is that the post-Cold War era is marked by complexity, uncertainty and 'unknown unknowns'. Such vague concepts can be quite frightening, as long as they are not considered in any real depth.

The threat to defence spending posed by the absence of threats to the country was first addressed by a group of analysts at the RAND Corporation in the early 1990s. James Winnefeld and other 'uncertainty hawks', in the words of Carl Conetta and Charles Knight, pioneered the idea that the new system was not in fact any safer, appearances notwithstanding.[16] 'Out with the old, in with the ?????' and 'Certitude vs. Uncertainty' were among Winnefeld's self-explanatory subheadings.[17] 'Uncertainty is the dominating characteristic of the landscape', wrote Paul Davis, editor of a 1994 RAND volume on defence planning that focused on the dire challenges posed by the collapse of the lone threat to American security.[18] It did not take long for US national-security-strategy documents to pick up the theme. 'The real threat we now face', according to the 1992 'National Military Strategy', 'is the threat of the unknown, the uncertain'.[19] The message has been consistent, in both official and unofficial outlets, for more than two decades. The 2005 'National Defense Strategy' elevated uncertainty (rather than, say, stability) to the position of the 'defining characteristic of today's strategic environment'.[20] In 1997 Secretary of Defense William Cohen said that 'while the prospect of a horrific, global war has receded, new threats and dangers – harder to define and more difficult to track – have gathered on the horizon'.[21] At a press conference five years later, in the days leading up to the war in Iraq, his successor Donald Rumsfeld warned about unknown unknowns, which were the threats that 'we don't know we don't know', which 'tend to be the difficult ones'.[22] Uncertainty hawks are now prevalent in the United Kingdom as well. The 2010 UK national-security-strategy document, titled 'A Strong Britain in an Age of Uncertainty', claims that, 'today, Britain faces a different and more complex range of threats from a myriad of sources', and that 'in an age of uncertainty, we are continually facing new and unforeseen threats to our security'.[23] Such claims are rarely questioned, much less subjected to any kind of scrutiny. That the world of today is more complex, and therefore less predictable and knowable, than that of prior eras has entered into the realm of belief, accepted without the need for further justification.[24]

Analyses downplay the dangers of the past

The claims of uncertainty hawks contain a number of consistent elements. First and foremost, one of the more frightening aspects of unidentifiable threats is that little can be known about their relative levels of intensity.

Unknown unknowns might be rather benign, catastrophically severe or somewhere in between. For many observers of US foreign policy, the possibility that unseen threats are exceptionally dangerous simply cannot be ruled out. 'At present, Americans confront the most confusing and uncertain strategic environment in their history', writes prominent historian and strategist Williamson Murray. 'It may also be the most dangerous to the well-being of their republic.'[25] 'Known knowns' can be measured, understood and combatted; those left to the imagination quickly expand to ominous proportions. 'To make any thing very terrible, obscurity seems in general to be necessary', Edmund Burke noted centuries ago. 'When we know the full extent of any danger, when we can accustom our eyes to it, a great deal of the apprehension vanishes.'[26] The dangers posed by unknown unknowns, perhaps because of their obscurity, tend to appear unlimited and especially terrible.

Secondly, since the present is so uncertain and frightening, these analyses tend to downplay the dangers of the past. Such intangible threats are strategically meaningless unless presented comparatively; presumably, emphasising them is meant to imply that the current era is more complex, uncertain and unknowable than other epochs. The modern-day global security environment presents an 'increasingly complex set of challenges' in comparison to those that have come before, according to the 2012 US 'Defense Strategic Guidance'.[27] Nostalgia for the Cold War – a simple, straightforward, even less dangerous era – is depressingly common in the US strategic community. The US left a 'time of reasonable predictability [for] an era of surprise and uncertainty', claimed the 2006 'Quadrennial Defense Review Report'.[28] Although the assertion that the Cold War was predictable might surprise those who waged it, to the strategists who came afterward the struggle against the Soviets seems to have been relatively uncomplicated, even quaint, nuclear danger notwithstanding.

Uncertainty and complexity have technological roots. The third theme of claims by uncertainty hawks relates to the technological roots of uncertainty and complexity. They argue that the proliferation of science and advanced technology provides the enemies of the future with far greater potential for mayhem. The evolution of technology, therefore, is ominous not only for US national security, but for the peace and stability of the world. The

US National Intelligence Council predicted in 1996 that 'accelerating rates of change will make the future environment more unpredictable and less stable'.[29] Weapons proliferation is the most troubling aspect of this, but the potentially destabilising effects of general scientific advancements should not be underestimated. The 2006 'Quadrennial Defense Review Report' suggested that the US needed to pay attention not only to 'catastrophic' technologies that future enemies might employ but also to those that are merely 'disruptive'.[30] Few topics obsess US planners as much as cyber warfare, with the result that the US Cyber Command was created in 2009.[31] 'The world is applying digital technologies faster than our ability to understand the security implications and mitigate potential risks', warned a report of the US Intelligence Community in 2013. 'Compounding these developments are uncertainty and doubt as we face new and unpredictable cyber threats.'[32] Sociologists have long understood that technological change tends to be accompanied by increases in anxiety and predictions of ill effects to come.[33] Since the speed of that change has never been greater, it should perhaps come as no surprise that the anxiety it has generated is greater as well.[34]

Fourthly, the rise of intangible threats has found a receptive audience in the American strategic community due in large part to its traditional concern, perhaps even obsession, with surprise attack. For decades, a variety of observers have argued that a powerful, unreasonable fear of surprise has been a central part of US strategic culture since at least Pearl Harbor.[35] The attacks of 9/11 seemed to suggest that dangers can arise virtually out of the blue. Arnold Wolfers observed decades ago that the nations that tend to be most sensitive to threats 'have either experienced attacks in the recent past or, having passed through a prolonged period of an exceptionally high degree of security, suddenly find themselves thrust into a situation of danger'.[36] Periods of apparent calm are not comforting to those societies conditioned to believe that surprise attacks can materialise out of nowhere. A seemingly safe world, where the sources of those inevitable surprises remain obscure, can seem more frightening than one with obvious dangers.

Finally, the obsession with the intangible prevents proper consideration of what is probably the most important force-planning question: how much is enough? How many 'super-carriers' are enough to address a complex future, for instance? How many F-22s, cyber warriors or spy satellites does the US need to keep its people safe from unknown unknowns? A security environment characterised primarily by drastic 'unknowables' offers no guidance to those seeking to construct military forces. When danger is limited only by imagination, states will invariably purchase far more than they need, wasting money on weapons systems that will never be used in the hopes of addressing threats that they do not yet perceive.

As long as human rationality remains bounded, incorporating a certain degree of flexibility will remain part of any sagacious strategy. Those making planning decisions, however, must take probabilities into account, while establishing priorities. While anything is possible, if we are to believe the cliché, surely not everything is plausible. Even if there are no limits to the potential dangers that the human mind can manufacture, there will always be very definite boundaries on the specific threats that reality contains. Despite the assertions of uncertainty hawks, the current strategic environment has proven to be not only rather stable and predictable, but benign for the West. No new strategic threats have arisen out of the blue, whether small groups of psychotics – international intelligence services were well aware of al-Qaeda prior to 9/11 – or major peer competitors. Indeed, it is nearly impossible to imagine how the latter could possibly emerge without the US having fairly substantial warning. Serious threats cannot rise in secret.

Goldman wrote that, 'unlike the prior interwar period, the uncertainty engendered by the end of the Cold War shows few signs of abating'.[37] In this, she is essentially correct, even if her analysis is backward. The lack of identifiable, tangible, immediate threats to US security has caused strategists to look towards intangible, unidentifiable, future dangers, and this shows little sign of changing. This age of uncertainty, however, is an age of relative safety. Until the day comes when American strategists are forced to replace vague threats with concrete ones, the basic security of the US is assured.

Beyond denial: the turn inward

What would a chess player do if an opponent simply stood up and left the table? Would it make sense to continue on with the same amount of effort, concentrating instead on the capabilities of his or her own pieces? This is essentially what the US has done since the collapse of the Soviet Union. Rather than change its outlook or level of preparation to match the evolving dangers of the world, Washington merely changed the direction of its strategic gaze, turning its focus inward. The resulting, post-Cold War conception of strategy takes no other side into account (since none exists), which has drastically, and counterproductively, altered the way the US plans and constructs its military.

The most basic effect of this turn inward has been on the way in which strategists regard their central concept. Although there never has been a universally accepted definition, strategy has traditionally incorporated some conflict, or at least its potential, against a foe.[38] The imperative of taking the preferences and actions of the 'other' into account is what separates strategy from mere planning.[39] One does not need a strategy to drive home from work, nor to walk next door to buy a sandwich – unless, of course, one anticipates traffic, or people also trying to buy that sandwich who may interfere with the process. Chess and international security are inherently strategic endeavours because there are other actors simultaneously attempting to accomplish their own, often conflicting goals. Without an enemy, or at least other actors, there is no need for strategy in the traditional sense.

In the late 1980s, US strategists began to redefine the concept, severing the traditional link between strategy and the enemy. One of the first to do so was Arthur Lykke of the US Army War College, who wrote in 1989 that strategy was better thought of as the ways in which states used their power to pursue their objectives.[40] Risk arises when those three components are not properly balanced. The actions of others barely registered in Lykke's conception. To be strategic, one needed only to ask three questions, all of which could be answered by looking inward: what is to be done? How is it to be done? What resources are required to do it?[41]

Lykke's conception of strategy has become ubiquitous in the US strategic community. 'In essence', summarised Mackubin Owens of the US Naval War College in 2007, 'strategy describes the *way* in which the available *means* will be employed to achieve the *ends* of policy'.[42] No longer is interaction with, and the attempt to react to and influence, the other the essence of the concept; no longer does Washington need to ask itself what its enemies and rivals are likely to do in response to its actions. As long as ends are properly identified, and ways and means sagaciously chosen in their pursuit, the mission has been accomplished. 'The challenge for the strategist', write Derek Reveron and James Cook, is not to take the potential actions of others into account, but to 'coordinate the various levers of national power in a coherent or smart way'.[43] To those with a bit of historical perspective, such as eminent strategist Lawrence Freedman, this new but well-established conception 'barely counts as strategy'.[44] At the very least, it is a new way to conceive of the subject, one that has impoverished strategic thinking in a country already too willing to ignore the rest of the world. Strategy that fails to take others into account is not only a contradiction in terms but harmful to those decisions based upon it.

Washington turned its focus inward

The second result of the turn inward has been a fundamental alteration of the Pentagon's approach to force planning. Until two decades ago, the US had followed what was known as a 'threat-based' approach, which focused first and foremost on responding to the capabilities of potential opponents, anticipating their likely actions and devising ways to counteract them. This model was rendered obsolete by the removal of plausible enemies. Since then, the military has followed a 'capabilities-based' approach to force planning, in which the actions of rivals (or even their existence) are essentially irrelevant. Decisions on which capabilities to develop are now determined by perceived weaknesses in US defences that, if they are apparent to us, could be exploited by a future enemy. What such an enemy could do now is not as important as what we can imagine it doing in the future. As Rumsfeld argued, after the collapse of the Soviet Union a new approach was necessary, one that 'focuses less on who might threaten us, or where, and more on how we might be threatened and what is needed to deter and defend against such threats'.[45] In other words, the actual threats posed by the outside world are not as important for the purposes of planning as the vulnerabilities that US strategists can identify (or imagine) in their own armour. Wise planning should proceed as if there were peer competitors continually probing US defences for weakness, even if no such competitor actually exists.

As a result of capabilities-based planning, the United States is now adding a new generation of attack submarines to its fleet, despite the fact that the older generation – which remains the best in the world – was never used in the role for which it was designed. The mere fact that no other navy has even one super-carrier will not stop the US from replacing each of its 11 with all-new models, at a cost of $13 billion each.[46] The US Air Force was determined to add new generations of both air-superiority (F-22) and ground-support (F-35) fighters, no matter what the rest of the world did. Stealth ships, upgraded battle tanks and space weapons may someday be useful, we are told, even if they are not now.

This transformation in approaches to force planning did not occur accidentally, nor without debate. In the early 1990s, Les Aspin, then-chairman of the House Armed Services Committee, championed the continuation of traditional planning models, arguing that by using their logic a great deal of money could be saved in the absence of major threat. Secretary of Defense Dick Cheney opposed him, arguing that focusing on identifiable dangers (or lack thereof) rendered the US vulnerable to those as-yet-unidentified threats that might arise in the future.[47] Cheney maintained that the US ought to create and maintain the best military it could, rather than be limited by challengers of the present, or by the ability to predict the challengers of the future. After all, a high jumper does not stop trying to achieve greater heights just because the competition cannot keep pace.

Capabilities-based planning was another notion championed early on by analysts at RAND. Winnefeld and some of his colleagues led the way in encouraging the Department of Defense to break away from the 'tyranny of scenario plausibility' and turn the focus inward: 'the scenarios that are over the horizon – yet nevertheless make a sudden preemptive strike on today's comfortable assumptions – lie in the category of unanticipated surprises'.[48] The Pentagon seized upon capabilities-based planning with enthusiasm, in part because it helped justify the continuation of enormous defence budgets, but also because it fit nicely with a defence posture focused on uncertainty. Davis emphasised that 'the notion of planning under uncertainty appears in the very first clause' of his definition of capabilities-based planning because it fit nicely with a defence posture focused on uncertainty. The approach 'has the virtue of encouraging prudent worrying about potential needs that go well beyond currently obvious threats'.[49] Worrying about needs that go beyond threats is only prudent to those following the inward-looking, capabilities-based model that has come to dominate Pentagon planning since the end of the Cold War.

The *Millennium Challenge* exercise from the summer of 2002 is a clear example of capabilities-based planning in action. That war game, which was one of the biggest in the history of the US military, gave all the services a chance to test new technologies that had rolled off the high-tech assembly line in preceding years. Given the date, one might assume that the fictional enemy would have been Iraq, one of the other members of the 'Axis of Evil', or perhaps even China or Russia. None of those states had the potential to give US capabilities the correct kind of test, however, so the game's enemy was the country with the second-most advanced military: Israel.[50] The US spent $250 million simulating a war against the Israelis, an event that most would probably consider unlikely.

Capabilities-based planning led directly to one of the most notorious force-planning failures in American history. The US went into Iraq with the army it had, to paraphrase Rumsfeld, not the army it needed. Had force planners concentrated their energies on external threats rather than internal capabilities, they may well have considered the possibility that irregular enemies would not use advanced technology to challenge US power in the wars to come. Unfortunately, the long list of weapons that were in the US arsenal did not include much that would help against improvised explosive devices, such as armed personnel carriers with heavily armoured undersides. The army would have to wait until years of combat had passed, and thousands of lives were lost, before the Pentagon planned in response to real, pressing threats.

No rational planner would suggest that the US military should cease striving to remain the best that it possibly can be, no matter what other states are doing. The task of the strategist, however, is to assess realistic risks and allocate scarce resources according to the most likely threats of the future. Capabilities-based planning makes insufficient effort to assess probabilities, and as a result entails enormous costs, in both resources and opportunity, for the US.

Conflating means with ends

Since the new conception of strategy now common in US defence circles emphasises matching ends, ways and means, one might assume that, at the very least, those components have been well considered in the post-Soviet era. Unfortunately, this has not proven to be the case. Another effect of threatlessness on US defence planning has been a habitual conflation of means and ends, often in ways that can quickly become dangerous. A collection of concepts traditionally seen as ways to accomplish goals – influence, presence, credibility, even alliances – have all too often become the ends of policy in themselves, raising the possibility of conflict in the process.

The US has an obsession with credibility

The first example is one of the most pervasive ideas. Influence in foreign capitals has always been a goal of states, but it has historically been pursued as a means with which to pursue interests in times of both peace and crisis. Today, influence is increasingly pursued for its own sake, under the apparent perception that it will be useful someday, even if its utility is rarely considered, much less articulated. Once freed from tangible outcomes, or strategic purpose, the quest for influence can dramatically expand the scope of US involvement abroad. The massive US investment in security cooperation and assistance, for instance, is largely intended to increase its influence. By one count, the US places its commissioned and non-commissioned officers in more than 150 countries to serve a variety of purposes, one of which is certainly to influence events, whatever they may be.[51] The 1992 'National Military Strategy' justifies global deployments by explaining that they 'lend credibility to our alliances' and promote US influence and access.[52] What exactly such influence can hope to accomplish is rarely discussed, since it is not really at issue. Influence is valuable in itself, and is pursued for its own sake.

There is also a danger of conflating means and ends regarding 'access'. Instead of being a tool or capability that could allow for the realisation of national goals, access has been elevated to an end in itself, primarily by naval and air-force strategists. One of the hot new organising concepts for the Pacific, for example, is the so-called 'Air–Sea Battle' concept, which is specifically designed to counter potential Chinese attempts to shut off access to (or employ the dreaded 'area-denial' capabilities in) nearby seas.[53] Although details of the concept remain classified, in essence Air–Sea Battle encourages greater cooperation between the US Navy and Air Force in order to deny China the ability to keep American ships out of its littoral seas. The 2012 'Defense Strategic Guidance' warned that 'state and non-state actors pose potential threats to access', and pledged that the United States 'will seek to protect freedom of access throughout the global commons'.[54] The development of Air–Sea Battle, as well as another new joint-operating concept entirely devoted to access, is proceeding without much discussion of means and ends. Access has been awarded value all its own.

Assuring economic access has been an enduring US interest in Asia, dating back to Commodore Matthew Perry's mission to Japan and the Open Door policy in China. In these instances, access was valuable because it opened markets, which was the real goal of the policy. Today's strategists refer to the economic benefits of access or the protection of allies as afterthoughts rather than as the central purpose of policymaking. Why Beijing would decide to cut off international trade and essentially bring its economy to a grinding halt is hardly clear, but it does not need to be if the focus is on access itself. None of this is to downplay the tactical or operational importance of freedom of action, but that freedom must remain connected to larger strategic ends in order to have meaning. Once disconnected from such ends, as much thinking surrounding Air–Sea Battle is, ensuring access can drive choices by itself. To the extent that Washington values access for its own sake, rather than as part of a broader strategy to protect free trade, problems will arise.

Another vital interest of the US, at least as defined by the willingness to spill blood in its pursuit, is credibility. According to conventional wisdom in the policy world – which, it deserves noting, is nearly unanimously rejected by scholars – credibility earned through displays of resolution can help states achieve goals in the future by affecting the calculations of others.[55] During the Cold War, the US fought to preserve its credibility with regularity, in the belief that it was sending messages regarding its determination to defend its interests to the Soviet Union, allies and those countries on the fence.[56] This obsession with credibility outlived the Soviet Union, despite the fact there is no longer an enemy poised to take advantage of irresolution, nor an alternative power towards which US allies or third parties could tilt.[57] While it is far from clear that credibility ever had any real utility, it is certainly meaningless when there is no enemy to receive the messages the US tries to send. Today, the logic behind the obsession with credibility, or what Stephen Walt calls the 'credibility fetish', is rarely articulated or examined.[58] Credibility is pursued for its own sake, not so much as a tool to make future interests easier to address, but as an interest in itself.

The credibility imperative has been particularly visible during the past year. When US President Barack Obama drew a rhetorical 'red line' in Syria and then hesitated to back up the threat, critics charged him with the kind of irresolution that encourages challenges. Putin's adventurism in eastern Ukraine is only the most prominent example of the effects of diminished US credibility, according to this line of thought. Former Vice President Cheney asserted that there is 'no question' that Putin believes Obama is weak, and that weakness encouraged Russian aggression.[59] This criticism, which comes mostly but not exclusively from the most hawkish voices in the marketplace of ideas, also suggests that resolve and strength could somehow have deterred this action in the first place. Such critics would do well to remember one of the most basic observations of political psychology: actors routinely exaggerate their influence over the decisions of others.[60] The crisis in Ukraine – to the extent that it is actually a crisis for the US – has regional dynamics that unfolded irrespective of Washington's actions. There is little reason to believe that American credibility factored into Moscow's calculations any more than it did during the 1970s.[61]

As a general rule, there is little to fear from loss of credibility. When the Reagan administration pulled US troops out of Lebanon following the 1983 barracks bombing, to take but one of many examples, hawks were predictably apoplectic. 'If we are driven out of Lebanon, radical and rejectionist elements will have scored a major victory', Secretary of State George Shultz said in briefings on Capitol Hill. 'The message will be sent that relying on the Soviet Union pays off and that relying on the United States is a fatal mistake.'[62] Michael Ledeen was more explicit: 'our defeat in Lebanon will encourage our enemies, in the Middle East and elsewhere', he wrote. 'In all probability, we shall pay a disproportionate price for our Lebanese failure', from the Middle East to Central America, where Soviet-sponsored guerrillas would be disastrously encouraged. As always, US allies and potential friends would be powerfully disillusioned, including the Egyptians, whom Ledeen felt would 'increasingly distance themselves from the Camp David agreement'.[63] Fortunately for the United States, the Soviet Union's influence in the Middle East did not increase, its guerrilla allies did not change their behaviour and the Egyptians did not abandon their treaty commitments. The fears generated by lost credibility proved, as they usually are, baseless.[64]

The fears proved baseless

The final example of the conflation of means and ends involves one of the centrepieces of the US security structure. Arbatov was hardly the only person to be surprised when NATO not only survived the collapse of the Soviet Union but grew. Expansion had liberal and realist supporters, all of whom agreed that, in order to survive, the Alliance had to change, in both its missions and composition. For liberals, expansion represented a way to stabilise countries in the former Soviet bloc and integrate them into Europe.[65] The relatively few realist supporters appreciated the consolidation of gains from the Cold War, just in case future Russian leaders were to foster ideas about rising again. Expansion helped to give the Alliance a new *raison d'être*, a way to prevent the loss of momentum that could easily occur following the removal of its former purpose. To use a phrase common at the time, NATO had to 'expand or die'.[66] The Alliance that had once been a primary tool for keeping the Soviets out of Western Europe (and the Americans in, and the Germans down, in the well-known formulation) was in the 1990s transformed into an end in itself. Colin Powell summarised this thinking, and the confusion of means for ends, in the title of a 2004 piece published in *Foreign Affairs*: 'A Strategy of Partnerships'.[67] Partnerships no longer served the goals of the strategy; they became the goals of the strategy.

When there are no pressing goals to accomplish, or threats to be countered, inertia can ensure that the means previously employed take on the appearance of ends. As a result, US policymakers may feel pressured to fight the Chinese over access, or to intervene in Syria to preserve credibility, or to expand NATO further in order to maintain the viability of the

Alliance. The elevation of means into ends in the absence of threat may be understandable, but that does not make it wise. Blurring the distinction has confused US strategic thinking to the point that, in some cases, unnecessary confrontation has become more likely.

The formulation of post-Soviet policy

Threatlessness has had other, more predictable effects on the formulation of foreign and national-security policy, a few of which are worthy of brief mention. Elimination of the traditional strategic imperative has raised the standing of non-strategic considerations in the policy process. Domestic political and budgetary concerns in particular now drive decisions in ways that they never would have during the Cold War.

In states where no central, all-encompassing enemy demands the focus of strategists, domestic factors become more important in the making of foreign policy. Members of Congress in particular do not have to worry about the potential negative impact of parochial or ethnic-orientated influence on policy. When US national security is simply not threatened, they are free to promote the interests of lobbies without fear of serious strategic consequence. As a result, a variety of domestic lobbies have enjoyed a much greater degree of influence on foreign policy in the post-Cold War, low-threat period.[68] The US tilted decisively towards Armenia in the early 1990s, for example, as the Armenian diaspora asserted itself. During the Cold War, national interests occasionally clashed with the interests of the Israel lobby; today, lawmakers compete to be most obsequious to the American Israel Public Affairs Committee. In the absence of urgency from without, decisive influence comes from within. The US finds itself obsessing over trivia, such as formal recognition of the 1915 massacres in Turkey as genocide, or irrationalities, such as the continuing, pointless embargo on Cuba.[69]

The post-Cold War era could easily be read as a 25-year case study in organisational behaviour. As anyone familiar with Morton Halperin's writings would have expected, the protection of resources became a central concern of the massive defence bureaucracy originally constructed to fight the Soviets.[70] In the 1990s, defenders of the budgetary status quo argued that the US needed to be prepared to fight two simultaneous regional conflicts, which would require approximately the level of spending that occurred during the Cold War. Without that capability, which came to be known as 'two major theatre wars', potential enemies might take advantage of a situation in which US forces were tied down elsewhere to launch their own offensives. The two theatres under consideration were kept officially vague but were widely acknowledged to be the Middle East and Northeast Asia. If the US had to deal again with Iraqi President Saddam Hussein, this thinking went, the North Koreans might well take advantage of the opportunity to attack southward. The mere fact that such a sequence of events had never happened, or that this is generally not why countries decide to invade their neighbours, did not seem to bother supporters of this argument, whose primary purpose was to avoid the dreaded 'peace dividend' that might have been logically expected to follow the removal of the main threat to the West.

Fiscal imperatives will drive security decisions when not challenged by those of national security. Military spending, for instance, is commonly described in terms of percentage of GDP, usually in order to argue that the US is not spending as much as it could, or even to imply that there is an optimal level for proper force planning. Often, the connection is made quite explicitly, as in 2009 when US Senator James Inhofe introduced a bill that would have committed the US to devoting 4% of its GDP to defence in perpetuity, an idea endorsed by a large number of analysts.[71] The bill died, but the sentiment lives on, and the metric has become widely accepted.

Such blatant use of the budget to guide strategy is perhaps a good place to conclude this examination of the pathological effects of the end of the Cold War on US national-security thought. When otherwise serious analysts can argue that a certain level of spending must be maintained without reference to the external environment – nearly advocating spending for its own sake – or to how the US economy performs, for that matter, all pretence of strategy has been abandoned. Such arbitrary, spectacularly non-strategic goals for US military spending would not be needed if threats existed that needed to be addressed. The post-Cold War world does indeed contain threats, as it turns out, just not to the security of the US: it is the military budget that has been under siege, and its defenders have reacted with arguments that seem logical, as long as they are not subjected to much sustained, strategic analysis.

* * *

The Soviet Union did not survive the Cold War, but neither did the American ability to think clearly about strategy. Arbatov's warning to Washington might not have come true in every one of its particulars, but the overall effect of the removal of its enemy has indeed been detrimental to the formulation of US grand strategy. Attempts to chart a way forward in an era of essential threatlessness have suffered from a variety of under-considered, shallow and dangerous ideas that have come to dominate national-security policy for more than two decades. As a result, the US worries more, and spends more, than is necessary to achieve its goals.

During the Cold War, threat helped create an enormous strategic community; now that it is over, that strategic community has helped create threat. Those who worry about uncertainty, complexity and undetectable dangers evince a clear nostalgia for simpler times, when all the US had to fret over was an aggressive totalitarian enemy with millions of troops and thousands of nuclear weapons. Those with less selective memories, however, might recall that the Soviet Union was not only tangible and unpredictable, but much more dangerous to Western interests than the unknown unknowns that apparently keep modern-day US planners awake at night.

The US won the Cold War but somehow feels less safe. Washington would do well to remember the advice of one of its clearest thinkers, George Kennan: 'in so far as we feel ourselves in any heightened trouble at the present moment, that feeling is largely of our own making.'[72] The present moment is less troubled for the US than any that have come before, even if we do not always seem to realise it.

Notes

1 Georgi A. Arbatov, 'It Takes Two to Make a Cold War', *New York Times*, 8 December 1987, http://www.nytimes.com/1987/12/08/opinion/l-it-takes-two-to-make-a-cold-war-963287.html.

2 George F. Kennan, *The Cloud of Danger: Current Realities of American Foreign Policy* (Boston, MA: Little, Brown and Company, 1977); James Chace and Caleb Carr, *America Invulnerable: The Quest for Absolute Security from 1812 to Star Wars* (New York: Summit Books, 1989); John A. Thompson, 'The Exaggeration of

American Vulnerability: The Anatomy of a Tradition', *Diplomatic History*, vol. 16, no. 1, January 1992; Dana H. Allin, *Cold War Illusions: America, Europe and Soviet Power, 1969–1989* (New York: St. Martin's Press, 1994); Robert H. Johnson, *Improbable Dangers: U.S. Conceptions of Threat in the Cold War and After* (New York: St. Martin's Press, 1994); Michael C. Desch, 'America's Liberal Illiberalism: The Ideological Origins of Overreaction in U.S. Foreign Policy', *International Security*, vol. 32, no. 3, Winter 2007–08; A. Trevor Thrall and Jane K. Cramer, *American Foreign Policy and the Politics of Fear: Threat Inflation Since 9/11* (Abingdon: Routledge, 2009).

3 The concept of the 'super-empowered individual' was injected into the discussion by Thomas Friedman. See Thomas Friedman, *The Lexus and the Olive Tree* (New York: First Anchor Books, 2000).

4 Douglas Jehl, 'C.I.A. Nominee Wary of Budget Cuts', *New York Times*, 3 February 1993, http://www.nytimes.com/1993/02/03/us/cia-nominee-wary-of-budget-cuts.html.

5 Andrew J. Bacevich, *American Empire: The Realities and Consequences of U.S. Diplomacy* (Cambridge, MA: Harvard University Press, 2002), p. 118.

6 As discussed during a not-for-attribution talk at the US Naval War College in 2007.

7 Daniel Wirls makes a similar point in *Irrational Security: The Politics of Defense from Reagan to Obama* (Baltimore, MD: Johns Hopkins University Press, 2010), p. 42.

8 The empirical and theoretical literature on this phenomenon is immense and growing, as one would expect. For some of the most up-to-date data and evidence, see Monty G. Marshall and Benjamin R. Cole, *Global Report 2014: Conflict, Governance, and State Fragility* (Vienna, VA: Center for Systemic Peace, 2014); and Human Security Report Project, *Human Security Report 2009/2010: The Causes of Peace and the Shrinking Costs of War* (New York: Oxford University Press, 2011). Summaries, extrapolations, explanations and analyses can be found in Richard Rosecrance, *The Rise of the Virtual State: Wealth and Power in the Coming Century* (New York: Basic Books, 1999); John Mueller, *Retreat from Doomsday: The Obsolescence of Major War* (New York: Basic Books, 1989); John Mueller, *The Remnants of War* (Ithaca, NY: Cornell University Press, 2004); Robert Jervis, 'Theories of War in an Era of Leading-Power Peace Presidential Address', *American Political Science Review*, vol. 96, no. 1, March 2002, http://www.apsanet.org/media/PDFs/PresidentialAddresses/2001AddrJERVIS.pdf; Christopher J. Fettweis, *Dangerous Times?: The International Politics of Great Power Peace* (Washington DC: Georgetown University Press, 2010); Richard Ned Lebow, *Why Nations Fight: Past and Future Motives for War* (New York: Cambridge University Press, 2010); Joshua S. Goldstein, *Winning the War on War: The Decline of Armed Conflict Worldwide* (New York: Penguin Books, 2011); and Steven Pinker, *The Better Angels of Our Nature: A History of Violence and Humanity* (New York: Viking, 2011).

9 One of the most recent works to

point this out, and try to explain it, is Jacques E.C. Hymans, *Achieving Nuclear Ambitions: Scientists, Politicians, and Proliferation* (New York: Cambridge University Press, 2012).

10 Michael J. Mazarr, 'The Rise and Fall of the Failed-State Paradigm: Requiem for a Decade of Distraction', *Foreign Affairs*, vol. 93, no. 1, January–February 2014.

11 Mark W. Zacher, 'The Territorial Integrity Norm: International Boundaries and the Use of Force', *International Organization*, vol. 55, no. 2, Spring 2001, pp. 215–50; Anna Simons, 'The Death of Conquest', *National Interest*, no. 71, Spring 2003, pp. 41–9; Tanisha M. Fazal, *State Death: The Politics and Geography of Conquest, Occupation, and Annexation* (Princeton, NJ: Princeton University Press, 2007).

12 See John Mueller, 'Embracing Threatlessness: Reassessing U.S. Military Spending', in Michael Gerson and Alison Lawler Russell (eds), 'American Grand Strategy and Sea Power', Center for Naval Analysis, November 2011, http://www.dtic.mil/dtic/tr/fulltext/u2/a553727.pdf.

13 Colin S. Gray, 'Clausewitz Rules, OK? The Future is the Past – with GPS', in Michael Cox, Ken Booth and Tim Dunn (eds), *The Interregnum: Controversies in World Politics, 1989–1999* (New York: Cambridge University Press, 1999), p. 182.

14 Colin S. Gray, *Weapons Don't Make War: Policy, Strategy and Military Technology* (Lawrence, KS: University Press of Kansas, 1993), p. 105.

15 Emily Goldman, *Power in Uncertain Times: Strategy in the Fog of Peace* (Stanford, CA: Stanford University Press, 2011), p. 1. Emphasis in original.

16 Carl Conetta and Charles Knight, 'Inventing Threats', *Bulletin of the Atomic Scientists*, vol. 54, no. 2, March April 1998. See also Benjamin H. Friedman and Harvey M. Sapolsky, 'You Never Know(ism)', *Breakthroughs*, vol. 15, no. 1, Spring 2006.

17 James A. Winnefeld, *The Post-Cold War Force-Sizing Debate: Paradigms, Metaphors, and Disconnects* (Santa Monica, CA: RAND Corporation, 1992), p. 12. Number of question marks in the original.

18 Conetta and Knight, 'Inventing Threats', p. 34.

19 US Joint Chiefs of Staff, 'The National Military Strategy of the United States', January 1992, p. 4.

20 US Department of Defense, 'The National Defense Strategy of the United States of America', March 2005, p. 2.

21 William S. Cohen, 'Quadrennial Defense Review: The Secretary's Message', *DISAM Journal*, Summer 1997, http://www.disam.dsca.mil/pubs/INDEXES/Vol%2019_4/Cohen.pdf.

22 US Department of Defense, 'DoD News Briefing – Secretary Rumsfeld and Gen. Myers', 12 February 2002, http://www.defense.gov/transcripts/transcript.aspx?transcriptid=2636.

23 HM Government, 'Securing Britain in an Age of Uncertainty: The Strategic Defence and Security Review', October 2010, pp. 3–4, https://www.gov.uk/government/uploads/system/uploads/attachment_data/file/61936/national-security-strategy.pdf. As a point of comparison, the word 'uncertainty' does not appear in the 'European Union Security Strategy',

which in many ways does a better job of describing the post-Cold War world. European Council, 'A Secure Europe in a Better World: European Security Strategy', 12 December 2003, http://www.consilium.europa.eu/uedocs/cmsUpload/78367.pdf. See also Christopher J. Fettweis, 'Free Riding or Restraint? Examining European Grand Strategy', *Comparative Strategy*, vol. 30, no. 4, 2011.

24 Michael J. Gallagher, Joshua A. Geltzer and Sebastian L.v. Gorka, 'The Complexity Trap', *Parameters*, vol. 42, no. 1, Spring 2012.

25 Williamson Murray, 'Thoughts on Grand Strategy', in Williamson Murray, Richard Hart Sinnreich and James Lacey (eds), *The Shaping of Grand Strategy: Policy, Diplomacy, and War* (Cambridge: Cambridge University Press, 2011), pp. 32–3.

26 Corey Robin, *Fear: The History of a Political Idea* (New York: Oxford University Press, 2004), p. 72.

27 US Department of Defense, 'Sustaining U.S. Global Leadership: Priorities for 21st Century Defense', January 2012, p. 1, http://www.defense.gov/news/defense_strategic_guidance.pdf.

28 US Department of Defense, 'Quadrennial Defense Review Report', February 2006, p. iv, http://www.defense.gov/qdr/report/report20060203.pdf.

29 US Joint Chiefs of Staff, 'Joint Vision 2010', July 1996, p. 8, http://www.dtic.mil/jv2010/jv2010.pdf.

30 US Department of Defense, 'Quadrennial Defense Review Report'.

31 Derek S. Reveron, *Cyberspace and National Security: Threats, Opportunities, and Power in a Virtual World* (Washington DC: Georgetown University Press, 2012).

32 James R. Clapper, 'Worldwide Threat Assessment of the US Intelligence Community', US Intelligence Community, 12 March 2013, p. 1, http://www.dni.gov/files/documents/Intelligence%20Reports/2013%20ATA%20SFR%20for%20SSCI%2012%20Mar%202013.pdf.

33 For discussion of the effects of technological change on military organisations, see Jacques Ellul, *The Technological Society* (New York: Knopf, 1964).

34 Thomas Rid, *Cyber War Will Not Take Place* (London: C. Hurst & Co., 2013).

35 The literature on this is quite extensive. Good places to start include Richard K. Betts, *Surprise Attack: Lessons for Defense Planning* (Washington DC: Brookings Institution Press, 1982); John Lewis Gaddis, *Surprise, Security, and the American Experience* (Cambridge, MA: Harvard University Press, 2004); and Charles F. Parker and Eric K. Stern, 'Blindsided? September 11 and the Origins of Strategic Surprise', *Political Psychology*, vol. 23, no. 3, September 2002.

36 Arnold Wolfers, *Discord and Collaboration: Essays on International Politics* (Baltimore, MD: Johns Hopkins University Press, 1962), p. 151.

37 Goldman, *Power in Uncertain Times*, p. 125.

38 See Hew Strachan, 'The Lost Meaning of Strategy', *Survival*, vol. 47, no. 3, Autumn 2005. For a discussion of the traditional approach, see Thomas C. Schelling, *The Strategy of Conflict* (Cambridge, MA: Harvard University

Press, 1960).

39 See Lawrence Freedman, *Strategy: A History* (New York: Oxford University Press, 2013), p. xi.

40 Arthur F. Lykke, Jr, 'Toward an Understanding of Military Strategy', in Arthur F. Lykke, Jr (ed.), *Military Strategy: Theory and Application* (Carlisle, PA: US Army War College, 1989), pp. 3–8.

41 These questions, and a general discussion of Lykke's influence, can be found in H. Richard Yarger, 'Toward a Theory of Strategy: Art Lykke and the Army War College Strategy Model', in J. Boone Bartholomees, Jr (ed.), *Theory Of War And Strategy*, Fourth Edition (Carlisle, PA: Strategic Studies Institute, 2010).

42 Mackubin Thomas Owens, 'Strategy and the Strategic Way Of Thinking', *Naval War College Review*, vol. 60, no. 4, Autumn 2007, p. 111. Emphasis in original. For other prominent, similar descriptions of strategy, see J. Boone Bartholomees, Jr, 'A Survey of the Theory of Strategy', in Bartholomees, Jr (ed.), *Theory Of War And Strategy*; and Robert H. Dorff, 'A Primer in Strategy Development', in Joseph R. Cerami and James F. Holcomb, Jr (eds), *U.S. Army War College Guide to Strategy* (Carlisle, PA: Strategic Studies Institute, 2001), p. 11.

43 Derek S. Reveron and James L. Cook, 'From National to Theater: Developing Strategy', *Joint Force Quaterly*, no. 70, 2013, p. 113.

44 Freedman, *Strategy*, p. xi. See also the brief discussion on p. 633, footnote 2.

45 Donald H. Rumsfeld, 'Transforming the Military', *Foreign Affairs*, vol. 81, no. 3, May–June 2002, p. 24.

46 Ronald O'Rourke, 'Navy Ford (CVN-78) Class Aircraft Carrier Program: Background and Issues for Congress', Congressional Research Service, 31 July 2014, http://fas.org/sgp/crs/weapons/RS20643.pdf.

47 For a review of this, see James A. Winnefeld, 'The Post-Cold War Force-Sizing Debate: Paradigms, Metaphors, and Disconnects', RAND Corporation, 1992, http://www.rand.org/content/dam/rand/pubs/reports/2007/R4243.pdf.

48 *Ibid.*, p. 34. See also Paul K. Davis (ed.), *New Challenges for Defense Planning: Rethinking How Much Is Enough* (Santa Monica, CA: RAND Corporation, 1994); and Paul K. Davis, 'Analytic Architecture for Capabilities-Based Planning, Mission-System Analysis, and Transformation', RAND Corporation, 2002.

49 Davis, 'Analytic Architecture for Capabilities-Based Planning, Mission-System Analysis, and Transformation', p. 2.

50 General Paul Van Riper discussed the exercise in Julian Borger, 'Wake-up Call', *Guardian*, 6 September 2002, http://www.theguardian.com/world/2002/sep/06/usa.iraq. For details of the exercise, see US Joint Forces Command, 'MC02 Final Report'. On the use of Israel as the primary enemy, see 'Battle Plan Under Fire', *Nova*, PBS, 4 May 2004, http://www.pbs.org/wgbh/nova/transcripts/3110_wartech.html.

51 Derek S. Reveron, *Exporting Security: International Engagement, Security Cooperation, and the Changing Face of the U.S. Military* (Washington DC: Georgetown University Press, 2010), p. 2.

52 US Joint Chiefs of Staff, 'The National Military Strategy of the United States', p. 7.

53 Jonathan W. Greenert and Norton A. Schwartz, 'Air–Sea Battle', *American Interest*, 20 February 2012, http://www.the-american-interest.com/articles/2012/2/20/air-sea-battle/; Greg Jaffe, 'U.S. Model for a Future War Fans Tensions with China and Inside Pentagon', *Washington Post*, 1 August 2012, http://www.washingtonpost.com/world/national-security/us-model-for-a-future-war-fans-tensions-with-china-and-inside-pentagon/2012/08/01/gJQAC6F8PX_story.html.

54 US Department of Defense, 'Sustaining U.S. Global Leadership', p. 9. See also Greenert and Schwartz, 'Air–Sea Battle'.

55 For good discussions of credibility in international affairs, see Robert Jervis and Jack Snyder, *Dominoes and Bandwagons: Strategic Beliefs and Great Power Competition in the Eurasian Rimland* (New York: Oxford University Press, 1991); Jonathan Mercer, *Reputation and International Politics* (Ithaca, NY: Cornell University Press, 1996); and Daryl G. Press, *Calculating Credibility: How Leaders Assess Military Threats* (Ithaca, NY: Cornell University Press, 2005).

56 Robert J. McMahon, 'Credibility and World Power: Exploring the Psychological Dimension in Postwar American Diplomacy', *Diplomatic History*, vol. 15, no. 4, October 1991.

57 On the importance of credibility in the post-Cold War world, see Christopher J. Fettweis, 'Credibility and the War on Terror', *Political Science Quarterly*, vol. 122, no. 4.

58 'Fetishizing credibility', according to Walt, 'is one of the reasons American diplomacy has achieved relatively little since the end of the Cold War'. Stephen M. Walt, 'Why Are U.S. Leaders so Obsessed with Credibility?', *Foreign Policy*, 11 September 2012, http://www.foreignpolicy.com/posts/2012/09/11/the_credibility_fetish.

59 Dick Cheney, remarks made on CBS's *Face the Nation*, 9 March 2014, available at http://www.cbsnews.com/videos/dick-cheney-on-ukraine-no-question-putin-believes-obama-is-weak/.

60 The classic explanation of this phenomenon can be found in Robert Jervis, *Perception and Misperception in International Politics* (Princeton, NJ: Princeton University Press, 1976).

61 Soviet adventurism in the third world did not rise in the 1970s compared to earlier eras, when US credibility was presumably higher. Ted Hopf, *Peripheral Visions: Deterrence Theory and American Foreign Policy in the Third World, 1965–1990* (Ann Arbor, MI: University of Michigan Press, 1994).

62 Lou Cannon and Don Oberdorfer, 'Standing Fast: "Vital Interests" of U.S. at Stake', *Washington Post*, 25 October 1983.

63 Michael Ledeen, 'The Lessons of Lebanon', *Commentary*, vol. 77, no. 5, May 1984, pp. 21–2.

64 For more explanation of these (perhaps counter-intuitive) points, see Christopher J. Fettweis, *The Pathologies of Power: Fear, Honor, Glory, and Hubris in U.S. Foreign Policy* (New York: Cambridge University Press, 2013).

65 James B. Steinberg and Philip H. Gordon, 'NATO Enlargement:

Moving Forward; Expanding the Alliance and Completing Europe's Integration', Brookings Institution, November 2001, http://www.brookings.edu/research/papers/2001/11/globalgovernance-gordon.

66 Zbigniew Brzezinski, 'NATO – Expand or Die?', *New York Times*, 28 December 1994, http://www.nytimes.com/1994/12/28/opinion/nato-expand-or-die.html.

67 Colin L. Powell, 'A Strategy of Partnerships', *Foreign Affairs*, vol. 83, no. 1, January–February 2004.

68 John Newhouse, 'Diplomacy, Inc.: The Influence of Lobbies on U.S. Foreign Policy', *Foreign Affairs*, vol. 88, no. 3, May–June 2009.

69 William M. LeoGrande, 'The Cuba Lobby', *Foreign Policy*, 11 April 2013, http://www.foreignpolicy.com/articles/2013/04/11/the_cuba_lobby_jay_z.

70 Morton H. Halperin, *Bureaucratic Politics and Foreign Policy* (Washington DC: Brookings Institution Press, 1974).

71 Supporters include Baker Spring, Mackenzie Eaglen, James Jay Carafano, Mackubin Thomas Owens and Martin Feldstein. Baker Spring, Mackenzie Eaglen and James Jay Carafano, '4 Percent of GDP Defense Spending: Sustained Spending, Not Economic Stimulus', Heritage Foundation, 26 January 2009, http://www.heritage.org/research/reports/2009/01/4-percent-of-gdp-defense-spending-sustained-spending-not-economic-stimulus; Mackubin Thomas Owens, 'A Balanced Force Structure to Achieve a Liberal World Order', *Orbis*, vol. 50, no. 2, Spring 2006; Martin Feldstein, 'The Underfunded Pentagon', *Foreign Affairs*, vol. 86, no. 2, March–April 2007. For a critique, see Travis Sharp, 'Tying US Defense Spending to GDP: Bad Logic, Bad Policy', *Parameters*, vol. 38, no. 3, Autumn 2008.

72 Samuel F. Wells, Jr, 'Sounding the Tocsin: NSC 68 and the Soviet Threat', *International Security*, vol. 4, no. 2, Autumn 1979, p. 128.

Mastering the Endgame of War

Dominic Tierney

In 1941 Japan weighed the merits of attacking the most powerful country in the world: the United States. It was a war of choice, and Tokyo had time to carefully consider the decision. Japanese leaders debated the best date to strike Pearl Harbor. And they also thought through the potential short-term effects. But Tokyo barely considered the military endgame: the final stages of a campaign in which an armistice is negotiated, hostilities cease and a new post-war order emerges.

Japan knew that the long-term prognosis for a war against the US was uncertain at best, given America's vast advantage in resources. Still, Japanese leaders hoped that early battlefield victories, the nation's superior fighting spirit and a protracted war of attrition would somehow wear down the will of the Americans and produce a favourable peace. As Japanese military leaders wrote in a document prepared for the imperial conference of 6 September 1941,

> we cannot exclude the possibility that the war may end because of a great change in American public opinion … At any rate we should be able to establish an invincible position … Meanwhile, we may hope that we will be able to influence the trend of affairs and bring the war to an end.[1]

Dominic Tierney is Associate Professor of Political Science at Swarthmore College, Pennsylvania, Senior Fellow at the Foreign Policy Research Institute, and Contributing Writer at the *Atlantic*. This essay develops several sections in his book *The Right Way to Lose a War: America in an Age of Unwinnable Conflicts* (Little, Brown and Company, forthcoming in 2015).

Survival | vol. 56 no. 5 | October–November 2014 | pp. 69–94 DOI 10.1080/00396338.2014.962794

Japanese Prime Minister Tojo Hideki echoed this sentiment shortly after with a reference to Kyoto's Kiyomizu Temple, a Buddhist shrine that juts out over a cliff edge. He concluded that 'there are times when we must have the courage to do extraordinary things – like jumping, with eyes closed, off the veranda of the Kiyomizu Temple.'[2] But, lacking a clear plan to conclude the conflict, Japan leapt into the dark, and initiated a war that would end with its major cities reduced to ashes.

Throughout history, statesmen have plunged countries into war without thinking through the military endgame. When fighting looms, leaders often focus on the initial rounds rather than the achievement of ultimate strategic success.[3] The US may be particularly prone to neglect the conflict endgame. American officials paid little heed to the long-term consequences of invading Afghanistan and Iraq during 2001–03, and failed to plan effectively for post-combat stabilisation. This final stage has been referred to as 'Phase IV' of a war, following Phase I, deterrence and engagement; Phase II, initial operations to seize the initiative; and Phase III, major combat missions.[4]

Preparing for the conclusion of war is a critical part of any sound strategy that connects ends and means. Carl von Clausewitz advised against taking the first step in war 'without considering the last'.[5] Basil Liddell Hart wrote: 'it is essential to conduct war with constant regard to the peace you desire.'[6] According to Henry Kissinger, 'the test of policy is how it ends, not how it begins.'[7] The failure to prepare for post-conflict stabilisation in Iraq led to the death of thousands of American soldiers and tens of thousands of Iraqi civilians, and the expenditure of hundreds of billions of dollars.

Why does Washington struggle to master the endgame of war? And can its record be improved? Relatively little has been written about the conclusion of war, despite its importance. Indeed, far more scholarship is devoted to how wars begin than how they end.[8] Ineffective US planning for the military endgame results from the interaction of two variables: a psychological bias of overconfidence and a cultural bias against nation building. The first variable is a positivity bias that causes leaders to exaggerate the odds of success in wartime. The second is a negativity bias that creates an aversion to using the military for stabilisation operations. The synergy between these dynamics encourages the belief that extensive nation-building operations will be both unnecessary and unwise.

One solution to these challenges is to reverse-engineer victory. Instead of planning ahead chronologically, from Phase I to Phase IV, Washington should start at the end, identifying a final state that represents strategic success and then working backwards. Reverse-engineering victory may mitigate the effects of both overconfidence and scepticism towards nation building, encourage creative thinking, and reveal unexpected opportunities and challenges.

The American way of battle

Bradford Lee's examination of US war termination from the First World War until the 1991 Gulf War led him to conclude that Washington 'had considerable difficulty in bringing political rationality and military creativity to bear upon the strategic logic of war termination'.[9]

Part of the problem is that US military planning tends to neglect ultimate political goals. According to Russell Weigley, the American way of war is more a way of battle, one which focuses on winning engagements rather than turning military success into strategic success.[10] Frederick Kagan describes the American vision of war as a 'target set' that ignores 'how, exactly, one defeats the enemy and what the enemy's country looks like at the moment the bullets stop flying'.[11]

Another issue is that the US fails to adequately plan for failure. When conflict looms, American officials avoid being distracted by painful 'what if?' scenarios, such as those where the campaign deteriorates and US forces face an entrenched insurgency. Washington suffers from tunnel vision, and focuses mainly on implementing the first moves in its chosen strategy for victory.

These problems are evident in US war games. American air-strikes against Iraq in 1998 raised the prospect of an ultimate showdown with Iraqi President Saddam Hussein. But General Anthony Zinni, then head of US Central Command, saw a problem: 'it struck me then that we had a plan to defeat Saddam's army, but we didn't have a plan to rebuild Iraq.' In 1999 Zinni organised a war game, called *Desert Crossing*, to examine the contours of a post-Saddam Iraq. The exercise predicted a host of problems in stabilising the country, including 'rival forces bidding for power', fragmentation 'along religious and/or ethnic lines', and an upsurge in 'Iran's anti-Americanism'.[12]

Zinni asked different parts of the US government, including the Department of State and the Department of Commerce, to help prepare for the stabilisation of Iraq. As he recalled, the answer was: 'not interested. Would not look at it.'[13] A few years later, when war with Iraq seemed at hand, Zinni, who by that time had retired, told US Central Command that it needed to 'dust off Desert Crossing'. The reply was: 'what's that? Never heard of it.' In just a few years, according to Zinni, the corporate memory 'was gone'.[14]

War games conducted under the George W. Bush administration tended to neglect the endgame. In 2002 the US military carried out simulated regime-change missions against a fictional country called 'Nair' (which combined features of Iran and Iraq). Comfortingly, the games ended in a decisive US victory.

But according to Huba Wass de Czege, a retired brigadier-general who participated in the exercises, the simulations were based on a flawed conception of victory. They ended when the US achieved success on the battlefield rather than when Washington attained its political goals. Wass de Czege stated that the exercises 'tend to devote more attention to successful campaign beginnings than to successful conclusions'. They finish when American control of strategic locations looks like 'a matter of time', or, in other words, when 'victory seems inevitable to us (not necessarily to the enemy)'. The result is a 'blind spot at the back-end of campaigns'.[15]

American war games also tend to neglect scenarios of military failure. A 1971 review of education in the US Army, for example, found that war games and other exercises were 'generally euphoric in nature – the US Army always wins with relative ease'.[16] Wass de Czege has written that, in more recent war games, US forces greatly underestimated 'the difficulty of concluding such campaigns promptly'. In reality, he argues, 'coalitions tend to fray as optimistic expectations fade and the achievement of strategic aims is delayed ... the enemy's definition of winning promptly becomes not losing, or delaying defeat until the coalition tires of pursuing its original strategic ends'.[17]

In summer 2002, the US military carried out a simulation called *Millennium Challenge*. This was one of the largest war games in history: a massive $250-million exercise that involved more than 13,000 personnel and was designed to test America's capacity to defeat a major country in the Middle East.[18] As the simulation unfolded, Lieutenant-General (Retd) Paul Van Riper, commander of the enemy forces, employed asymmetric tactics to defeat the US. Van Riper sidestepped American electronic surveillance by delivering orders via motorcycle messenger. When a US fleet gathered for the invasion, Van Riper struck first with cruise missiles and a swarm of suicide bombers in speedboats, destroying 16 US warships.

At this point, the Pentagon had an opportunity to explore the consequences of military failure by letting the simulation run its course. Instead, the game was suspended, the American fleet 'came back to life' and new rules were introduced to ensure victory for the US. Van Riper was told to reveal the location of some of his units, and to turn off his air defences so that American troops could land safely. Rather than continue the sham, Van Riper quit in protest, stating that 'it was in actuality an exercise that was almost entirely scripted to ensure an [American] "win".'[19]

War games neglected the endgame

The failure to plan effectively for endgames soon became evident in practice as well. A US Army review criticised the American campaign in Afghanistan: 'the lack of a war plan or theatre campaign plan has hindered operations and led to a tactical focus that ignores long-term objectives.'[20] Thomas Pickering, former under-secretary of state for political affairs, said that, in the 2001 invasion of Afghanistan, 'we had a failure to define with precision and clarity what our objectives are. The danger is not knowing where we want to go, and seeking to achieve much more than we can possibly achieve.'[21] Isaiah Wilson described the mission in Afghanistan as a 'battle victory' followed by 'strategic stalemate'.[22]

The negative consequences of poor planning were even greater for the subsequent war in Iraq. Preparations for the conflict prioritised the regime-change phase and neglected efforts to stabilise the country after the initial battles had ended. The official US Army history of the campaign concluded: 'it is questionable whether ... [US officials] conducted a thorough, coordinated, and realistic evaluation of the probable force levels required for Phase IV based on the realities of the new Iraq that were emerging in front of them'.[23]

During 2002–03, there was considerable inter-agency debate in Washington about the governmental structure of post-war Iraq, involving the Department of State, the Department of Defense and Central Command, particularly at the level of deputy secretaries. The US also prepared carefully for the early rounds of the Iraq War, and even readied for negative scenarios that never became reality, such as a massive humanitarian crisis.[24]

But a series of connected problems emerged in the planning for post-Saddam Iraq that proved highly damaging to US interests. Firstly, the final plan for Phase IV was decided very late in the process. President George W. Bush's initial major briefing on post-conflict issues occurred in January 2003, just weeks before the invasion.[25] During the same month, US Army Lieutenant-General (Retd) Jay Garner was approached to head the Office of Reconstruction and Humanitarian Assistance (ORHA), the post-war Iraqi administration. Garner described his organisation as being 'glued together over about four or five weeks' time. [We] didn't really have enough time to plan.'[26]

In early March, the policy for post-war governance in Iraq was finally agreed on. Washington rejected the idea of creating a provisional government of Iraqi exiles, fearing that this would hand over too much power to untested individuals. Instead, US officials endorsed the Iraqi Interim Government, which would relinquish a degree of sovereignty to Iraqis immediately and then steadily transfer additional control. By this point, however, the war was about to begin.[27]

Secondly, civilian and military principals paid far less attention to the post-war phase than to more immediate concerns, such as pre-war diplomacy at the United Nations and initial military operations. According to Wilson, the plan was

> resourced and directed toward the attainment of a limited military object (toppling of Saddam) instead of a more comprehensive political object. We essentially planned our way into a fight with Saddam instead of planning a way toward a better state of peace with the Iraqi people.[28]

Tommy Franks, then-head of US Central Command, told the deputy secretary of defence where his priorities lay: 'you pay attention to the day *after*, I'll pay attention to the day *of*.'[29] But civilian leaders also neglected the day after. Nine days before the war began, Garner gave his only high-level briefing on post-war issues. Bush and senior National Security Council officials seemed uninterested, and asked no questions.[30]

On 14 March, Secretary of Defense Donald Rumsfeld told Garner: 'I haven't given you the time I should have given you. Quite frankly, I just have been so engulfed in the war that I just didn't have time to focus on everything that you're doing.'[31] Rumsfeld evidently saw Phase IV stabilisation operations as distinct from 'the war', rather than something that should be integrated into every stage of the military plan. Anthony Cordesman has referred to this as the 'rebuilding effort begins after the war ends syndrome'.[32]

Thirdly, the war plan was based on unrealistic assumptions, and there was a lack of contingency planning for scenarios of failure. Officials believed that security could be quickly turned over to Iraq's police and army units, the country's oil revenues would cover most of the post-war costs, and US force levels could draw down to around 30,000 troops by September 2003.[33]

The special inspector general for Iraq reconstruction concluded there were 'no established plans to manage the increasing chaos' in Iraq. As a result, 'when Iraq's withering post-invasion reality superseded [official] expectations, there was no well-defined "Plan B" as a fallback and no existing government structures or resources to support a quick response.'[34] John Abizaid, head of US Central Command during 2003–07, stated that, 'in Iraq, we saw a lack of clarity on war-ending conditions. There was a heroic assumption that it would be quick and easy. The time horizon was not extended far enough to cover the possibility of an insurgency.'[35]

Fourthly, the plan was changed dramatically before it could be implemented. On 6 May 2003, Garner's replacement, Paul Bremer, had lunch with Bush, who granted his envoy broad powers to stabilise Iraq. Bremer promptly abandoned the Iraqi Interim Government, and turned the Coalition Provisional Authority (the successor to the ORHA) into a direct occupying power that would rule by decree. This sudden shift in US policy over lunch is testament to the lack of forethought and coordination that went into preparation for the post-Saddam era.[36]

The war in Iraq was therefore a well-orchestrated regime-change mission followed by an improvised stabilisation operation. American troops were not trained to set up police and judicial authorities in Iraq, nor to handle the wave of looting and violence that spread across the country. Garner's ORHA was under-resourced and quickly overwhelmed by the mounting instability. Bremer's Coalition Provisional Authority was also hobbled by a lack of trained personnel, and had limited reach outside Baghdad. As Iraq unravelled, Washington's tactical success turned into a strategic defeat.[37]

The fog of war

Why does the US struggle with the endgame of conflict? Perhaps inattention to the final stages of a campaign is simply a rational response to the fog of war. After all, conflict is not a precise science with fixed laws. It is more like an art, or a social science based on probabilities. Military campaigns are inherently complex, and there is usually doubt about the opponent's capabilities and intentions. Indeed, Leo Tolstoy saw history as 'a succession of "accidents" whose origins and consequences are, by and large, untraceable and unpredictable'.[38]

Given this uncertainty, any plan for the endgame of war could be based on an illusion. History is littered with blueprints for victory that did not survive contact with the enemy. Therefore, it may be reasonable to focus finite resources on the initial and relatively predictable stages of war, and to keep the nation's options open for the 'untraceable and unpredictable' events to come. If decision-makers are not tied to a fixed plan, so the argument goes, they can see how the chips fall and adapt more easily to unexpected circumstances and the actions of the other side. One member of the military staff who planned the invasion of Iraq concluded that

> both the planners and the commander had been schooled to see fighting as the realm of war and thus attached lesser importance to post-war issues ... Only a fool would propose hurting the war fighting effort to address post-war conditions that might or might not occur.[39]

But there is no rational explanation for the wider US failure to plan for endgames. America's experience in Afghanistan and Iraq – or, indeed, Japan's experience in the Second World War – suggests that inattention to the endgame starkly undermines state interests. It is extremely difficult to improvise the final stages of a war. National militaries are large and unwieldy organisations that do not change course efficiently. The US Army, for example, took years to adapt to the Iraqi insurgency.

Furthermore, post-war stabilisation can be the most difficult phase of war and may therefore be worthy of greater attention than initial combat operations. Building a new political order in Iraq was always likely to be more challenging than toppling Saddam's sclerotic regime. American officials received – and largely ignored – many warnings about the probable difficulties involved in owning Iraq, from organisations such as the CIA, the Defense Intelligence Agency, the US Army War College, the RAND Corporation and the United States Institute of Peace. One US intelligence assessment of January 2003 claimed that Ba'athists 'could forge an alliance with existing terrorist organizations or act independently to wage guerrilla warfare against [Iraq's] new government or coalition forces'.[40]

Although the fog of war complicates planning for the endgame of conflict, countries do have some capacity to predict war outcomes and prepare. If they did not, the use of force would be fundamentally irrational. In recent years, however, Washington has not employed its available planning resources efficiently or effectively.

It is true that, in certain campaigns, the US has had little time to plan for Phase IV. On 10 September 2001, few American officials were focused on Afghanistan. Three months later, the US was responsible for the country. But there was no such excuse in the case of Iraq. The overthrow of Saddam was a war of choice, and Washington had plenty of time to prepare for Phase IV.

If America's neglect of the endgame cannot be seen as a rational response to the fog of war, what is the explanation? A variety of dynamics may play a role in encouraging Washington's short-term mindset. Debates over post-war Iraq became bogged down in inter-agency divisions between the Department of State and the Department of Defense.[41] The latter ultimately took the lead in planning for Phase IV, but lacked the necessary expertise and capabilities in many areas of civilian reconstruction.[42] Individual personalities may also have impeded long-term strategic thinking. Franks was largely uninterested in the wider political goals of the war, and retired almost as soon as major combat operations ended. According to one US officer, Franks 'really was comfortable at the tactical level'.[43]

But these dynamics cannot account for a systemic failure to plan for endgames, nor explain why Washington prepared effectively for the initial steps of the Iraq War, only to neglect the finale. A more fundamental answer lies in the interaction of two variables: a psychological bias towards overconfidence, and a cultural and institutional aversion to nation building.

Overconfidence

The psychological bias of overconfidence can significantly impede planning for the endgame of war. Psychologists have found that mentally healthy people tend to exaggerate their perceived capabilities, overestimate their control over events and exhibit excessive optimism about the future – features that are collectively labelled as positive illusions or overconfidence. A survey of 1m American high-school students found that 70% rated themselves as above the median in leadership ability. Similarly, around 80% of Americans claim to be above the median in driving skill. There is an extensive literature on overconfidence, which covers a wide variety of subjects, issues and methodologies.[44]

Positive illusions can significantly heighten the risk of war. If leaders exaggerate the odds of military success, they may be more enthusiastic about seizing the sword. Stephen Van Evera has argued that overconfidence is 'a potent and pervasive cause of war', while Geoffrey Blainey has described it as 'crucial to an understanding of war'.[45]

Overconfidence can also encourage poor planning for the military endgame. If leaders assume that the final stages of war will be easy, they may not pay as much attention to the conclusion. Before the invasion of Iraq, US officials exhibited overconfidence about the post-war phase, including the ease of establishing security, the degree of Iraqi popular support for the intervention, and the capacity of Iraq's government, police and army to administer the country and enforce law and order. Deputy Secretary of Defense Paul Wolfowitz's comments in February 2003 symbolised the administration's mindset: 'we're not talking about the occupation of Iraq. We're talking about the liberation of Iraq ... Therefore, when that regime is removed we will find [the Iraqi people] ... basically welcoming us as liberators.'[46] A RAND study of 2005 found that, in pre-war planning, 'post conflict stabilization and reconstruction were addressed only very generally, largely because of the prevailing view that the task would not be difficult.'[47]

Positive illusions are often evident on the eve of war. As cultural historian Wolfgang Schivelbusch argues, 'nations are as incapable of imagining their own defeat as individuals are of conceiving their own death.'[48] But three sources of variation may heighten the odds that the US will be overconfident about the endgame of war.

Firstly, overconfidence varies between cultures, and Americans may be particularly prone to positive illusions about their abilities. Scholars suggest that self-enhancement of individual capabilities is more acceptable and beneficial in the US relative to other countries. Psychologists David Armor and Shelley Taylor write that 'Americans are widely regarded as the most optimistic people on earth.'[49] James Stavridis, former supreme allied commander in Europe, has said that 'US military culture is not particularly compatible with failure planning.' One reason is 'the culture of "can-do", "we will succeed", or, as Colin Powell put it, "perpetual optimism is a force multiplier."'[50]

Secondly, people may be more prone to overconfidence about the final stages of war relative to the initial rounds. Construal level theory in psychology holds that actors will tend to judge immediate tasks based on their feasibility, and distant endeavours based on the desirability of the goals. Future scenarios' separation from the present often causes people to rely on vague, abstract or simplistic mental constructs when considering them, and to thereby fall prey to overconfidence. Individuals ask fewer tough questions about distant events, and often see what they want to see. According to Aaron Rapport, 'temporal distance encourages people to downplay or even ignore the feasibility of their long-term objectives.'[51]

Applied to war planning, officials are likely to consider near-term events in a relatively cool-headed manner and the final stages of the campaign with an overconfident mindset. As expected, US planners were fairly cautious in their preparations for regime change in Iraq. But this wariness largely disappeared when it came to thinking about post-war Iraq. According to the special inspector general for Iraq reconstruction, 'the U.S. government planned for the worst-case humanitarian scenario while it simultaneously planned for the best-case reconstruction one.'[52]

Thirdly, overconfidence is prone to spike at a particularly inopportune moment for effective planning: the point at which war is first perceived as imminent. The Rubicon Model of Action Phases in psychology suggests that decision-making follows a series of distinct stages, each of which activates a particular mindset, or cognitive orientation. A 'deliberative' mindset dominates the pre-decisional phase, when different policy options are weighed. At this point, actors judge issues fairly objectively in a bid to make the best selection. An 'implemental' mindset dominates the post-decisional phase, when the focus shifts to enacting the selected option. Actors in an implemental mindset become committed to the chosen course of action and exhibit heightened levels of overconfidence. In the words of psychologists Heinz Heckhausen and Peter Gollwitzer, people become 'narrow-minded partisans of their plans of action'.[53]

Decision-making about war is therefore expected to follow the same sequence. When leaders believe that a war is possible but not certain, they will weigh the potential outcomes in a relatively wary manner. At this stage, planners may pay attention to worst-case scenarios, and vigorously debate the merits of different military options. But when war is seen as imminent, decision-makers will switch to an implemental mindset, which triggers overconfidence. They will worry less about the feasibility of the proposed strategy, and avoid making contingency plans for possible failure. Instead, planners will strongly support the chosen course of action, and focus on taking the initial steps in the plan for victory.[54]

The switch to an implemental mindset may have influenced US war plans. In 1999, when the prospects for an invasion of Iraq were uncertain, Zinni's war game examined the challenges of post-conflict stabilisation in a cautious manner. Washington's 1998 plan for the invasion of Iraq, OPLAN 1003-98, called for the use of 400,000 troops.[55] But, in 2002, when a conflict seemed inevitable, US war games exhibited overconfidence about the campaign, and planners dramatically scaled down the size of the invasion force.[56]

Aversion to nation building

The second dynamic that inhibits effective US planning for the endgame of war is a cultural aversion to nation building. America's public, political leaders and military are all sceptical about using force for stabilisation operations, including counter-insurgency and peacekeeping.

Public support for nation-building missions is consistently lower than that for interventions aimed at checking the aggression of foreign states.[57] Whereas Americans tend to view conventional inter-state wars (such as the world wars or the 1991 Gulf War) as righteous crusades, they often see nation-building operations (such as those in Vietnam, Somalia and post-2003 Iraq) as grim quagmires.[58]

In part, public scepticism stems from Washington's very real struggles with nation building. But the public often disapproves of nation building even when the mission succeeds, as shown by its response to the peacekeeping missions in Bosnia and Kosovo during the 1990s.[59] Such operations lack the 'good-versus-evil' moral clarity of many inter-state wars, and dredge up painful memories of Vietnam. Americans on the left sometimes see nation building as a dangerous form of imperialism, while those on the right often view it as the kind of nefarious social engineering associated with 'big government'.[60]

The US military also traditionally favours conventional inter-state war over nation building. Weigley wrote that the US repeatedly engaged in counter-insurgency campaigns but, each time it did, 'had to relearn appropriate tactics at exorbitant costs', and viewed the experience as 'an aberration that need not be repeated'.[61] Following the Vietnam War, the US Army decided that it would never fight guerrillas again, and went so far as to destroy its notes on counter-insurgency. American officials began planning incessantly for an inter-state showdown with the Soviet Union in Europe. After the Cold War ended, the US military continued to neglect nation building and counter-insurgency. Stabilisation missions were dismissed as 'military operations other than war', or MOOTWA. One chairman of the joint chiefs of staff reportedly said: 'real men don't do mootwa'.[62]

In 2007 Robert Gates, then secretary of defence, said that, after Vietnam, 'the Army relegated unconventional war to the margins of training, doctrine, and budget priorities'. As a result, 'it left the service unprepared to deal with the operations that followed: Somalia, Haiti, the Balkans, and more recently Afghanistan and Iraq – the consequences and costs of which we are still struggling with today'.[63]

This aversion to nation building can impede effective planning for the endgame of war. The desire to avoid stabilisation operations may promote the vision of war as a target set designed to eliminate enemy forces, rather than to create the conditions for ultimate political success. And, having neglected training for post-conflict operations and failed to learn the lessons of past counter-insurgency missions, the US military has reduced its ability to prepare for the consequences of regime change.

The George W. Bush administration, for example, came into office belittling nation building as armed social work and Clinton-style do-goodery. 'Let me tell you [what] I'm worried about', said Bush the day before the 2000 election. 'I'm worried about an opponent who uses "nation-building" and "the military" in the same sentence.'[64] Rumsfeld claimed that US nation-building missions, such as that in the Balkans, created a culture of foreign dependence. In their place, he advocated a model of US military 'transformation' based on agile, technologically advanced warfare and 'small-footprint' regime-change operations.

In both Afghanistan and Iraq, the Bush administration's aversion to nation building undermined planning for the endgame by encouraging the belief that extensive stabilisation operations would be imprudent and unnecessary. After overthrowing the Taliban regime in Afghanistan, the US resisted anything that resembled nation building. In 2002 only 8,000 US soldiers and 4,000 international troops were stationed in Afghanistan, a country then inhabited by more than 20m people. As a result, Washington failed to create an effective government in Kabul, and allowed the Taliban to recover.[65]

Similarly, American scepticism about nation building in Iraq was a major barrier to achieving long-term political goals. Bush sought to remove Saddam without getting bogged down in a drawn-out stabilisation operation. Rumsfeld consistently pressed for a reduction in US troop levels and a transfer of responsibility to the Iraqis, stating 'if you're not willing to take your hand off the bicycle seat, the person will never learn to ride.'[66]

The US military's aversion to nation building may also have eroded effective planning in Iraq. According to Conrad Crane, 'the American military would rather not deal with [stabilisation operations], or would like to quickly hand them off to other US government agencies or international organizations.'[67] Franks was scornful of the task of post-war stabilisation in Iraq. In April 2003, the military needed a name for the new combined joint task force that would oversee the stabilisation of the country. He suggested 'CJTF-1369, unlucky cocksuckers'.[68]

Optimism and scepticism

The interaction between a positivity bias (overconfidence) and a negativity bias (an aversion to nation building) may play a crucial role in explaining America's inadequate planning for endgames. An exaggerated belief in success combined with an allergy to stabilisation operations supports the vision of war as liberation, in which Phase IV operations will be relatively straightforward, the target population will yearn to be free and any prolonged US presence will be detrimental. In effect, scepticism about nation building channels overconfidence by promoting the belief that post-war stabilisation can somehow be circumvented. Officials therefore decline to explore the requirements of nation building in detail or consider how to handle negative scenarios, including those that involve sectarian tensions or a potential insurgency.

If either of these dynamics were missing, the same pattern of ineffective planning for the endgame might not be evident. Overconfidence without an aversion to nation building could cause positive illusions to take a different form, perhaps manifesting as the belief that a 'large-footprint' nation-building mission would succeed. Alternatively, scepticism about stabilisation operations without overconfidence could have deterred Washington from invading Iraq, out of fear that it would become bogged down in a protracted nation-building operation.

The synergy between overconfidence and scepticism about stabilisation operations led US officials to conclude they could achieve the best of both worlds, regime change and the democratisation of Iraq, without the need to tie down American troops in a lengthy nation-building mission. As Pickering said, the White House believed that 'military victory would produce its own rewards magically, out of the clouds'.[69]

Reverse-engineering victory

There is no simple solution for a problem caused by deep-rooted psychological and cultural factors. Instead, a number of complementary approaches might be attempted. Washington could set up institutional structures that encourage critical debate about the endgame of war, for example, by creating a formal devil's advocate, or senior official tasked with criticising the proposed strategy and ensuring that a wider range of perspectives reach the president's ear.[70] Washington could also try to plan for conflict ahead of time, before it assumes an implemental mindset in which overconfidence is likely to skew decision-making.

Furthermore, Stavridis stated: 'we should do more deliberate planning for potential failure' by systematically studying past debacles.[71] This advice echoed the review of US Army education in 1971:

> A strong element of every curriculum should be historical studies which frankly analyze unsuccessful American military efforts … [including] an objective discussion of what we did, what went wrong, and why. This single action would do more to establish credibility for our instruction than any other known to me.[72]

Washington also needs to think more creatively about the endgame. The traditional way to plan for the final stage of a conflict is to engineer victory by identifying national goals and then creating a road map that details the route towards this end state. In a regime-change mission, officials can move progressively from Phase I to Phase IV.

An alternative approach is to reverse-engineer victory, by working backwards from Phase IV. Cuban chess player José Raúl Capablanca once said: 'in order to improve your game, you must study the endgame before everything else, for whereas the endings can be studied and mastered by themselves, the middle game and the opening must be studied in relation to the endgame.'[73] Capablanca's strategy was to work backwards from checkmate and then secure a small positional edge early on – say, three pawns to two on one side of the board – that ultimately proved decisive.

Working backwards from success is an established idea in other domains as well. One of the principles of game theory is 'backward induction', or starting out with the final move, then looking at the next-to-last decision and so on, before finally discovering what you should do at the beginning. Similarly, the first step in building a house is to create a blueprint by imagining the completed structure and then working backwards from the final stage.

War, of course, is very different to chess, simple game-theory models or construction. But the same core advice holds true: the opening and intermediate stages of a military campaign should be studied in relation to the endgame. Several analysts have briefly noted the potential for working backwards in wartime planning. A RAND study of the Iraq War suggested in passing that

> planners must start with strategic guidance from the civilian leadership on where they want to be, strategically, when the war ends. They can then work backward to points of major conflict, shaping plans for those in ways that contribute to the larger and longer-term strategic goal.[74]

Gideon Rose also noted in passing that, instead of thinking forward from Phase I to Phase IV, we should 'reverse the direction of the sequence'. According to Rose, 'this easy fix would focus attention on the desired end result as the starting point for all war planning, with the earlier stages understood as having significance only as building blocks of or preparatory stages for the final outcome.'[75]

Although not quite an 'easy fix', reverse-engineering victory holds considerable promise as a tool of military planning. Planners should first visualise the desired end state in as much detail as possible, asking 'what is America's geographic area of control?'; 'what does the target country's political system and economy look like?'; and 'what is the timeframe for achieving these goals?' Before invading Iraq, Washington might have outlined a plausible conception of the country as a reasonably democratic and stable ally by, say, 2006.

Planners can then work backwards from this future vision in stages, breaking down the path into short-term actions and milestones. With Iraq, Washington could have planned for the intermediate stages, such as overseeing elections, creating effective security forces and so on – always specifying which American assets needed to be in place at particular points in time, and how they should be used.

Washington cannot script the entire campaign

Reverse-engineering victory requires analysts to ask many of the same questions that they would for a traditional, forward-looking plan, such as 'what are the respective strengths of the combatants?'; 'what is each side's potential for mobilising resources?'; and 'what role will external actors play?' Crucially, the vision of a path back from the end state is a creative thought exercise rather than a precise route to be followed. Washington cannot script the entire campaign, nor follow the proposed course precisely. Intelligence on the target country may be limited. The fog of war, unexpected events and the enemy's response all create added uncertainty. And the objectives of each side often change during the fighting, according to the fortunes of war.

But the exercise of reverse-engineering victory offers several valuable benefits. Firstly, it encourages planners to focus on the ultimate political objective. Strategy is about efficiently working towards clear goals, or knowing the destination before the journey begins. With traditional attempts to engineer victory, the present is cast in bright light while the end state is usually murky. Planners are therefore tempted to prioritise the initial steps that can be clearly identified, and to hope that everything works out in the end. By contrast, reverse-engineering victory encourages officials to illuminate the finale by imagining it in detail. The approach is therefore an antidote to short-termism. It habituates planners to thinking about ultimate strategic success, and not just about victory in individual battles.

For example, in both Iraq and Afghanistan, there should from the start have been a broader central goal: the creation of a reasonably stable and representative regime. If this had been the focus from day one, the Bush administration might have provided additional resources for post-war stabilisation, or even avoided war in Iraq altogether.

Secondly, reverse-engineering victory can mitigate the effects of overconfidence. The exercise provides a reality check by encouraging planners to think more critically about whether their objectives are feasible, and, if they are, the concrete steps needed to achieve them. As seen in Iraq and Afghanistan, post-war stabilisation may be the most difficult phase of a campaign. Placing the greatest barriers to success at centre stage could reduce the odds of positive illusions.

The tendency to create a mental construct of the future based on wishful thinking (as described in construal level theory) may also be reduced by reverse-engineering victory. The process encourages actors to map out the construct in greater detail, thereby contextualising the endgame, and making it less vague and abstract. It may also help to guard against the negative effects of an implemental mindset by preventing actors from simply ignoring questions of how ultimate success will be achieved.

Thirdly, reverse-engineering victory can alleviate problems caused by an aversion to nation building. The exercise encourages planners to think carefully about what is truly required for post-war stabilisation. Working backwards might have produced more detailed and precise thinking about the nature of the post-Saddam Iraqi government.

The notion of 'Phase IV' promotes the idea that stabilisation efforts are a distinct and secondary endeavour that occurs after the main fight. Efforts to create order and governance, however, should begin as soon as the first shot is fired. Douglas Feith, under-secretary of defence for policy at the time of the Iraq invasion, recognised a 'major error' in that 'across the board, administration officials thought that postwar reconstruction would take place *post* – that is, after – the war.'[76]

Reverse-engineering victory can limit this problem by promoting the perception of war fighting and stabilisation as intertwined activities. By working backwards, planners may recognise that major combat operations are a building block in achieving their ultimate political goals. Phase III (major military acts) is viewed not as a successor to Phase II (initial operations to seize the initiative), but in terms of how it facilitates Phase IV (post-combat stabilisation).

Fourthly, the exercise can reveal unexpected obstacles, challenges or opportunities. Working backwards may show that it is fairly straightforward to identify certain steps, such as implementing a plausible timetable for elections during the stabilisation phase. Before the invasion of Iraq, for example, planners could have recognised that, in order to install a representative government in Baghdad by the end of 2006, the country would need to hold national elections in 2005. And the process may identify steps that are hard to plan for with any confidence, such as building regional political support for a new government. These uncertainties should then be factored into the decision of whether to wage war.

Reverse-engineering victory may also indicate that a seemingly inconsequential move early in the campaign could turn out to be critical later on. By working backwards from a representative government in Iraq, planners might have found that allying with a minor local leader in the immediate aftermath of regime change would have ultimately reaped a dividend as the political arena opened up.

The exercise is more or less speculative depending on the length, complexity and difficulty of the military campaign. In a fairly straightforward operation, officials may be able to follow the broad contours of the proposed road map with some confidence. The US typically outmatches its opponents in military power and can often expect the opening rounds of a conflict to go relatively smoothly. When fighting powerful opponents, or in conflicts involving extensive post-war stabilisation, the steps will be more problematic to map out precisely. But, in such scenarios, the exercise remains important – indeed, it may be more important – in terms of identifying potential challenges and uncertainties.

Traditional forward-looking planning and reverse-engineering victory are complementary tools. Together, they create two paths: from the origin to the destination, and from the destination to the origin. Comparing and integrating the two routes may reveal the optimum course. Washington may even use the 'red team, blue team' approach by setting up independent groups to think forward to victory, and backwards from victory. Once the two paths have been created, they can be integrated into the final war plan.

* * *

Despite its vast intelligence and military resources, the US has struggled to master the endgame of war. Overconfidence and an aversion to nation building have combined to promote a short-term mentality that downplays preparations for the finale of conflict. This combination of beliefs is likely to shape future military campaigns. Positive illusions are an integral part of human psychology, and may be particularly prominent among Americans. An aversion to nation building is also deeply embedded in broader American culture, and is evident today in the Obama administration. In 2012 the Pentagon announced: 'U.S. forces will no longer be sized to conduct large-scale, prolonged stability operations.'[77] Obama's 'pivot' from the Middle East to the Asia-Pacific is really a turn away from nation building in places such as Iraq, and towards inter-state rivalry with opponents such as China.

One solution to America's endgame problem is to reverse-engineer victory, by identifying the conditions for ultimate political success and then working backwards from the end state. This exercise forces planners to look at the military campaign from a new angle. It encourages officials to ask difficult questions, and spurs imaginative thinking. It also provides a test of the proposed use of force. If the process of creating a plausible path from the end state is too difficult, policymakers may need to rethink the whole endeavour.

Of course, reverse-engineering victory could itself succumb to the biases of overconfidence and an aversion to nation building. But the exercise may be less prone to these problems than alternative planning tools. Starting at the end places the stabilisation phase front and centre, and encourages greater consideration of what is truly required in terms of nation building.

In working backwards, planners should not embrace rigid long-term thinking. Attempting to follow a fixed path regardless of the changing environment will invite disaster. War is a collision between opposing forces and rarely follows a simple script. Military policy will need to be adapted as conditions change. The path backwards will not be the war plan, but it can inform the war plan. By balancing long-term planning with short-term flexibility, the US can avoid leaping into the dark.

Acknowledgements

The author would like to thank Ryan Grauer, Dominic Johnson, Amy Oakes and Aaron Rapport for their helpful comments.

Notes

1 Fred Charles Iklé, *Every War Must End*, Second Edition (New York: Columbia University Press, 2005), p. 4.

2 Ian Kershaw, *Fateful Choices: Ten Decisions that Changed the World, 1940–1941* (New York: Penguin, 2007), pp. 352–3.

3 Iklé, *Every War Must End*.

4 Conrad C. Crane, 'Phase IV Operations: Where Wars are Really Won', *Military Review*, vol. 85, no. 3, May–June 2005, p. 11.

5 Carl von Clausewitz (Michael Howard and Peter Paret, eds and trans), *On War* (Princeton, NJ: Princeton University Press, 1976), p. 584; Gideon Rose, *How Wars End: Why We Always Fight the Last Battle* (New York: Simon & Schuster, 2010).

6 B. H. Liddell Hart, *Strategy*, Second Edition (New York: Meridian, 1991), p. 353.

7 Henry A. Kissinger, 'Henry Kissinger: To Settle the Ukraine Crisis, Start at the End', *Washington Post*, 5 March 2014, http://www.washingtonpost.com/opinions/henry-kissinger-to-settle-the-ukraine-crisis-start-at-the-end/2014/03/05/46dad868-a496-11e3-8466-d34c451760b9_story.html.

8 On exit strategies see Iklé, *Every War Must End*; Rose, *How Wars End*; Richard Caplan (ed.), *Exit Strategies and State Building* (New York: Oxford University Press, 2012); and David M. Edelstein, 'Exit Lessons', *Wilson Quarterly*, vol. 33, no. 4, Autumn 2009, pp. 34–9. On war termination, see Elizabeth A. Stanley, *Paths to Peace: Domestic Coalition Shifts, War Termination and the Korean War* (Stanford, CA: Stanford University Press, 2009); and H.E. Goemans, *War and Punishment: The Causes of War Termination and the First World War* (Princeton, NJ: Princeton University Press, 2000).

9 Bradford A. Lee, 'Winning the War but Losing the Peace?: The United States and the Strategic Issues of War Termination', in Bradford A. Lee and Karl F. Walling (eds), *Strategic Logic*

and Political Rationality (Portland, OR: Frank Cass, 2003), p. 265.

10 Russell F. Weigley, *The American Way of War: A History of United States Military Strategy and Policy* (New York: Macmillan, 1973). See also Crane, 'Phase IV Operations'.

11 Frederick W. Kagan, 'War and Aftermath', *Policy Review*, August–September 2003. See also Emile Simpson, *War from the Ground Up: Twenty-First Century Combat as Politics* (Oxford: Oxford University Press, 2012).

12 US Central Command, 'Desert Crossing Seminar: After Action Report', 2 July 2004, http://www2.gwu.edu/~nsarchiv/NSAEBB/NSAEBB207/Desert%20Crossing%20After%20Action%20Report_1999-06-28.pdf.

13 Leslie Evans, 'Straight Talk from General Anthony Zinni', UCLA International Institute, 14 May 2004, http://www1.international.ucla.edu/article.asp?parentid=11162.

14 *Ibid*. See also Roger Strother, 'Post-Saddam Iraq: The War Game', National Security Archive, 4 November 2006, http://www2.gwu.edu/~nsarchiv/NSAEBB/NSAEBB207/index.htm.

15 Huba Wass de Czege, 'Wargaming Insights', *Army*, March 2003, pp. 36–44, http://www3.ausa.org/webpub/DeptArmyMagazine.nsf/byid/CCRN-6CCS7T?OpenDocument&Print=1; Fred Kaplan, *Daydream Believers: How a Few Grand Ideas Wrecked American Power* (Hoboken, NJ: John Wiley & Sons, 2008), pp. 47–8; Fred Kaplan, *The Insurgents: David Petraeus and the Plot to Change the American Way of War* (New York: Simon & Schuster, 2013), pp. 59–60.

16 Eliot A. Cohen and John Gooch, *Military Misfortunes: The Anatomy of Failure in War* (New York: Free Press, 2006), p. 38.

17 Wass de Czege, 'Wargaming Insights'.

18 Julian Borger, 'Wake-up Call', *Guardian*, 6 September 2002, http://www.theguardian.com/world/2002/sep/06/usa.iraq.

19 Sean D. Naylor, 'War Game Rigged?', *Army Times*, 16 August 2002; Fred Kaplan, 'War-Gamed', *Slate*, 28 March 2003, http://www.slate.com/articles/news_and_politics/war_stories/2003/03/wargamed.html.

20 Thomas E. Ricks, *The Generals: American Military Command from World War II to Today* (New York: Penguin Press, 2012), pp. 400–1.

21 Interview with Thomas Pickering, 3 January 2014.

22 Isaiah Wilson, 'America's Anabasis', in Thomas G. Mahnken and Thomas A. Keaney (eds), *War in Iraq: Planning and Execution* (New York: Routledge, 2007), p. 13.

23 Donald P. Wright and Timothy R. Reese, *On Point II – Transition to the New Campaign: The United States Army in Operation IRAQI FREEDOM, May 2003–January 2005* (Fort Leavenworth, KS: Combat Studies Institute Press, 2008), p. 142.

24 Stephen Benedict Dyson, 'What Really Happened in Planning for Postwar Iraq?', *Political Science Quarterly*, vol. 128, no. 3, Autumn 2013, pp. 455–88; Nora Bensahel et al., *After Saddam: Prewar Planning and the Occupation of Iraq* (Santa Monica, CA: RAND Corporation, 2008).

25 Aaron Rapport, 'The Long and

Short of It: Cognitive Constraints on Leaders' Assessments of "Postwar" Iraq', *International Security*, vol. 37, no. 3, Winter 2012–13, p. 148.

26 Ivo H. Daalder and James M. Lindsay, *America Unbound: The Bush Revolution in Foreign Policy* (Washington DC: Brookings Institution Press, 2003), p. 151; David L. Phillips, *Losing Iraq: Inside the Postwar Reconstruction Fiasco* (Boulder, CO: Westview, 2005), pp. 131, 138; Bensahel et al., *After Saddam*, pp. xxii, 17, 60–3.

27 Dyson, 'What Really Happened in Planning for Postwar Iraq?', p. 469.

28 Wilson, 'America's Anabasis', p. 11.

29 Tommy Franks, *American Soldier* (New York: Harper Collins, 2004), pp. 440–1; Rose, *How Wars End*, p. 3; Bob Woodward, *Plan of Attack* (New York: Simon & Schuster, 2004); Dyson, 'What Really Happened in Planning for Postwar Iraq?'.

30 Rapport, 'The Long and Short of It', p. 158; Michael R. Gordon and Bernard E. Trainor, *Cobra II: The Inside Story of the Invasion and Occupation of Iraq* (New York: Pantheon Books, 2006), p. 161; Bob Woodward, *State of Denial: Bush at War, Part III* (New York: Simon & Schuster, 2006), pp. 130–6.

31 Woodward, *State of Denial*, pp. 149–50.

32 Anthony H. Cordesman, 'Planning for a Self-Inflicted Wound: US Policy to Reshape a Post-Saddam Iraq', Center for Strategic and International Studies, 31 December 2002, http://www.comw.org/warreport/fulltext/0212cordesman.pdf.

33 Bensahel et al., *After Saddam;* David A. Lake, 'Two Cheers for Bargaining Theory: Assessing Rationalist Explanations of the Iraq War', *International Security*, vol. 35, no. 3, Winter 2010–11, pp. 7–52; Gordon and Trainor, *Cobra II*; George Packer, *The Assassins' Gate: America in Iraq* (New York: Farrar, Straus and Giroux, 2005); Phillips, *Losing Iraq*.

34 Special Inspector General for Iraq Reconstruction, *Hard Lessons: The Iraq Reconstruction Experience* (Washington DC: US Government Printing Office, 2008), pp. 323–4; Gordon and Trainor, *Cobra II*, pp. 142–50.

35 Interview with John Abizaid, 8 August 2013.

36 Dyson, 'What Really Happened in Planning for Postwar Iraq?', p. 478.

37 Joseph E. Stiglitz and Linda J. Bilmes, *The Three Trillion Dollar War: The True Cost of the Iraq Conflict* (New York: W.W. Norton & Co., 2008). For casualties in Iraq, see Iraq Body Count, http://www.iraqbodycount.org/.

38 For a discussion of this idea, see Richard K. Betts, *American Force: Dangers, Delusions, and Dilemmas in National Security* (New York: Columbia University Press, 2012), p. 243.

39 Rose, *How Wars End*, p. 2.

40 Rapport, 'The Long and Short of It', p. 164.

41 Dyson, 'What Really Happened in Planning for Postwar Iraq?'; Lee, 'Winning the War but Losing the Peace?'.

42 Bensahel et al., *After Saddam*, p. 239.

43 Thomas E. Ricks, *Fiasco: The American Military Adventure in Iraq* (New York: Penguin Press, 2006), p. 127.

44 Daniel Kahneman and Jonathan Renshon, 'Hawkish Biases', in A. Trevor Thrall and Jane K. Cramer, *American Foreign Policy and the Politics of Fear: Threat Inflation Since 9/11* (New

York: Routledge, 2009), pp. 79–96; Dominic Johnson, *Overconfidence and War: The Havoc and Glory of Positive Illusions* (Cambridge, MA: Harvard University Press, 2004); Shelley E. Taylor and Jonathon D. Brown, 'Illusion and Well-Being: A Social Psychological Perspective on Mental Health', *Psychological Bulletin*, vol. 103, no. 2, February 1988, pp. 193–210.

45 Geoffrey Blainey, *The Causes of War* (New York: Free Press, 1973), p. 35; Stephen Van Evera, *Causes of War: Power and the Roots of Conflict* (Ithaca, NY: Cornell University Press, 1999), p. 16.

46 US Department of Defense, 'Deputy Secretary Wolfowitz Interview with National Public Radio', 19 February 2003, http://www.defense.gov/transcripts/transcript.aspx?transcriptid=1937.

47 Ricks, *Fiasco*, p. 111.

48 Wolfgang Schivelbusch, *The Culture of Defeat: On National Trauma, Mourning, and Recovery* (New York: Picador, 2003), p. 6.

49 David A. Armor and Shelley E. Taylor, 'Situated Optimism: Specific Outcome Expectancies and Self-Regulation', in Mark P. Zanna (ed.), *Advances in Experimental Social Psychology*, Volume 30 (New York: Academic Press, 1998), p. 361; Johnson, *Overconfidence and War*.

50 Interview with James Stavridis, 16 September 2013.

51 Rapport, 'The Long and Short of It', p. 143.

52 Special Inspector General for Iraq Reconstruction, *Hard Lessons*, p. 31. In his study of military occupations, David Edelstein notes a consistent and often unwarranted degree of optimism about the likely success of nation building. David M. Edelstein, *Occupational Hazards: Success and Failure in Military Occupations* (Ithaca, NY: Cornell University Press, 2008).

53 Heinz Heckhausen and Peter M. Gollwitzer, 'Thought Contents and Cognitive Functioning in Motivational versus Volitional States of Mind', *Motivation and Emotion*, vol. 11, no. 2, June 1987, p. 103.

54 Dominic D.P. Johnson and Dominic Tierney, 'The Rubicon Theory of War: How the Path to Conflict Reaches the Point of No Return', *International Security*, vol. 36, no. 1, Summer 2011, pp. 7–40.

55 Strother, 'Post-Saddam Iraq: The War Game'.

56 It is hard to determine the exact point at which administration officials began to see war as certain, and to adopt an implemental mindset. In July 2002, Richard Haass, then the director of policy planning at the Department of State, realised that Bush had decided to confront Saddam. Nicholas Lemann, 'How It Came to War', *New Yorker*, 31 March 2003, http://www.newyorker.com/magazine/2003/03/31/how-it-came-to-war.

57 Bruce W. Jentleson and Rebecca L. Britton, 'Still Pretty Prudent: Post-Cold War American Public Opinion on the Use of Military Force', *Journal of Conflict Resolution*, vol. 42, no. 4, August 1998, pp. 395–417.

58 Dominic Tierney, *How We Fight: Crusades, Quagmires, and the American Way of War* (New York: Little, Brown and Company, 2010).

59 The US-led peacekeeping missions in the Balkans helped create reason-

able peace and stability in the region with no American casualties, but the US public remained sceptical. See Tierney, *How We Fight*, Chapter Eight.

60 *Ibid.*, Chapter Three.

61 Weigley, *The American Way of War*, p. 36.

62 James Traub, 'Making Sense of the Mission', *New York Times*, 11 April 2004, http://www.nytimes.com/2004/04/11/magazine/making-sense-of-the-mission.html; David Fitzgerald, *Learning to Forget: US Army Counterinsurgency Doctrine and Practice from Vietnam to Iraq* (Stanford, CA: Stanford University Press, 2013); Crane, 'Phase IV Operations', p. 17.

63 Speech Delivered by Secretary of Defense Robert M. Gates, Washington DC, 10 October 2007, http://www.defense.gov/speeches/speech.aspx?speechid=1181.

64 Terry M. Neal, 'Bush Backs into Nation Building', *Washington Post*, 26 February 2003.

65 David Rohde and David E. Sanger, 'How a "Good War" in Afghanistan Went Bad', *New York Times*, 12 August 2007, http://www.nytimes.com/2007/08/12/world/asia/12afghan.html.

66 Donald Rumsfeld, *Known and Unknown: A Memoir* (New York: Sentinel, 2011), p. 667; Linda Robinson, *Tell Me How This Ends: General Petraeus and the Search for a Way Out of Iraq* (New York: PublicAffairs, 2008).

67 Crane, 'Phase IV Operations', p. 12; Bensahel, et al., *After Saddam*, p. 48.

68 Rose, *How Wars End*, pp. 247, 268; Thomas E. Ricks, 'General Failure', *Atlantic*, 24 October 2012, http://www.theatlantic.com/magazine/archive/2012/11/general-failure/309148/4/.

69 Interview with Thomas Pickering, 3 January 2014.

70 However, the problem with a devil's advocate is that ritualised dissent may be discounted, and could even boost confidence in the original strategy by giving the impression that all options have been considered. An alternative idea is to form a 'murder board', or committee of notables tasked with finding flaws in a military plan and killing the idea. A single devil's advocate can be ignored; a whole choir of them is harder to disregard.

71 Interview with James Stavridis, 16 September 2013.

72 Cohen and Gooch, *Military Misfortunes*, p. 38.

73 Irving Chernev, *Capablanca's Best Chess Endings* (Oxford: Oxford University Press, 1978), p. v.

74 Bensahel, et al., *After Saddam*, p. 242.

75 Rose, *How Wars End*, p. 285.

76 Douglas J. Feith, *War and Decision: Inside the Pentagon at the Dawn of the War on Terrorism* (New York: HarperCollins, 2008), pp. 275–6; Bensahel, et al., *After Saddam*, p. xxviii.

77 US Department of Defense, 'Sustaining U.S. Global Leadership: Priorities for 21st Century Defense', January 2012, http://www.defense.gov/news/defense_strategic_guidance.pdf.

The Smart Revisionist

Jonathan Holslag

In what has become a tradition for new Chinese presidents seeking to confirm their peaceful intentions, Xi Jinping has put forward yet another ostensibly original security concept. Describing the approach as 'common, comprehensive, cooperative and sustainable', Xi has called on countries other than China to align their diverse security interests within a common project; avoid monopolising security affairs; work towards security without exclusive alliances; and tackle the full range of traditional and non-traditional threats.[1] In line with the new security concept of former President Jiang Zemin, and the idea of peaceful development espoused by his successor Hu Jintao, Beijing now cultivates the image of China as a status quo power that is restrained in its use of military force, willing to accept international norms and prepared to actively participate in international organisations. It also supports the notion of China as a constructive power that is inclined to cooperate and strike a compromise.

There is nothing new in Xi's security concept, however, and Chinese scholars have not reached a consensus in the renewed debate about grand strategy. The praise for Beijing's forward-looking leadership and ability to pursue such a strategy is therefore misplaced. Under previous leaderships, China was reactive rather than proactive, in both economic and security affairs. Beijing managed to be flexible, and to adjust without having to compromise on the four great aspirations that it had pursued since 1949. But it

Jonathan Holslag is Professor of International Politics at the Free University of Brussels.

Survival | vol. 56 no. 5 | October–November 2014 | pp. 95–116 DOI 10.1080/00396338.2014.962802

was the security environment that changed first, not China. This strategy of adaptation has been remarkably successful. Beijing has acquired military capabilities far stronger than those of its neighbours, while provoking only limited resistance. The true bearing of its great aspirations is increasingly clear: to fulfil them, China must become the most powerful country in Asia by far, and attain the power to deter other protagonists by force. The chance that its peaceful rise will continue is therefore small. Either China's growth will run into trouble or it will become harder to maintain the peace.

Rejuvenation

Most generations of Chinese leaders have come up with a new security concept. The approach of Mao Zedong and Zhou Enlai revolved around the five principles of peaceful coexistence. Among them, sovereignty, equality and mutually beneficial cooperation were a reflection of communist China's needs as a juvenile state, and an expression of its aversion to the meddling of the two superpowers. Deng Xiaoping complemented this with the insistence that territorial disputes were to be shelved to let cooperation in other areas progress; Taiwan and the mainland were to work towards a solution involving 'one country, two systems'; states were to focus on economic development instead of military power; and a harmonious neighbourhood was to be maintained to sustain China's rise. Even then, these ideas were not entirely new. Zhou and Mao had entertained them, but they became more feasible only in a later era. After Deng retired, the changes became increasingly modest. Jiang's generation further stressed the importance of international organisations and economic interdependence. Hu's peaceful development put more emphasis on global public goods and active participation in such groups. In keeping with these incremental steps, Xi's new security concept includes only minor innovations.

At the same time, there is no point of convergence in the debate among Chinese experts. Proposals for a more secure China sprawl in many directions. Peking University's Ye Zicheng described China's grand strategy as essentially the pursuit of sustainable development, and the establishment of a harmonious society and world, peaceful relations with neighbours and a normal relationship with the United States.[2] Duan Peijun, professor at the

Central Party School of the Communist Party of China, argued that the main objective of the grand strategy was to deploy Chinese resources efficiently in order to build a well-off society.[3] To Yu Zhengliang of Fudan University, it was more about devising a foreign policy that would mount an effective challenge to the US. Yu argued that China's foreign policy had to maintain its focus on Asia, then aim to establish a quasi-alliance with Russia, before expanding its influence in South America and Canada, and, finally, strengthening its position in the Middle East, Africa and Europe.[4] Yuan Peng, vice-president of the China Institute of Contemporary International Relations, insisted that grand strategy largely remained a matter of bolstering 'hard power', and was similar to a national-security strategy. He also stated that the foremost objective of the leadership was to create a well-off society by the centenary of the People's Republic, in 2049.[5] Zhu Feng of Peking University claimed that China needed a grand strategy mostly to advance its core interests. 'A peaceful rise', he wrote, 'does not blindly reject the legitimate use of force, but stresses that China not seek to change its structural position in the international system by force.'[6] A comprehensive discussion of grand strategy was undertaken by Men Honghua, another scholar at the Central Party School. He described it as the application of economic, military and cultural resources in pursuit of *fanwei he kongjian* (a larger development space) around China, Asia-Pacific leadership and a means to avoid international isolation. In the end, he asserted, China had to be able to fight several major powers at once.[7] For Hu Angang and Yan Yilong, scholars at Tsinghua University, China had to focus on its core interests and 'the great rejuvenation'. It should, they argued, develop an alternative to the United States' 'big stick' strategy – one that would revolve around peace, harmony, order and, preferably, the 'Chinese Dream'.[8]

Circumstance, not vision

There seem to be as many Chinese strategies as there are scholars discussing them. To some, China's strategy remains an economic one essentially focussed on rebalancing the domestic economy and improving industrial competitiveness. To others, it centres on the pursuit of esteem and 'soft power', as well as the promotion of the Chinese Dream. Still another group contends that China's current security strategy revolves around the development of great-power relations – that is, a new modus vivendi among the world's most influential states based on a recognition of China as one of them, along with mutual respect, military restraint and pragmatic coordination.

Although the contemporary debate cannot reveal much about China's security concerns and objectives, history can. In fact, China's most important aims have been clear since 1949. The first objective has been sustained control of strategic frontier lands such as Yunnan, Tibet, Xinjiang, Inner Mongolia, and so on. Officially, that has been achieved, but, in reality, these areas remain restive. The second goal has been to reinforce the position of the Communist Party at the centre of modern China by maintaining security, bringing back stability and promoting growth. The third aim has been to attain respect for China's sovereignty: on paper, by gaining diplomatic recognition; in practice, by resisting the interference of other great powers. The final objective has been to recover so-called 'lost territory': Taiwan, the disputed islands in the South China Sea, a large part of the East China Sea and areas of contested borderland in the Himalayas.

China has moved from one excess to the other

These goals have been remarkably static during the past 65 years, running as a red line through most Chinese policies. Yet the policies themselves, and the ways in which China has coordinated its use of resources, have been dynamic, even erratic. China's leadership is often credited with possessing great visionary qualities in its use of economic resources. But the reality is more complicated. The first Five-Year Plan led to excessive dependence on the Soviet Union, which supplied most of the technological know-how that Beijing required and financed 4% of China's official budget.[9] The second major reform was the Great Leap Forward, which ended in disaster. The third was one of import substitution, which caused large trade deficits (by 1984, the trade deficit in capital goods was equal to 170% of China's GDP).[10] That was followed by opening up, which led to an uncomfortable dependence on foreign investors. The fifth reform was, accordingly, an effort to develop national champions as an alternative, but the vast investments in industry this required made China more dependent on exports.[11] This was followed by a policy of aggressive financial support for exports. As a result, in 2013, foreign loans (to allow other countries to purchase Chinese products) and export-tax rebates equalled 3.4% of China's GDP.[12]

It is unclear what the next stage will be. The government promises yet another rebalancing, this time away from exports and investments, and towards consumption. But whether this will work remains to be seen. The slowdown of 2013–14 has not been accompanied by a rebalancing.[13] China's economic policies have thus moved from one excess to the other, a pattern that was not always anticipated. In the mid-1980s, for example, the party leadership came to the conclusion that the first stage of the opening-up had led to excessive dependence on Japan. As Vice-Premier Li Peng put it, 'China should rely mainly on its own products instead of importing large amounts of equipment.'[14] By the late 1990s, the leadership had concluded that the effort to persuade foreign companies to produce more inside China had important downsides, and that Chinese companies were increasingly outmatched by their competitors. This realisation led Beijing to call for the creation of '30–50' large state companies able to compete with foreign giants.[15]

Similarly, it would be hard to describe China's foreign policy of recent years as a proactive shift towards integration with global society. Since the early 1970s, China has indeed been eager to strengthen its relations with the rest of the world, in search of diplomatic recognition, economic opportunity, security and status. But it often leant against an open door, as the rest of the world tried as least as hard to strengthen ties with China. Consider Japan in the 1960s: Tokyo was almost desperate to develop relations with Beijing, despite China's revolutionary turmoil. Even before the dust settled and the pro-Soviet camp of Lin Biao disappeared, Washington spearheaded rapprochement via Secretary of State Henry Kissinger's secret diplomacy with Beijing. Subsequent diplomatic progress facilitated American overtures to Southeast Asian countries and a rapprochement with South Korea. The problem of the Soviet Union resolved itself. The federation's decay in the 1980s allowed Beijing to extract humbling concessions from Moscow, such as the withdrawal of troops from Mongolia. It only had to wait for the collapse to turn the tables completely. In all these developments, other states took the initiative, something that was also true for China's accession to regional organisations such as the Association of Southeast Asian Nations (ASEAN), the Asia-Pacific Economic Cooperation forum and the Asian Development Bank. In the 1980s, it was ASEAN that invited China to participate in trade fairs and, later, a greater level of political dialogue.

However tempting it is to regard China's integration with the rest of the world as a product of its proactive leadership, this is not the case. The evolution of Chinese military posturing has not been different in that regard. Chinese leaders' concern about overburdening the economy with large military budgets was present from the start. Important party members warned that intervention in the Korean conflict could further weaken China. One year into that war, Mao considered pulling his troops back, but was overruled by Moscow. In subsequent armed conflicts (with Taiwan, India and the Soviet Union), Beijing consistently tried to avoid long, escalating confrontations. The government was ultimately allowed to trim the military budget – from official spending levels of more than 10% of GDP in the 1960s to around 2% in the last two decades – by the change in its security environment: improving relations with the US, the concomitant assurances about Taiwan, the weakening and collapse of the Soviet Union, and so on.[16] This trend occurred despite a rapid rise in personnel costs and the fact that the military also had to relinquish many of its most treasured assets, which ranged from hotels to arms factories. Military doctrines also adjusted to revolutions in warfare spearheaded by the two superpowers. So too did the scope of Beijing's military aspirations. Even if Mao had already insisted that China become a naval power, the country's navy was only deployed on an important mission when expanding maritime trade made this necessary. As had happened with most trading powers in the past, the flag followed trade. Mission creep rather than grand strategy shaped the behaviour of the People's Liberation Army.

Flexibility without compromise

For all the attribution of visionary and forward-looking qualities to Beijing, China has been more reactive than proactive. Yet it reacted in a way that allowed for deeper integration with the international community, changed

Chinese society and led to important adjustments in its norms and standards. China shifted from ideological radicalism to political pragmatism. It changed from offensive struggle to defensive military restraint. It moved from the sidelines of international organisations to the centre stage. There is no denying that China has become more peaceful, cooperative and constructive as an international actor. And the price that it had to pay was modest. Beijing managed to adjust without having to compromise on its four central aspirations. It made some concessions on less important disputed regions, such as the mountainous areas also claimed by Central Asian countries and small parts of the land border with Vietnam and Myanmar. On all the important contested territories, however, it did not budge an inch. Border negotiations with India remain deadlocked. A swap of the eastern sector, called Arunachal Pradesh, for the western sector, named Aksai Chin, would be beneficial to both sides, but China continues to stick to its claim over both parts, does not want to compromise over smaller areas in the central sector and continually pushes for the maximal interpretation of the Line of Actual Control, even where historical borders are not clearly defined. Beijing has taken a similar position on the South and East China seas. Its claims have not changed for decades, with the possible exception that some Chinese officials seem to have replaced the infamous 'nine-dashed line' in the South China Sea with a slightly more nuanced delineation of the exclusive economic zone around some of the larger islands, a definition that still asserts Chinese control over most of the waters.

The same is true with regard to arms-control and security issues. For example, China has signed up to, and abided by, the nuclear Comprehensive Test-Ban Treaty.[17] But, like other states, it has done so without giving up its ability to continually improve its nuclear weapons. In fact, the treaty has been a major incentive for China to develop more advanced simulation programmes, and to thereby improve its capacity to build a more powerful nuclear deterrent. China has also joined the Non-Proliferation Treaty.[18] From the available information, it appears that it has put a brake on the export of nuclear-weapons systems, even to Pakistan. It has thus adjusted, but this came only after the most critical know-how had been delivered to its three strategic partners: North Korea, Pakistan and Iran. Having done so, it became reluctant to join Western countries in pressuring these states to relinquish their nuclear-weapons programmes. In the case of Pakistan, it went on to supply significant dual-use technology for civilian power plants that are being developed by Chinese contractors. This is not to say that China is alone in such a practice, but it does mean that Beijing's signature on the Non-Proliferation Treaty should not be regarded as an important gesture of adjustment. China has also signed up to agreements with Southeast Asian countries to promote peace and stability, such as the Declaration on the Conduct of Parties in the South China Sea (in 2002) and the Treaty of Amity and Cooperation in Southeast Asia (in 2003). The country has shown restraint in the use of its military since signing these accords, but has merely continued a trend apparent since the end of its 1988 naval battle with Vietnamese forces over Johnson South Reef in the Spratly Islands.[19] At the same time, Beijing has shown its resolve in different ways, sending in constabulary agencies, deploying an oil rig, and keeping its rapidly expanding and modernising Southern Fleet at hand primarily to display Chinese power. The sheer size of China's naval build-up, however, and its increasingly robust naval exercises reveal a widening gap between the promise of restraint and the power of its capabilities.

China's integration with the global trade regime came with painful economic reforms, but led to unparalleled gains in revenue, technology, experience and access to foreign markets. Since its accession to the World Trade Organization (WTO) in 2001, China has effectively lowered most of its tariff barriers.[20] However, it has gone on to support its exports in different ways: by preventing the rapid appreciation of its currency, encouraging the transfer of trillions of dollars from Chinese households to the corporate sector, and handing out hundreds of billions of dollars more in export credit and tax rebates. Technically, it is hard to see these policies as a violation of the international trade rules that China signed up to. Moreover, Chinese officials correctly state that other major countries also intervene in trade through financial and industrial policy. China has thus turned to free trade without compromising its industries, and is taking an offensive interest in promoting free trade to advance its exports. Beijing is also gradually gaining the confidence to go beyond the current rules of the WTO. It has, for instance, proposed a new trade agreement with ASEAN states that would liberalise investment rules and the services market.[21] It can afford to do so because it has become stronger, and it is the strong that profit from free trade.

Nor has membership of regional organisations constrained Beijing's freedom of action when defending its interests. China has joined a growing number of such groups, actively participated in their meetings, proposed new initiatives on security and trade, and even invested in their institutional capacity. So, if membership and participation are the benchmarks, China has again adjusted. But this has not forced it to compromise on its four great aspirations. In fact, it has helped to advance them. The cover of regional organisations, such as ASEAN and the Shanghai Cooperation Organisation, has allowed China to mitigate the distrust of its smaller neighbours; promote its trade interests; develop some military confidence-building measures; push initiatives to combat piracy and terrorism further up the agenda; and still play on the divisions between other members when they attempt to form a front against Beijing. In this way, it has deflected criticism of its allegedly unfair competitive practices and South China Sea policies through ASEAN, and warded off complaints about its construction of a dam on the Mekong River via the Asian Development Bank's Greater Mekong Subregion programme.[22] China's behaviour in the last few decades could therefore be described as 'flexibility without compromise'.

Beijing is gradually gaining confidence

Beijing's acceptance of some international organisations and increased cooperation with other countries does not mean that it accepts the global order. The repercussions of the four strategic aspirations, the core of its grand strategy, remain that it has to profoundly change the international order and thus the distribution of power. Control over its frontier lands has already allowed China to secure huge resources in terms of population, energy, farmland, fresh water, and more. Together, these make China's potential for power larger than that of other major Asia-Pacific states, such as India and Japan. The party's desire to maintain control by turning China into a high-income country implies that its economy must become larger than all others, and that it must acquire even more resources.[23] Japan would be dwarfed by such growth. Only India has the demographic potential to match China, but it lags way behind economically, and many of its natural resources are smaller. China will require greatly strengthened economic power to fulfil its fourth aspiration: the recovery of lost territory. Given the resolve of other Asian countries to stick to their claims, the reunification of the motherland ultimately requires China to be able to win wars with its neighbours, eventually even those allied with the US. Beijing's grand strategy might resemble that of a status quo power, but the attainment of its great aspirations will inevitably require that it change the structure of the Asian order, become the largest power in the region and gain the ability to shape the behaviour of its neighbours.

Success

It is a misconception that revisionism concerns only military aggression or efforts to destroy the existing order of international relations, institutions and rules. In essence, revisionism is a desire to change the international order, which has implications for the distribution of power. Such a stance creates a situation in which the conservative interests of the incumbent powers, the status quo countries, are as much of a problem as the ambitions of the revisionist. China has been a revisionist power in a status quo guise. Its great aspirations demand that it revise the structure of the regional order. It is hard to blame China for having this goal. Its attempts to become a rich country are understandable, as are its efforts to control the frontier lands. They reflect a desire for restoration and security. Yet the search for security is a search for power. Even though Beijing's claim on almost all of the South and East China seas is more difficult to justify, its claims on various islands often make as much sense as those of other countries. But the prospect of a China that towers above the rest of Asia is frightening. A pre-eminent China would challenge the privileges of the strong, particularly Japan and the US, and become more able to shape the terms of interaction with weaker states. The Chinese leadership has been aware of that dilemma since the outset. Mao reassured Asia that China would never become a hegemonic power. Deng even proclaimed that, were China to gain such ambitions, other countries would have the right to overthrow it. At the same time, Mao and Deng still seemed to surmise that China would face more resistance as it grew, and that conflict would merely be postponed.

That uncertainty has never entirely disappeared. Jiang spoke of a period of strategic opportunity that China had to seize in order to grow.[24] He and other politicians of the third generation also stressed the global trend of peace and cooperation, yet confirmed China's persistent concern about the intentions of the US; the privileges of the West in terms of wealth and the capacity to set international norms; and the revolutions in military affairs. The fourth generation put even greater emphasis on a peaceful rise and, indeed, used it as the central narrative of its foreign policy. Under Hu and Prime Minister Wen Jiabao, Beijing seemed almost to assume that it could win the battle without fighting, and fulfil its great aspirations simply by surmounting resistance with trade. They continued to refer to major strategic uncertainties and challenges, but their pledges to peace became even more unwavering and were accompanied by equally energetic participation in a sprawl of dialogues and exchanges.

The claim of a peaceful rise often seemed to be so pervasive that officials came to believe in it themselves. It has been very difficult to measure this evolution accurately, of course, but many leaders gave the impression that they had indeed become acclimatised to the principles of peace and cooperation. State Counsellor Dai Bingguo, for instance, could be very firm in negotiations, but relentlessly sought options to diffuse tensions and prevent stalemates. Wen made it his trademark to launch emotional pleas for cooperation, both in public and in private. The foreign minister of the time was almost the embodiment of mild-mannered diplomacy. Young diplomats often seemed to be genuinely convinced that China had it right and was earnest in its peaceful intentions, but also that interlocutors in Tokyo and Washington did not always understand the country.

China's peaceful rise of recent decades has been self-made. It has become routine to praise Beijing's achievement of lifting hundreds of millions of citizens out of poverty. That accomplishment is even more remarkable in light of China's environment. In 2000 the country generated 14% of Asia's GDP and had 37% of its population.[25] In 2012 those proportions had changed to 37% and 35% respectively. This period saw a rise in per capita GDP of 9% in

China, and 5% in Asia as a whole. China's exceptional gains were even more obvious in trade. In 2000 it accounted for 12% of Asia's exports. By 2012 this figure had reached 36%.[26] This still masks the fact that China focused on increasing its share in manufacturing. In 2012 it generated 41% of exported manufactured goods and 52% of exported, labour-intensive manufactured goods – the kinds of products that developing countries need to produce in order to trigger labour-intensive growth.[27]

China did all that while continuing to enjoy peace. The last soldier to die on a Chinese border was an Indian guard who lost his way in the Himalayan mist in 1989.[28] Even if the US continued to show resolve in protecting its interests, none of the other Asia-Pacific powers resorted to military force to stop China's rise, or to oppose its territorial claims. At the same time, China's own military capabilities expanded rapidly. Its share of Asian defence spending increased from 4% in 1990 to 35% in 2013.[29] The country's official defence expenditure is now by far the largest of any Asian state, and is only slightly less than that of Japan, India and South Korea combined.[30] This has resulted in larger investments in human resources, with troops receiving higher salaries and better training.[31] It has also allowed for larger investments in equipment. In 2013, China spent an estimated $56–60bn on military research, development and acquisition.[32] At the beginning of the century, China relied entirely on imports for advanced weapons; 13 years later, it had indigenised the development and production of most key systems and, importantly, subsystems such as engines, sensors, data links and missiles. China commissioned more fighter jets, navy ships and military satellites than all of its neighbours put together.[33] As a result, Beijing could dramatically increase its military presence along its border and in adjacent seas. Its armed forces have also gained the ability to raise the costs for its challengers, probably enough to gain the upper hand in short conflicts with Taiwan and other neighbours over the South China Sea.

The smart revisionist

China's rise has been revisionism at its best: assiduous and efficient instead of noisy and antagonistic. But the contradiction between its revisionist ambitions and promises of harmony remain obvious. What, then, explains the lack of a challenge to its ascent? On the one hand, this has followed from the leadership's success in making strategic choices and responding to domestic and international changes. The focus on economic growth proved the most efficient way to fulfil its four aspirations, and Beijing has found a formula for making rapid gains. It opened its huge labour reservoir to foreign investors and subsequently transferred a large part of its incomes into public infrastructure, industrial capacity, strategic assets abroad and bonds in important consumer markets. It also struck a balance between economic nationalism and globalism. Foreign investors were welcomed, but Beijing made sure that their know-how was transferred to national companies and that those firms retained their market share. The benefits of this approach could be seen between 2003 and 2012, during which time the share of foreign-owned industries in China's output and profits shrank back to 23%.[34]

This success has also allowed Beijing to cultivate economic expectations in other countries. China has presented itself as an investment opportunity, an emerging investor and, thanks to its middle class, a growing market for exports. At the same time, however, it has pushed many of these countries into large trade deficits and the role of raw-materials supplier. In 2003, 119 of China's 174 trade partners had a trade deficit with the country; this figure had risen to 123 by 2013.[35] Raw materials accounted for 78% of their exports to China in 2003, and 86% in 2013.[36] These unequal trade relations were managed by efficient economic diplomacy, which cultivated relations with the domestic interest groups that gained from the trade: mostly large companies invested in China, raw-materials suppliers and governments given various forms of credit to purchase Chinese goods and services. In 2013 China's distributed external credits and loans worth more than $165bn.[37]

Beijing adopted a discourse of mutual gain, but made sure that the benefits it received were greater. True, its citizens made an important financial sacrifice by lending vast sums to export markets, in the form of export credit and purchases of government bonds, but this was expected to enhance China's market share and competitiveness in the long run. Credit always came with an important condition: access. As with many other Chinese economic policies, there was a false perception of generosity in this approach. In free-trade negotiations with other Asian states, few of China's concessions affected its own exporters. In accepting international rules, it always made sure that they did not imperil the country's vital interests. The accommodations Beijing made in negotiations over land borders were very small and often even misleading, certainly in comparison to its tough position on more important claims in adjacent seas and on the contested border with India. Equally, codes and declarations designed to restrain the use of military force in these areas were never allowed to curb the manoeuvrability of the People's Liberation Army.

Beijing also managed to strike a balance between hard and soft power. Most of the time, China robustly countered the behaviour of other states that could harm its great aspirations. As a result, there were moments when it was perceived as unconstructive, assertive or aggressive. But Beijing often prevented the growth of that perception. Again, this was a matter of sham concessions, that is limited gestures that did not affect its important interests. It was also a matter of communication. In many tense situations, China offered to set up official dialogues, working groups and confidence-building initiatives, which, in turn, resulted in new discussions and measures but seldom produced genuine solutions to important problems. Furthermore, when confronted on territorial, security or commercial quarrels, China proved adept at setting the resolute parties against less determined stakeholders.

However, the particular nature of China's security environment was at least as important as the alleged ingenuity of its grand strategy. A study of the deepening relations between China and the rest of the world reveals that many diplomatic breakthroughs were initiated not because of Beijing's initiative but due to the policies of the other party. That was the case with Japan's pragmatic attitude during and after the Cultural Revolution; the US in the run-up to the diplomatic revolution of 1971; the overtures of many Southeast Asian countries after that event; and the humbling concessions made by the Soviet Union in the decade before its collapse. The idea that China engaged with the world is mistaken. Most of the time, it was the world that came to China.

It was also important that China's neighbours did not yet face an inescapable choice between resisting Beijing or joining it, between balancing or jumping on the bandwagon. Therefore, the Asian strategic landscape remained too multipolar. Despite the cultivation of economic expectations, in 2013 China accounted for only 15% and 11% of its neighbours' exports and foreign stock investments respectively. For most countries, there were thus still enough opportunities to diversify economic relations. Similarly, China's 2013 defence budget only accounted for 16% of Asian defence spending when Russia and the US were counted as powers in the region.[38] As a result, there was not yet a major threat emanating from China's military modernisation, particularly while the US maintained its military dominance of the Asia-Pacific. This is probably one of the reasons that China has recognised Washington's stabilising role; as Wang Yiwei put it, 'the challenge of Chinese foreign policy in the future is to avoid American decline from happening too fast.'[39]

China has also benefited from the divides within and among other Asian states. Within countries, Beijing has been able to balance different economic interest groups, and has had the opportunity to play off China-friendly parts of the political elite against Sinophobic nationalists and others. Beijing has ruthlessly exploited splits between other Asian states on issues such as territorial disputes and trade relations. And there has been an inevitable misalignment of security concerns among countries close to China and those farther away. This has allowed Beijing to step up its cooperation with capitals outside of Asia when tensions rise in its neighbourhood, and to thereby retain a degree of manoeuvrability.

Dilemmas

If China has been successful in advancing its interests, this is because it has prioritised economic growth, proven able to avoid conflicts without making large concessions and, most of all, enjoyed a security environment that allows for sufficient manoeuvrability. But it has not yet attained its objectives, and there are several indications that the easy part of China's rise might be over. Firstly, there has been a decline in economic growth, profit margins, the performance of stock markets and consumer confidence. Despite Chinese officials' claims to the contrary, slowing growth is not the result of efforts to make development more durable. Again, there has been a slowdown without a rebalancing. The share of China's GDP allocated to investments has continued to increase, at the expense of consumption, and many of these investments are troubled. The spree of investment in urban real estate has outpaced the rate at which people have settled in Chinese cities. The rise in manufacturing investment has outstripped domestic demand. And the industrial sector's dependence on exports grew from 13% in 2003 to 34% in 2013.[40]

This trend is of huge importance to China's economy. The trade surplus in manufactured goods accounted for 11% of China's GDP in 2013, up from 4% in 2003.[41] As a result, the Chinese government is set to introduce many new policies to offset the impact of rising wages on the competitiveness of its labour-intensive factories, shift manufacturing to more advanced industries, and support exporters with measures that range from export credit to exchange-rate intervention. However, this comes at a moment when its trade partners expect it to trim surpluses. Large Asian economies such as India, Indonesia, Japan and Russia have all expressed their frustration about the imbalance in trade relations. Between 2009 and 2013, neighbouring countries imposed 95 new anti-dumping duties that affected China, 34 of which were specifically aimed at Beijing.[42]

China's leaders are under greater pressure

China's leaders are under greater pressure to share the benefits of the country's growth, not only from their own citizens but also from other states. This tension manifests itself in a much more complicated political climate. Many of China's neighbours are plagued by social uncertainty, growing public dissatisfaction with governance and dwindling political trust. As a result, some of these states hover between increasing electoral fragmentation and a new enthusiasm for strong, populist leaders. Fragmentation can provide Beijing with an opportunity to play on the internal divisions to assert its interests, but populist leadership has certain disadvantages, especially when it coincides with increasingly negative perceptions of China.

The latter dynamic is particularly apparent in the governance styles of Japanese Prime Minister Shinzo Abe, Indian Prime Minister Narendra Modi and Philippine President Benigno Aquino III. These leaders not only show a greater tendency to balance against China, but also to push it back in territorial disputes. Banking on strong public support, Abe has done everything he can to counter China's growing presence around the Senkaku/Diaoyu Islands, and threatened to expel any Chinese force that lands there. His administration has accelerated programmes to boost Japanese military capabilities in the East China Sea. In the run-up to the 2014 Indian elections, Modi frequently railed against Chinese expansionism and swore that he would not 'bow down' to China in the dispute over Arunachal Pradesh, stating that 'I swear in the name of this soil that I will never allow the state to disappear.'[43] Campaign or no, Modi's stance set the markers for a tougher policy. Aquino has gone to great lengths to resist Beijing's ambitions in the South China Sea and internationalise the dispute over the Spratly Islands, and has announced $1.8bn in defence spending to 'resist bullies entering our backyard'.[44] It remains to be seen whether these leaders will be able to balance Chinese power effectively, but their intention to do so has certainly become more pronounced.

China also faces growing challenges in Taiwan. The more Taiwan and the mainland increase their economic cooperation, official exchanges and contact between citizens, the less the Taiwanese support reunification. Polls conducted by the Taiwanese Mainland Affairs Council showed that, between 2003 and 2013, support for independence grew from 16% to 19%, and support for an indefinite status quo rose from 17% to 24%. During the same period, the share of Taiwanese respondents who thought that cross-Straits relations had developed too fast went up from 23% to 33%.[45] Many Chinese experts have described Taiwan's student-led Sunflower Movement as a purely internal problem involving frustrated youngsters. However, the group's spring 2014 protest against a new trade deal with the mainland was one of the first such large-scale rallies in a long time, and sparked criticism within the Democratic Progressive Party about its new tendency towards moderation in relations with Beijing.

Resistance to Chinese plans for the recovery of lost territory is thus growing, and coincides with more assertive balancing efforts among many of China's neighbours. These states have also become more determined to weave a web of security partnerships around China. At least 20 new defence agreements were signed between 2009 and 2013, a period in which concerns about China's alleged military assertiveness grew quickly. Vietnam stood at the centre of many of these arrangements, negotiating ten new military-cooperation accords, while Japan and South Korea signed five each. Most of these new plans focused on maritime security, and several were accompanied by statements of concern about tensions in the South China Sea. This evolution was highlighted by the fact that China only concluded one defence agreement (with Indonesia) during this period.

There is growing reason to doubt the effectiveness of peaceful development as a policy in service of China's four great aspirations. Firstly, development itself is becoming much more uncertain, as the leadership struggles to address imbalances in the economy. Secondly, it is progressively less likely that Beijing's unshakeable desire to reunify the motherland will be fulfilled in a peaceful way. Two decades of growing economic cooperation have not erased distrust between China and its neighbours, several of which have an increasingly negative attitude towards Beijing. In the same vein, the approach of shelving territorial disputes and increasing the Chinese presence in disputed areas has not lessened the resistance or resolve of other claimants. In light of all this, a situation is arising in which Beijing is expected to make more concessions to show its benign intentions just as it becomes less willing to do so, and in which China is perceived as a growing threat just as it increasingly sees its neighbours in the same way. The future of China's peaceful rise will depend not only on whether its neighbours act assertively, but also on Beijing's ability to keep a cool head in response to the trend towards balancing.

Will China falter?

The only fixed aspects of China's foreign policy are its four great aspirations, and Beijing's eagerness to pursue them. Everything else has continually changed: the way in which resources have been deployed in pursuit of these aspirations, and in which the leadership has sought to coordinate their use, both at home and abroad. Peace is not the crux of Beijing's strategy. Of course, China would benefit from a rise that did not require it to expend resources on costly wars, but it would be wrong to conclude that Beijing has made major concessions to maintain the peace. The cooperation that developed in recent decades resulted more from the desire of other countries to establish closer relations with China than from Beijing's diplomatic overtures. In border negotiations, international organisations and economic-reform initiatives, the Chinese government has always been rather successful in preventing concessions that would imperil its great aspirations.

Now, there is gradually rising tension between these aspirations and the ideal of fulfilling them without a fight. Indeed, the more China grows, the less its central aims seem compatible with a peaceful rise. The main point is that, if China already has a grand strategy, it is a revisionist one. Whatever adjustments Beijing makes to its policy tools and stratagems, the effect of fulfilling its great aspirations would be to fundamentally change the international order by making China the most powerful country in Asia. That does not bode well for most of its neighbours, nor for rival Asia-Pacific powers such as the US. Such a change would inevitably entail a weakening of their position, privileges and security, and would make it far harder for them to defend their territorial claims in disputes with Beijing. China's dominance of Asia would force them deeper into the kind of unequal economic partnerships increasingly prevalent today.

China's revisionism is not some evil scheme rising from the deep caverns of the Communist Party. Many of its aspirations are understandable, and resemble those that other rising powers have held. But the fears of other countries are equally justified, and the resulting rise in tension has more and more in common with the preludes to great-power conflicts of the past.

Notes

1 Xi Jinping, 'Jiji Shuli Yazhou Anquan Guan Gong Chuang Anquan Xin Jumian', speech at CICA Summit, 21 May 2014, http://www.mfa.gov.cn/mfa_chn/zyxw_602251/t1158070.shtml.

2 Ye Zicheng (ed.), *Inside China's Grand Strategy: The Perspective from the People's Republic* (Lexington, KY: University Press of Kentucky, 2010).

3 Duan Peijun, 'Zhanlue Dao Da: Zhanlue De Shiye Bianhuan', *Guanmin Ribao*, 26 June 2012.

4 Zhengliang Yu, 'Guanyu Zhonggguo Dazhan Lue De Sikao', *Quishi*, 13 July 2013.

5 Yuan Peng, 'Xin Shiqi Zhongguo De Da Zhanlue', *Xiandai Guoji Guanxi*, no. 5, 2013, pp. 1–9.

6 Zhu Feng, 'Weihu Hexin Liyi Jidai Wai Jiaoda Zhanlue', *Remin Lutan*, 18 September 2012.

7 Men Honghua, 'Guanyu Zhongguo Dazhan Lue De Lixing Sikao', *Aisi Xang*, 8 March 2014.

8 Hu Angang and Long Yanyi, 'Zhongguo Dazahan Lue: Tongchou Liang Ge Daju Yu Tianshi Dili Renhe', *Renmin Ribao*, 30 June 2013.

9 CIA, 'Economic Intelligence Report No. 75', 1959, p. 3.

10 UN Comtrade Database, http://comtrade.un.org/db/.

11 In 2013 the trade surplus in manufactured goods accounted for 13% of China's GDP. UNCTAD database, http://unctadstat.unctad.org/wds/ReportFolders/reportFolders.aspx?sCS_ChosenLang=en; World Development Indicators database, http://databank.worldbank.org/data/views/variableSelection/selectvariables.aspx?source=world-development-indicators.

12 State Administration of Foreign Exchange database, available at http://www.safe.gov.cn/wps/portal/english/.

13 'Report on the Work of the Government', speech delivered by Li Keqiang, Beijing, 14 March 2014, http://news.xinhuanet.com/english/special/2014-03/14/c_133187027.htm.

14 Yong Deng, 'Chinese Relations with Japan: Implications for Asia-Pacific Regionalism', *Pacific Affairs*, vol. 70, no. 3, Autumn 1997, p. 379.

15 'All Strength to China's Industrial Sector', Reuters, 5 July 2001.

16 David Shambaugh, *Modernizing China's Military: Progress, Problems, and Prospects* (Berkeley, CA: University of California Press, 2002), p. 184.

17 Wendy Frieman, *China, Arms Control, and Non-Proliferation* (Abingdon: Routledge for the IISS, 2004), pp. 38–61.

18 *Ibid.*, pp. 7–38. See also Yuan Jingdong, 'China's Pragmatic Approach to Non-Proliferation Policy in the Post-Cold War Era', in Suisheng Zhao (ed.), *Chinese Foreign Policy: Pragmatism and Strategic Behavior* (New York: M.E. Sharpe, 2003), pp. 151–79.

19 Ralf Emmers, *Cooperative Security and the Balance of Power in ASEAN and the ARF* (Abingdon: Routledge, 2003), pp. 12–138.

20 Hui Feng, *The Politics of China's Accession to the World Trade Organization: The Dragon Goes Global* (Abingdon: Routledge, 2005).

21 China Institute for Reform and Development, 'Jiakuai Dazao Zhongguo Dong Meng Zi Mao Ou Shengji Ban', *Xinhua*, 27 February 2014.

22 Selina Ho, 'River Politics: China's Policies in the Mekong and the Brahmaputra in Comparative Perspective', *Journal of Contemporary China*, vol. 23, no. 85, 2014; Sebastian Biba, 'China's Continuous Dam-building on the Mekong River', *Journal of Contemporary Asia*, vol. 42, no. 4, 2012.

23 The World Bank defines a high-income country as one in which gross national income per capita exceeds $12,745. World Bank, 'Country and Lending Groups', http://data.worldbank.org/about/country-and-lending-groups.

24 Wang Jisi, 'China's Search for a Grand Strategy', *Foreign Affairs*, vol. 90, no. 2, March–April 2011.

25 China also had 35% of Asia's labour force. World Development Indicators database.

26 UNCTAD database.

27 *Ibid.*

28 'India Closes Most Roads to Nepal in Trade Dispute', Reuters, 26 March 1989, http://www.nytimes.com/1989/03/26/world/india-closes-most-roads-to-nepal-in-trade-dispute.html.

29 Author's calculations based on Stockholm International Peace Research Institute Military Expenditure Database, available at http://www.sipri.org/research/armaments/milex/milex_database.

30 IISS, *The Military Balance 2014* (Abingdon: Routledge, 2014).

31 Zhou Yang, 'E Chen Zhongguo Wangpai Feixingyuan Nian Fei Xiaoshi Shijie Jiliu', *Huanqiu Ribao*, 13 January 2014; 'Meiti: Chen Wo Kongjun Feixingyuan Nian Feixing Xiaoshi Shu Da 200 Jiejin Meijun', *Xinhua*, 7 February 2012.

32 Tai-Ming Cheung (ed.), 'The Chinese Defence Economy Takes Off', University of California Institute on Global Conflict and Cooperation, pp. 78–81, http://www-igcc.ucsd.edu/assets/001/504355.pdf.

33 Author's calculation based on IISS, *The Military Balance 2014*.

34 National Bureau of Statistics of China database, http://www.stats.gov.cn/english/statisticaldata/AnnualData/.

35 UNCTAD database.

36 *Ibid.*

37 State Administration of Foreign Exchange balance of payments database, http://www.safe.gov.cn/wps/portal/english/Data/Payments.

38 Author's calculations based on Stockholm International Peace Research Institute Military Expenditure Database.

39 Howard W. French, 'A Voice of Dissonance on American Decline', *International Herald Tribune*, 14 September 2006, http://www.nytimes.com/2006/09/14/world/asia/14iht-letter.2811843.html.

40 Author's calculation based on World Bank, World Development Indicators database, available at http://data.worldbank.org/data-catalog/world-development-indicators. (Industrial-export dependence calculated by dividing the trade surplus of manufactured goods by total manufacturing output.)

41 *Ibid.*

42 World Trade Organization anti-dumping database, http://www.wto.org/english/tratop_e/adp_e/adp_statindex_e.htm.

43 'Modi in Arunachal: China Should Shed Expansionist Mindset', *Times of India*, 22 February 2014, http://timesofindia.indiatimes.com/india/Modi-in-Arunachal-China-should-shed-expansionist-mindset/articleshow/30844702.cms.

44 'Manila Boosts Military to Resist "Bullies" as Ties with Beijing Sour', Agence France-Presse, 21 May 2013, http://www.scmp.com/news/asia/article/1242849/philippines-boosts-military-resist-bullies.

45 Mainland Affairs Council, Republic of China (Taiwan), 'Unification or Independence?', http://www.mac.gov.tw/public/Attachment/41161531382.gif; Mainland Affairs Council, Republic of China (Taiwan), 'The Pace of Cross-Strait Exchanges', http://www.mac.gov.tw/public/Attachment/41161532124.gif.

Germany's Commercial Realism and the Russia Problem

Stephen F. Szabo

Russia's annexation of Crimea and its attempts to destabilise Ukraine resemble traditional geopolitics and have prompted references to a 'new Cold War', but this comparison overlooks the transformation in the nature of international affairs brought about by globalisation, and its implications for Berlin's relationship with other Western capitals, as well as Moscow. We are in an era of commercial realism, and Germany is the kind of prototypical geo-economic power that challenges the old type of military-based power embodied by the United States and Russia. Moscow's use of, and threat to use, military force in Ukraine are only part of the opening phase in a much longer game, one in which economic interdependence will be decisive. Not only have the West's assumptions about dealing with Russia been proven wrong, so has its conviction about where Germany will stand in this central challenge to the post-Cold War order in Europe. Berlin has been the key player in shaping Western policy towards Moscow, with some observers writing of a Russo-German Europe.[1] Washington and European capitals have increasingly relied on German Chancellor Angela Merkel to take the lead in mediation attempts with Russian President Vladimir Putin. The European sanctions regime that emerged in July 2014 was shaped by her leadership, after the destruction of Malaysia Airlines flight MH17 over Ukraine – an act widely blamed on Russian-backed separatists – spurred EU leaders to take a tougher stance with Moscow. Future European sanctions will only go as far as Berlin permits.

Stephen F. Szabo is Executive Director of the Transatlantic Academy, Washington DC, and the author of *Germany, Russia and the Rise of Geo-economics* (Bloomsbury, forthcoming in 2014).

Survival | vol. 56 no. 5 | October–November 2014 | pp. 117–128 DOI 10.1080/00396338.2014.962799

Germany's relationship with Russia is a case study in commercial realism, and has implications not only for its future role in Europe and beyond, but for the wider evolution of international politics. While not quite, 'it's the economy, Dummkopf', it comes close. Russo-German relations have been 90% economics, and driven by Germany's role as one of the world's leading exporters, yet one that is highly dependent on imports of natural resources, especially energy, to run its industrial-based economy. Developments in Ukraine may shift that calculation somewhat, but are unlikely to fundamentally alter the long-term nature of the relationship. Even if Russo-German relations do deteriorate, Berlin will continue to pursue a geo-economic policy with China and other emerging nations, which may be more important in terms of the future global order.

Germany has been an economic power since West Germany emerged from the ashes of the Second World War. Given both its newfound aversion to military force and that of its Western allies to a major German military role, Bonn's influence was exercised through the Deutschmark. This stood in marked contrast to London and Paris, which continued to emphasise military power that came to be anchored in their independent nuclear forces. West German economic diplomacy played a key role in the reunification of Germany and the country's development as Europe's pivotal power. But its growth as a geo-economic power was facilitated by the end of the Cold War. United Germany was not constrained by security dependence on the US, and markets in Eastern Europe were no longer off limits to German companies. The broader strategic dimension that had restricted the economic aspect of German policy was weakened. Following the departure of Russian forces from German soil, Berlin's defence budget was progressively reduced and the German private sector was allowed to develop further markets in Russia and China. Globalisation accelerated these trends. And Russia changed as well, developing a variant of a market economy that had many opportunities for German firms. Hundreds of thousands of Russians emigrated to Germany, and Russian energy companies became interlocked with German industry.

What is commercial realism?

Several traits define the commercially realist, or geo-economic, model of foreign policy.[2] Geo-economic powers define national interest largely in economic terms. This results in a move away from true multilateralism and towards a form of selective multilateralism, comprising bilateral approaches towards key economic partners. Business and finance, especially export-oriented commerce, play a dominant role in shaping foreign policy. Economic interests are given priority over others, such as the promotion of human rights and democracy. Finally, geo-economic powers use their economic influence as the principal means of imposing national preferences on other states.[3]

This type of power has caused a tectonic shift in German foreign policy, and has important implications. Firstly, it cedes overall grand strategy to business interests, especially those associated with the export market and natural resources, and reduces the role of political and administrative leaders in government. The model diminishes the influence of the Foreign Office and the Ministry of Defence, and enhances the power of the chancellor's office, the Ministry of Finance and the Ministry for Economic Affairs and Energy. The symbiosis between commerce and politics is deepened where German business has to deal with state-dominated economies, notably those of China, Russia and the Gulf states – all countries in which liberal commercial relations are not possible without political relationships. While Germany's trade with Poland, for example, is greater than that with Russia, economic relations with the latter have a qualitatively different political nature from those with open-market countries.

Secondly, a geo-economic approach clearly downgrades *Moralpolitik*, the concept of Germany as a normative power.[4] Berlin's reputation as a stable, reliable economic partner is paramount. In this sense, risk aversion, already a trait deeply embedded in German political culture, is reinforced, producing the '*Nein* nation', a Germany that increasingly says 'no' – to the US in Iraq, and to its European partners in Libya and Syria.[5]

Not only has the dependence of German security on the US greatly diminished, but the nature of hard security and of the military as an instrument of state influence has also been transformed. Despite Russia's actions in Ukraine, including its absorption of Crimea, German security policy will not be substantially altered. Defence spending will not be increased. When Minister of Defence Ursula von der Leyen suggested that NATO should provide more support to Alliance members who potentially faced Russian military aggression, she quickly had to pull back in the face of substantial resistance from the German public, parliamentarians and Vice-Chancellor Sigmar Gabriel, who criticised her for contributing to the escalation of tensions (although Gabriel later hardened his stance towards Russia, after the destruction of MH17). While Moscow's image has deteriorated a great deal, Russia is not regarded as a military threat by Germany's public or policymakers. The old roles of protecting the German homeland from invasion or of deploying forces for missions defined by NATO are clearly being downgraded by Berlin. Given the centrality of economic interests, especially trade, the military's primary role is to protect German access to raw materials, and to secure sea lines of communication and other key trading routes. In Edward Luttwak's formulation, 'methods of commerce are displacing military methods'.[6] While Germans can continue to comfort themselves that they are anti-militarist, even pacifist, and exceptional in their rejection of the use of military force à la the US, France and the United Kingdom, Germany's defence industry reaps the profits of being the world's third-largest arms exporter.[7] This is another change from the West German policy of limiting arms exports to regions troubled by conflict, especially the Middle East.[8]

Globalisation, with all of its broad implications, has reinforced these tendencies. Germany has begun to be pulled away from Europe as markets expand in Asia and elsewhere, and the European Union falters as a global competitor. In 2010, eurozone countries, including Germany, exported mostly to one another. By 2013, 60% of these exports left the common-currency area, including two-thirds of German exports.[9] Commercial networks are replacing state alliances in this new 'zero-sum world', in which competition for markets, technology and natural resources is accelerating, and emerging economies have a growing influence on German foreign policy.[10]

The Russian case

As Angela Stent observed in her recent study of US–Russia relations, Berlin and many other European capitals have more extensive economic ties with

Moscow than Washington does, and accordingly have a greater number of influential domestic stakeholders involved in these relationships.[11] Russo-German trade is worth more than €75 billion per year, with a German investment of around €19.5bn, and more than 6,000 German firms that have premises, in Russia. This is an exposure to Russia five times greater than that of American companies, which invest around $14bn in Russia annually, and export goods worth $11bn.[12] On the energy front, Germany receives more than one-third of its gas and oil from Russia, a share that was set to increase over the short-to-medium term in the wake of Merkel's decision to move away from nuclear power and towards renewable energy sources, the so-called *Energiewende*.[13] All of this has created a significant lobby of German businesses invested in Russia, including those represented by the influential Committee on Eastern European Economic Relations. The American equivalent, the US–Russia Business Council, is small by comparison, although firms such as Boeing, Exxon Mobil, General Electric and PepsiCo have substantial stakes in the Russian market. The organisation has met with US National Security Council staff, and individual companies have lobbied members of Congress and federal agencies, over their concerns about the sanctions, but on a much smaller scale than their counterparts in Berlin.[14]

Given that voters in Germany, like those in other Western countries, measure their government largely by its economic performance, all major German political parties have an electoral stake in good economic relations with Russia, on whose market more than 200,000 German jobs depend. An 8 August poll (taken after the loss of MH17) found that the number of Germans who supported sanctions on Russia had jumped to 70%. Still, only 49% said they would continue to back sanctions if the dispute were to have a negative effect on growth or jobs in Germany. The pollster, Richard Hilmer, concluded, 'the fact that almost 60% of people think Russia and Europe can be partners again in the long term shows there is still hope that conflict can be defused through diplomacy.'[15] It is crucial for an exporting power to maintain reliable lines of production and supply, and to be viewed by its suppliers and customers as a dependable partner that will not engage in sanctions and other forms of unpredictable behaviour. The imposition of sanctions on Russia was an important break with this tradition. Germany's dependence on imports of natural resources from countries with authoritarian and corrupt governments places real constraints on its role in promoting democratic reform and human rights.

In the case of Russia, there is an ongoing debate within Germany over the balance between values and interests, or 'silence for gas'.[16] This is an especially difficult issue for a country that overcame the legacy of the Nazi era by being a good global citizen and pursuing a foreign policy with strong normative overtones. German policymakers have tried to reconcile the tension between values and interests in Russia by stressing the legacy of Ostpolitik, the German version of detente and engagement with Moscow that Germans believe was key to the peaceful resolution of the Cold War divisions within Germany and Europe more widely. Frank-Walter Steinmeier spoke of a modernisation partnership with Russia in his first term as German foreign minister, from 2005 to 2009. His successor, Guido Westerwelle, made the case for *Wandel durch Handel* (change through trade). The German discourse on human rights and democracy in Russia intensified in the wake of three events: the rigged Russian parliamentary elections of December 2011, Putin's return to the presidency in 2012 and Moscow's domestic crackdown that followed the intervention in Ukraine. Yet the arguments about *Wandel durch Handel* and the need for continued engagement with Russia have prevailed, widening the gap between the prioritisation of the economic relationship and the public statements of Merkel, as well as those of others in her government and party.

Ukraine has pushed this tension to its limits, with Merkel delivering a number of tough speeches and warning Putin that his actions risk 'massive damage to Russia, both economically and politically'. While Germany was key to the EU's initial reluctance to impose sectoral sanctions, economic considerations also played an important role in the Russia policies of other European countries, including the UK (a magnet for rich Russians' money), France (whose sale of two *Mistral*-class amphibious assault ships to Moscow was not covered by the sanctions), Italy and the Netherlands. Facile comparisons with the Cold War ignore this geo-economic dimension, and disregard the new nature of the West's relationship with Russia and other economically important authoritarian states, such as China.

Beyond Russia

Overall, the German approach to Russia fits the geo-economic model, with the exception that Berlin did not use economic power to impose its preferences on Moscow until after the Ukraine crisis began. Even in this case, Germany was driven to impose sanctions by Russia's violation of the European security order and the downing of MH17, not by the state of authoritarianism in Russia. There was an unavoidable disruption of the overall strategic environment in Europe, one that directly threatened stability in the region.[17] If this approach is applied beyond Russia, Germany will continue to be driven by the economic interests that define its national interests.

The private sector will increasingly set the course that Germany takes in the world. Most studies of the evolving international system, including those by the US National Intelligence Council and the European Union Institute for Security Studies, conclude that corporations will play a larger role in a post-Westphalian world. As the latter organisation put it,

> non-state actors, in particular national and transnational civil society networks and private corporations, will play a critical role in the coming decades. Their power and influence will be greater than that of many states, and may lead to new forms of governance and civic action.[18]

This dynamic is particularly apparent in Germany because of the country's aversion to the use of force. Like military strength, however, economic influence is a form of 'hard power'. In the Second World War, Germany conquered Greece militarily, while today it influences key Greek economic, social and political decisions using its economic clout. There is certainly a qualitative and moral difference between the two approaches, but their effects are comparable.

Germany Inc. can have a global perspective and global relations, but can it have a foreign policy? Although Merkel has been justly criticised for her lack of strategic vision (in this, she is typical of most of the German political class), and despite the fact that German business leaders operate in a global environment every day, corporate chief executives rarely have a coherent and comprehensive view of the world. Joseph Nye has noted that economic power is difficult to wield on a global scale because the locus of decision-making is diffuse, at the level of firms and households.[19] While business leaders know what it takes to compete in a brutal global marketplace, their concerns are usually sectoral and limited. This is true despite the fact that many large firms adopt a long-term planning perspective. Daimler, Siemens and E.ON, for example, think at least ten years ahead – and an aircraft manufacturer such as Airbus considers the next 30 years. Equally, energy and infrastructure projects require huge investments with long-term returns. The exposure of firms to the world, in terms of their production and distribution chains (including the need to import almost all of their raw materials), makes them favour a careful approach: they create as few enemies as possible in order to maintain a reputation as a reliable business partner. Berlin has to prioritise business interests because of their centrality to election outcomes, and to Germany's international influence.

US–German tensions over Russia

Commercial realism has its limits. Germany has proven capable of acting against its short-term economic interests when they run up against sustained strategic concerns, as seen in its enforcement of Western sanctions on Iranian oil imports. However, this policy should be seen in light of several factors that do not apply to Berlin's relationship with Moscow: the negative image of Iran among the German public; the relatively small economic stake in relations with Tehran; anxiety about nuclear proliferation; and diplomatic pressure from Israel. Even so, American officials faced a hard slog in persuading their German counterparts to go along with the measures.

In the Ukraine crisis, Germany's commercial realism allows it only economic tools with which to respond to Russia's use of military power. Berlin's Russia strategy, like Washington's, is now in tatters. Both capitals will have to come up with new approaches. The discussion in the US seems to centre on those who favour a new containment strategy and an incremental, conditional approach to targeting the Russian economy, and those who would like to see a more aggressive sanctions policy, increased arms shipments to the Ukrainian government and further NATO deployments in eastern Poland and the Baltic states.[20] In Germany, a containment strategy and a shutdown in relations with Putin would be a non-starter not only because it would abandon the country's long-standing reluctance to use economic levers for political purposes in its dealings with other states, but also because of Russia's geographical proximity and the Ostpolitik legacy of engagement over confrontation. Some American policymakers are inclined to push Putin into a corner, in the hope that this will force him to give up on Ukraine, but this is not a viable option for their German counterparts. For Germany, Russia is not only a large neighbour, but a country in which its economic interests far outweigh those that it has in Ukraine. A settlement in Ukraine will require the Russians and the Germans to do all they can to prevent Putin from worsening the dilemma that he has created for himself.

Geo-economic Germany assumes that economics will trump the use of military force in the medium term, if not immediately, and that Russia's dependence on outside markets will eventually draw it back from further confrontation. While the German public and media are among Europe's most vocal critics of Putin, even surpassing those in Poland and the US, they also remain reluctantly realist on the use of sanctions, supporting the tough measures of July 2014 but fearing that they will harm the German economy.[21] Germany will continue to depend on Russian energy in the medium term, as neither American gas nor European resources can replace it for at least a decade. While there may be an adjustment to the *Energiewende*, it is unlikely that future German governments will reverse the move away from nuclear power as a means of lessening dependence on imports from Russia. Joe Kaeser, head of technology giant Siemens, told Putin of the firm's long-term commitment to investments in Russia in March 2014, the same month that US President Barack Obama travelled to Europe with the aim of persuading Merkel to support sanctions on Moscow. Gazprom remains on track to take over leading German gas-storage and -distribution company Wingas. It is significant that the sectoral sanctions were backed by the German business community, including the Committee on Eastern European Economic Relations and the Confederation of German Industry, but longer-term policy will be determined by the investment climate in Russia and Putin's actions in Ukraine. German firms will make every effort to limit the commercial damage, and will work with their Russian business partners to mend the relationship as soon as possible.

Merkel is also constrained by growing anti-Americanism in Germany that stems from the Snowden revelations and more recent disclosures about US spying in the country. Many Germans feel betrayed, and have lost faith in American policies. The depth of anger and mistrust is consistently underestimated in Washington, and makes it very difficult for Merkel to support Obama's approach to Moscow.[22] Despite the current unity on sanctions, there remains the prospect of a serious split between Washington and Berlin over Russia policy. During the Cold War, there were significant divisions over Soviet policy and detente, but West Germany always sided with Washington in the end because of the strategic imperatives that kept their disagreements in check. The first real sign of discord came in the debate over the US invasion of Iraq in 2003, when Chancellor Gerhard Schröder sided with Moscow and Paris against the George W. Bush administration. Schröder now sits on the board of Nord Stream, whose joint pipeline project with Gazprom was feted by Putin both as the Ukraine crisis loomed and after Crimea was annexed. Germans' frequent references to the events of 1914 in their discussion of the crisis reflect a concern that America will pull their country into an escalating conflict with Russia. This confluence of factors only increases the likelihood that commercial realism will continue to be the leitmotif of Germany's approach to Russia and other emerging powers, with unpredictable consequences for the German–American relationship.

Notes

1 Mitchell A. Orenstein, 'Get Ready for a Russo-German Europe', *Foreign Affairs*, 9 March 2014, http://www.foreignaffairs.com/articles/141018/mitchell-a-orenstein/get-ready-for-a-russo-german-europe.

2 'Commercial realism' is an adaptation of 'commercial realpolitik', a term developed by Rawi Abdelal in an unpublished paper written for Harvard Business School. Rawi E. Abdelal, 'The Profits of Power: Commercial Realpolitik in Europe and Eurasia', Harvard Business School, 20 September 2010, http://hbswk.hbs.edu/item/6505.html.

3 See Hans Kundnani, 'Germany as a Geo-economic Power', *Washington Quarterly*, vol. 34, no. 3, Summer 2011.

4 For more on Germany as a normative power, see Beverly Crawford, 'The Normative Power of a Normal State: Power and Revolutionary Vision in Germany's Post-Wall Foreign Policy', in Jeffrey Anderson and Eric Langenbacher (eds), *From the Bonn*

to the Berlin Republic: Germany at the Twentieth Anniversary of Unification (New York: Berghahn Books, 2010).

5 Abraham L. Newman, 'Flight from Risk: Unified Germany and the Role of Beliefs in the European Response to the Financial Crisis', in Anderson and Langenbacher (eds), *From the Bonn to the Berlin Republic*. A May 2014 survey found that some 60% of Germans preferred 'restraint' when it came to 'taking responsibility in international crises', compared to around 37% who favoured 'greater engagement'. This was a reversal of the results of 20 years earlier. See Körber-Stiftung, 'Die Sicht der Deutschen auf die Aussenpolitik', 6 May 2014; and Jochen Bittner, 'Wir Tun Doch Nix', *Die Zeit*, 1 April 2013, http://www.zeit.de/2013/13/Deutschland-Aussenpolitik.

6 Edward N. Luttwak, 'From Geopolitics to Geoeconomics', *National Interest*, no. 17, Summer 1990. For a broad survey of the concept, see Paul Aligica, 'Geo-economics as a Geo-Strategic Paradigm: An Assessment', *American Outlook Today*, 9 August 2002. In May 2010, then German President Horst Köhler stated in an interview that 'a country of our size, with its focus on exports and thus reliance on foreign trade, must be aware that ... military deployments are necessary in an emergency to protect our interests – for example when it comes to trade routes'. He was forced to resign in part because of these comments, which came too close to the truth. 'Controversy Over Afghanistan Remarks: German President Horst Köhler Resigns', *Der Spiegel*, 31 May 2010, http://www.spiegel.de/international/germany/controversy-over-afghanistan-remarks-german-president-horst-koehler-resigns-a-697785.html.

7 Stockholm International Peace Research Institute, 'The Top 20 Arms Exporters, 2009–2013', http://www.sipri.org/googlemaps/2014_of_at_top_20_exp_map.html.

8 This change was heavily criticised, and dubbed the 'Merkel Doctrine' in a December 2012 cover story in *Der Spiegel*. 'German Weapons for the World: How the Merkel Doctrine Is Changing Berlin Policy', *Der Spiegel*, 3 December 2012, http://www.spiegel.de/international/germany/german-weapons-exports-on-the-rise-as-merkel-doctrine-takes-hold-a-870596.html.

9 Claire Jones, 'Doubt Cast on German-led Exports Drive', *Financial Times*, 14 November 2013, http://www.ft.com/cms/s/0/24c28938-4d52-11e3-bf32-00144feabdc0.html#axzz3AMABMbQ7.

10 See Gideon Rachman, *Zero-Sum World: Politics, Power and Prosperity After the Crash* (London: Atlantic Books, 2010).

11 Angela E. Stent, *The Limits of Partnership: U.S.–Russian Relations in the Twenty-First Century* (Princeton, NJ: Princeton University Press, 2014), pp. 17–18.

12 Howard Schneider and Holly Yeager, 'U.S. Businesses Fear Russia Sanctions Could Put Billions at Risk', *Washington Post*, 8 March 2014.

13 Klaus Deuse, 'Just How Important is Russian Gas for Europe?', Deutsche Welle, 17 April 2014, http://www.dw.de/just-how-important-is-russian-gas-for-europe/a-17574004.

14 Schneider and Yeager, 'U.S. Businesses Fear Russia Sanctions Could Put

Billions at Risk'.

15 Harriet Torry, 'Germans Back Tougher Stance Toward Russia Over Ukraine – Poll', *Wall Street Journal*, 8 August 2014, http://online.wsj.com/articles/germans-back-tougher-stance-toward-russia-over-ukraine-poll-1407495865.

16 In the May 2014 survey, Germans said that the defence of human rights was the top priority of their country's foreign policy, and that the protection of economic interests abroad was the lowest, in stark contrast to the geo-economic nature of Berlin's actual approach. See Körber-Stiftung, 'Die Sicht der Deutschen auf die Aussenpolitik'.

17 Even in the Netherlands, which grieved over the loss of more than 150 Dutch citizens aboard MH17, there has been a clash between economic interests and support for the imposition of strong sanctions on Russia.

18 Alvaro de Vasconcelos (ed.), 'Global Trends 2030 – Citizens in an Interconnected and Polycentric World', European Union Institute for Security Studies, 27 April 2012, http://www.iss.europa.eu/publications/detail/article/espas-report-global-trends-2030-citizens-in-an-inter-connected-and-polycentric-world/. Anne-Marie Slaughter, former director of policy planning at the US Department of State, has also made this point: 'if you look at the role that companies are playing in the world … these are corporations that have to be part of the solutions of most of the top problems that are on the [US] secretary of state and president's list … Whether that is combating violent extremism, or climate change, or development of the global economy broadly, or global pandemics, those are not issues that can be solved only by governments … because they involve changing the individual behaviour on the ground. And who is on the ground? Well, foundations, [aid and advocacy groups] and corporations.' Shawn Donnan, 'Think Again', *Financial Times*, 8 July 2011, http://www.ft.com/cms/s/2/b8e8b560-a84a-11e0-9f50-00144feabdc0.html#axzz3AMABMbQ7.

19 Joseph S. Nye, Jr, *The Future of Power* (New York: PublicAffairs, 2011), p. 53.

20 Peter Baker, 'In Cold War Echo, Obama Strategy Writes Off Putin', *New York Times*, 19 April 2014, http://www.nytimes.com/2014/04/20/world/europe/in-cold-war-echo-obama-strategy-writes-off-putin.html.

21 Katharina Graça Peters, 'Umfragen zur Krim-Krise: Deutsche Zweifeln an Sanktions-Strategie', *Der Spiegel*, 20 March 2014, http://www.spiegel.de/politik/deutschland/umfragen-zur-krim-krise-deutsche-zweifeln-an-sanktions-strategie-a-959679.html.

22 Asked to identify the countries whose cooperation was most important to Germany, 61% of Germans named China, while 56% and 53% listed the US and Russia respectively. Körber-Stiftung, 'Die Sicht der Deutschen auf die Aussenpolitik'.

Italy's Forty Years' Crisis

Mark Gilbert

The era of Silvio Berlusconi is over. Italy will never again be represented on the world stage by an ageing businessman with a turbulent private life, a criminal record and pariah status among other European leaders. Power has passed into the hands of a kinetic young man with a pudding-bowl haircut, Matteo Renzi, whose self-proclaimed mission is to *rottamare* (junk) the old guard in Italian politics and to revive the country's institutions and economy.

Global markets have applauded Rome's change of tack. Italian government debt has become appetising again: helped by European Central Bank president Mario Draghi's promise to 'do whatever it takes' to prevent another sovereign-debt crisis in the eurozone,[1] the spread between German treasury bonds and their Italian equivalents has shrunk to 1.5 percentage points, enabling Italy to service its giant national debt more easily. The Italian stock market has also been on a roll: investors who bought blue-chip Italian companies at the end of last year have seen their portfolios increase by as much as one-third in 2014.

It is clear that Italian voters like Renzi. In May's European parliamentary elections, the Partito Democratico (PD), which Renzi leads, took 41% of the vote. One has to go back to the heyday of Christian Democracy (DC) in the 1950s to find a political party that commanded so large a segment of the electoral market. The PD's electoral success has earned Renzi kudos

Mark Gilbert is Professor of History and International Studies at SAIS Europe, the Bologna Center of the Paul H. Nitze School of Advanced International Studies, Johns Hopkins University.

Survival | vol. 56 no. 5 | October–November 2014 | pp. 129–142 DOI 10.1080/00396338.2014.962801

in Berlin and Brussels. Unlike French President François Hollande, whose Socialist Party was humiliated by the triumph of the Front National, or British Prime Minister David Cameron, whose coalition was thrashed by the United Kingdom Independence Party, Renzi took on anti-EU populists and won hands down. Comedian Beppe Grillo's 'Five Stars' movement (M5S) stalled at 21%, less than it gained in the landmark general election of February 2013. Berlusconi's Forza Italia recorded its worst share of the vote since the party was founded in 1994. Flushed with victory, Renzi claims that the time is ripe for a *governo del fare* (can-do government) able to implement sweeping reforms to the country's constitution, restructure its economy, and negotiate greater 'flexibility' in the austerity policies dear to Berlin and the European Commission. Italy took over the presidency of the EU in the second semester of 2014.

Yet a dose of healthy scepticism about Renzi's chances is in order. Like US President Barack Obama, Renzi has risen from relative obscurity to the top of national politics primarily because his undeniable rhetorical gifts have diffused fresh hope, first among the activists of his centre-left party and then more widely among voters disillusioned with the record of their rulers. But hope quickly turns sour when policy choices require painful change. Renzi might well prove to be an authentic leader capable of convincing Italians to accept unpopular choices. Certainly, beneath his undeniable charisma and external bonhomie lies a pronounced streak of ruthlessness. But he might also be no more than an 'institutional meteor' – the Italian label for politicians who briefly loom large in the public eye but then flare out upon contact with the unyielding atmosphere of Roman politics.

A sorry history

To understand Italy's present politics, one has to go back at least 40 years. In the mid-1970s, it briefly looked as though the Communist Party (PCI), led by Enrico Berlinguer, would overtake the DC to become the vital centre of the Italian political system. There were a number of reasons for the PCI's growth in support. Berlinguer was a moderate who was willing to support NATO. The DC, which had shown courageous leadership in the immediate post-war period, had degenerated by the mid-1970s into an agglomeration of warring factions unable to cope with the challenges thrown up by the country's passage to modernity. Many voters were willing to give the PCI a chance, rather than vote for the DC's venal style of government. Others, however, were still prepared to hold their noses against the stench of the DC's corruption and place a cross next to the same old names. Consequently, the DC won the 1976 elections with 38% of the vote, 4% more than the PCI. A government of 'national solidarity' was formed by DC boss Giulio Andreotti, with the PCI providing parliamentary support, but no ministers. (Washington was adamant that the PCI should not be trusted with executive power.) This so-called 'historic compromise' is relevant to contemporary Italian politics because it enabled the DC to defeat Red Brigade terrorism and survive the economic crisis of the 1970s without implementing major structural reforms to the country's economy and institutions, reforms that, even then, were badly needed. Italy continues to pay the price for this missed opportunity.

The PCI terminated the government of national solidarity in 1979. Its place as the DC's indispensable ally was taken by the Socialist Party (PSI), whose leader, Bettino Craxi, supported the siting of cruise missiles on Italian soil and became premier in June 1983. The DC and the PSI had the numbers to push through a platform of reforms. Instead, although Craxi talked the talk of a reformer, promising 'great reform' to the Italian state, he never walked the walk. The DC had no interest in changing a system that suited it, and both the PSI and Craxi personally soon learned to relish the perks of power.

What would a 'great reform' have looked like? Firstly, it would have meant constitutional changes to strengthen the powers of the government in Italy's bicameral parliamentary system. Secondly, it would have meant an electoral law that allowed voters to choose the government at the ballot box. Post-war Italy had a highly proportional electoral law that guaranteed a fragmented party system in which no one party could emerge triumphant. Voters cast their ballots and then the politicians haggled over the composition of the government and over which party (and which faction within the parties) would control the various *dicasteri*, or offices of state. Thirdly, a great reform would have attacked the worst abuses of patronage politics. In the 1980s, Italy's political parties held the country in an asphyxiating grip.

Their tentacles reached throughout the economy and society, with top jobs in state-owned companies, banks and cultural foundations being awarded only to individuals with political connections. RAI, the national broadcasting service, was a case in point: its three channels were explicitly shared out between the DC, the PSI and the PCI, and its news services broadcast overt propaganda on behalf of their political masters. RAI 2's promotion of a cult of personality around Craxi was reminiscent of the Eastern bloc, not of a modern, pluralist democracy.

Rather than embrace a reformist agenda, the PSI and the DC wasted the 1980s fighting an internecine war for greater power and patronage. Craxi's government (1983–87) was held hostage by the DC, and although the premier acquired a spurious reputation among sycophantic journalists for being a *decisionista*, he achieved little of substance. Successor governments headed by Giovanni Goria and Ciriaco De Mita, the DC's party secretary, were both sabotaged by Craxi's minions in parliament. A ceasefire was declared only in February 1989, when DC barons led by Andreotti ditched De Mita and came to terms with the PSI boss.

Berlusconi epitomised the epoch

What does all this have to do with Renzi and the challenges he faces today? The relevance of this history lies in the economic legacy bequeathed by the political parties' struggle for popularity and power. The single largest factor conditioning Italian politics today – the debt trap into which the country has fallen – was created when Renzi was still a schoolboy. At a time when Margaret Thatcher was imposing supply-side reforms on Britain, Ruud Lubbers was squeezing public spending until the pips squeaked in the Netherlands, and even François Mitterrand's goal of constructing socialism in France had given way to Bundesbank-imposed austerity, Italy was engaging in a binge of unproductive public spending. In borrowing terms, the 1980s were like war years – a decade in which the Italian state paid out 10% or more of GDP every year above what it raised in taxes. Much of this vast increase in expenditure (overall, the national debt rose from under 60% of GDP in 1980 to 121% in 1994[2]) was siphoned off by corruption, used to finance generous pensions (it was possible, in some cases, to retire after only

15 years' work, and pensions were based upon final salary, not contributions paid), or frittered away on the cost overruns of prestige projects.

This suicidal debt increase occurred despite the fact that taxes also increased sharply during the 1980s as a share of GDP, reaching 40% of national income by the early 1990s, a hitherto unheard-of figure. Taxes were raised disproportionately from the salary- and wage-earning classes, whose income could be taxed at source, leading to widespread tax evasion among entrepreneurs and professionals. In the dying days of the DC–PSI regime, the Italian state presided over an unjust redistribution of wealth from the middle class to those with good political connections, or to those who were living directly off politics. The 1980s became renowned as a decade of excess, producing millionaires whose antics rivalled those of Russian oligarchs and Chinese property dealers today. Besides Craxi himself, Silvio Berlusconi, with his media empire and jet-set lifestyle, was the man who best epitomised the entire epoch. (Craxi was, in fact, Berlusconi's political protector and sponsor.[3])

Such a state of affairs could not go on, especially when the end of the Cold War robbed Rome's politicians of their anti-communist rationale. Between 1990 and 1994, Italy experienced the worst crisis of any contemporary democracy since the collapse of France's Fourth Republic in 1958. The DC and the PSI were swept away in 1992–93 by corruption investigations in Milan, Venice and other cities, and by a crackdown on relationships between politicians and the mafia in the country's south. Thousands of politicians were investigated (over 2,500 by the Milanese prosecutors alone[4]) and most were either sentenced or took a plea bargain.

The turmoil in the political sphere spilled over into the markets: during the September 1992 crisis in the European Monetary System, only a savage austerity package, featuring tax raises and a levy on bank accounts, saved Italy's creditworthiness. The lira plunged against the German mark and Italy's formidable exporters were able to capitalise for the remainder of the decade on the advantage given to them by a devalued currency (Italy ran substantial trade surpluses in the mid-1990s). The memory of rapid economic growth brought about by the 1992 devaluation lives on; the fact that it suddenly made Italians poor relatives of the Germans is remembered less well.

What is not sufficiently appreciated outside Italy, however, is that the economic consequences of the end of the so-called 'First Republic' were enormous for the majority of Italian voters. When eurozone politicians preach the need for fiscal rigour to the Italians, they are ignoring – wilfully or otherwise – the fact that most Italian citizens feel that they have been enduring austerity since summer 1992. Since then, the Italian state, in order to keep the financial markets quiet, has been underinvesting in national infrastructure (and thus deflating the economy) and taxing too many of its citizens too highly. While Italians pay, as a percentage of national income, no more tax than most EU citizens, their hospitals, welfare provision, universities, roads and railways are for the most part worse, sometimes much worse, than in the rich countries of northern Europe. Those countries have invested their wealth wisely; Italy, when it was wealthy, squandered a patrimony. But it is no consolation to Signor Rossi (the archetypal middle-class Italian), when he contemplates his diminished pay check and considers his daughter's limited prospects for a fulfilling career, to know that Italy's northern European critics are correct in asserting that increased public spending is not the answer to Italy's problems.

Tarnished saviours

Voters naturally rebelled against the costs imposed by the party system's implosion and the moral squalor revealed by the judicial investigations in the 1990s. New forces, such as the Lega Nord, a populist party demanding autonomy from Rome for the then-vibrant economies of northern Italy, surged in the polls. As in the 1970s, the Communists – the PCI had split in 1991, with its progressive wing forming the Partito Democratico della Sinistra (PDS) and its diehards launching Rifondazione Comunista (PRC) – began to creep upwards in the polls, as Italians who had once been wary of the left concluded that they were the least awful alternative. It was to avoid a victory at the polls for the radical left that Berlusconi decided to *scendere in campo* (take to the field) as a political player, launching a new party, Forza Italia, in January 1994. In the short term, his gamble paid off: by April 1994, Berlusconi was premier, heading a coalition that included the Lega and also Alleanza Nazionale, effectively rebranded neo-fascists. Although his first government only lasted for a few months, it was one of the most remarkable electoral performances in post-war European history.

In the 1994 election campaign, Berlusconi depicted himself as a man of destiny who would save Italy from the ineptitude of squabbling politicians, a narrative that would remain unchanged for the next 20 years. The entire Italian right-wing – a motley crew of so-called liberals, reactionary Christian Democrats, former and actual fascists, the Lega Nord, and southern Italian notables with unfortunate acquaintances – was able to build an uneasy unity by backing Berlusconi's claim to be the *salvatore della patria*. Without him, they could never have assembled a winning coalition and obtained the fruits of government. For his more idolatrous followers (among them a group of female politicians in their forties, known collectively as the 'Amazons'), Berlusconi, like Mussolini, is always right, perhaps especially when he is obviously wrong. A saviour's judgment cannot be called into question.

At the same time that Berlusconi was presenting himself as a *toccasana* (remedy) for national renewal following the collapse of the early 1990s, a second remedy was being offered by the centre-left, by Catholic centrists and by influential professori with a pulpit in the national newspapers. That remedy was Europe. For many educated Italians, the Process (capital letters are obligatory) of European Integration is aimed at nothing less than the historical achievement of a federal United States of Europe, which will bring social justice to all Europeans. For men like Romano Prodi (premier in 1996–98 and then president of the European Commission, 1999–2004), Mario Monti (technocratic premier from November 2011 to April 2013 and former EU commissioner for the single market), Carlo Azeglio Ciampi (president of Italy in 1999–2006 and before that treasury minister under Prodi in 1996–98 and prime minister in 1993–94), Tommaso Padoa-Schioppa (Prodi's economy minister during his second premiership in 2006–08 and a member of the executive committee of the ECB before that), and current head of state Giorgio Napolitano, it is a matter of national pride that Italy be at the forefront of this process. As the speeches and books of these men make clear, building Europe means being on the side of human progress.[5]

Membership of the euro was expected to bring immediate, concrete economic benefits too. The neo-liberal character of the Maastricht Treaty was perceived as a *vincolo esterno* (outside constraint) that would compel Rome to follow budgetary discipline, implement necessary supply-side reforms and, in general, 'Europeanise' the state. Between 1996 and 1998, Prodi and Ciampi worked like Trojans to get Italy's accounts in order. A special tax was imposed on higher earners, and state-owned industries were privatised. These efforts paid off, and Italy was accepted into the euro-club in 1998. Prodi's parliamentary majority celebrated by sacking him a few months later.

Unfortunately for the improperly named Second Republic (that is, the period since the democratic collapse of the early 1990s), both putative saviours have been tarnished – Berlusconi irredeemably so. Although he was premier longer than any other statesman in the history of post-war Italy, serving as premier for five years between June 2001 and May 2006 and for over three years between May 2008 and November 2011, Berlusconi's accomplishments were negligible. Taxes went remorselessly up, not down, and public expenditure increased by unconscionable amounts; the national debt, despite the eurozone's low interest rates, inched upwards; the state bureaucracy remained elephantine; Italian schools and universities slid down the world's league tables; tax evasion was condoned by various amnesties; and an attempt at constitutional reform in 2006 was shot down by the Italian public in a referendum. National income – despite Berlusconi's empty boasts that Italy was 'the richest country in Europe'[6] – stagnated while he was in power. Despite the substantial majorities Berlusconi's coalitions enjoyed in parliament, his governments always seemed to be hanging by a thread. Far from being a chief executive making tough decisions in an efficient way, Berlusconi often had to act as mediator-in-chief between belligerents within his own coalition. Above all, hundreds of days were wasted on Berlusconi's own private affairs; on laws that succeeded in keeping him out of jail; and in frenzied speculation about his complicated sex life.

In 2011, Berlusconi's personal appetites, political failures and judicial woes finally caught up with him. His private life became embarrassingly public when he was accused of having sought to cover up the presence at a sex party at his country estate of a seventeen-year-old Moroccan immigrant nicknamed 'Ruby the Heartstealer' (a charge of which the Court of Appeal found him innocent in July 2014). Swamped with personal and political problems, Berlusconi's government lost the plot. Foreign owners of Italian debt began dumping bonds, the spread with German bonds widened dramatically, and a Greek-style crash loomed. Under pressure from horrified EU leaders, President Giorgio Napolitano told Berlusconi it was time to go.[7] The would-be saviour was condemned to four years' imprisonment for embezzlement in July 2013 and is currently facing additional criminal charges of a serious nature, including the accusation that he bribed an opposition senator with €3 million to bring down the government of Romano Prodi in 2006. Although his hardcore supporters continue to insist that he alone can revive Italy, railing against the 'judicial terrorism' of which they believe he has been a victim, Berlusconi will never be premier again. (Forza Italia remains a political force of some weight, and is giving conditional parliamentary support to the Renzi administration.) The enchantment that led millions of middle-class Italians to support his premiership has been broken.

Politicians lived in a fools' paradise

The tarnishing of the European project has been less lurid. It is now widely asserted that the EU's commitment to fiscal rigour has been the primary cause of Italy's economic stagnation, and that only exit from the single currency can save the Italian economy from more decades of slow or non-existent growth. More than 50% of Italians think EU membership is a bad thing, an unprecedented number.[8] The truth is that, unlike in Britain, Italians have never had a grown-up conversation about the merits of euro membership. The country joined the single currency as a leap of faith, without serious discussion of its merits and demerits.

In hindsight, it is clear that euro membership saved Italy from a brutal millennium devaluation. Eurozone convergence towards German bond yields made it easier for Italy to finance its public debt and put off shock therapy. On the other hand, the fact that the *vincolo esterno* turned out to be less of a corset than a pair of elasto-pants allowed Italy's politicians to live in a fools' paradise. The post-euro decade should have been Italy's chance to sweat off its excesses in the gym; instead, it will be remembered as a period in which the political class sat on the sidelines and gossiped idly about Berlusconi's crimes and misdemeanours while others pounded the treadmills. The debt disaster of the 1980s was compounded by a culpable failure to take hard decisions in the 2000s.

Yet Italy's political elites have been adroit in shifting the blame for stagnation on to Brussels. 'If only we had been allowed to breach Brussels' restrictions on deficit spending,' they protest, 'we would have been able to revive economic activity'. Such anti-EU propaganda, which also plays on latent anti-German sentiment, has been a mainstay of the Lega Nord's political discourse since the late 1990s, and has permeated Berlusconi's populist newspapers, *il Giornale* and *Libero*, for nearly as long. A less populist, more radical-chic version of the same blame game can also be found on the left. Italy's trade unions, along with many of its progressive politicians, are viscerally opposed to labour-market reforms, privatisation and reduced public spending, even though they are nominally enthusiasts for European integration. They square the circle by arguing that 'Europe' has become a neo-liberal perversion of its original goal: a *socialist*, or at any rate a socially progressive, United States of Europe.

A prodigal son

Italy's present plight, therefore, is the product of two generations of inadequate (when not actually criminal) political leadership. Ordinary Italians, who pay their taxes and work in schools, factories, farms and hospitals, are not to blame. One of the reasons why Renzi rose to power so quickly, in a country where under-50s had previously played only marginal political roles, is that there has been a nationwide revolt of the guiltless, who have become aware since 2008 that they and their children may have to pay – possibly for decades to come – for their rulers' ineptitude.

Grillo's M5S represents the Jacobin strain of this revolt: its adherents regard all politicians as vermin and are almost hysterically determined that their own elected representatives remain untainted by the venality and corruption of the *palazzo*. Renzi-ism takes a softer, though similar, line. Its supporters believe that politics is not necessarily evil, but has for too long been in the hands of a 'caste' of people who have made a good living from it and who have lost any desire to bring about real changes in peoples' lives.

The contempt of the PD's younger activists for the mediocrity of the generation of centre-left leaders who let Berlusconi prevail and who colluded in the economic disaster of the last 30 years is palpable.

Renzi has harnessed this contempt and made it the driving force of his rise to the top. First, he decried the 60-somethings that had led the centre-left since the early 1990s (a *lèse-majesté* that infuriated them); he then deposed Pier Luigi Bersani, the PD's likeable but serially unsuccessful leader; and finally, in February 2014, after he had been elected leader of the PD in a nationwide primary, Renzi stabbed his able predecessor as premier, Enrico Letta, in the front, accusing him of not pushing the reform agenda hard enough. Throughout this Machiavellian rise to the top, which has left a residue of resentment among the PD's old guard and the party apparatchiks that Renzi has eclipsed, the Florentine former boy scout has wielded his dagger with all the certainty of one who knows he has right on his side.

The fact that Renzi-ism is essentially an act of generational rebellion is an important one that Italy's EU partners would do well to grasp. The Germans, Finns and Dutch delight in depicting the Italians (not to mention the peoples of the other Mediterranean member states) as wastrels who need to get a grip and live within their means. Italians, especially young adults and the early middle-aged, regard themselves as the unlucky heirs of a gang of spendthrifts who must now reverse the state of chronic decline bequeathed to them. The Renzi generation thinks that Italy should be treated as a prodigal son, one who will, once he has eaten his fill of the fatted calf (that is, been given a degree of 'flexibility' within the EU's rigid fiscal pact), return to the family farm and work for its prosperity alongside his more prudent brothers and sisters. In their own imagination at least, the *Renziani* are bringing closure to Italy's 40 years of crisis.

Will they succeed? The first six months of the *governo del fare* has been a procession of missed targets. A set-piece reform of the constitution, designed to eliminate perfect bicameralism and replace the Senate with a chamber of representatives from the regions and major cities, was undermined by Renzi's internal opponents within the PD; by the principled opposition of eminent jurists for whom the Italian Constitution, forged in 1947 by the Christian Democrats and the Communists as a symbol of the values of a post-fascist nation, is the 'most noble in the world' (*la costituzione più bella del mondo*); and by a cross-party cohort of senators who wish to keep their seats at all costs. A complementary reform of the electoral law has run into a similar wall of opposition. On the constitutional reform, however, Renzi has shown his mettle. Perhaps sensing that his opponents within his own party would kill his programme as a whole if he showed weakness on the constitutional question, Renzi has brooked no compromises as the reform has made its way through parliament.

On the economic side, despite a helpful tax cut for lower-income earners, consumption remains depressed, the national debt (now at €2.17 trillion, or 135% of projected 2014 GDP[9]) continues to expand, and incipient deflation is making both problems worse. Italy remains one spike in bond yields away from a catastrophe of Greek dimensions.

Italy's neighbours need to think very hard about how they intend to treat Rome in the next few months. If the countries of northern Europe continue to press the case for rigour in an insensitive way, they will run the risk of diverting the generational rebellion in Italy against the institutions of the EU itself. There is still a powerful current of pro-EU feeling in Italy: Renzi and his youthful team of ministers were schooled on textbooks that presented the EU as the culmination of Western civilisation.[10] But their sense of victimhood is more visceral, and could easily be directed at Europe. Since Renzi took over the presidency of the EU he has peppered his speeches with populist-sounding attacks on the 'Europe of bureaucrats'.[11] There may be more of this rhetoric to come if Brussels' monetarist ideology strangles the *governo del fare's* plans in the cradle.

Renzi is ultimately a product of Italy's decline. Had Italy been more successful in the last 40 years, Renzi would now be deputy mayor of Florence, presiding over civil weddings and the committee on parking permits. But Italy has not been successful. For two generations, its leadership has mortgaged the country to the hilt, evaded its responsibility to future generations, and cultivated a political culture that for moral squalor has few, if any, equals among developed nations. Renzi had the political nous to ride the wave of rebellion that this state of affairs has belatedly generated, drawing on his considerable charisma (and ruthlessness) to make himself the figurehead of a generation. What is not clear, however, is whether he will amount to anything more than an able opportunist with an intuitive grasp of his peer-group's grievances. One hopes that he will. Italy's political class has steered *il bel paese* to a point where either renewal will take hold, or decline will quicken. Given Italy's economic weight in Europe, and its history of chronic political instability, it is in nobody's interest that its decline should become a rout.

Notes

1 Mario Draghi, 'Speech by Mario Draghi, President of the European Central Bank at the Global Investment Conference in London', 26 July 2012, http://www.ecb.europa.eu/press/key/date/2012/html/sp120726.en.html.

2 Maura Francese e Angelo Pace, *Il debito pubblico italiano dall'Unità a oggi. Una ricostruzione della serie storica* (Rome: Banca d'Italia, 2008), p. 28.

3 Easily the best book on Craxi is Simona Colarizi and Marco Gervasoni, *La Cruna dell'ago: Craxi, il partito socialista e la crisi della repubblica* (Rome: Laterza, 2006).

4 See Gianni Barbacetto, Peter Gomez and Marco Travaglio, *Mani pulite: La vera storia* (Milan: Mondadori, 2012).

5 See, for example, Padoa-Schioppa, *L'Europa: Forza Gentile* (Bologna: Il Mulino, 2001); and Romano Prodi, *Europe As I See It* (Cambridge: Polity, 2000). President Napolitano's collected speeches on the EU are available at http://www.quirinale.it/elementi/Continua.aspx?tipo=Discorso&key=2821.

6 'Berlusconi: Siamo il Paese più ricco d'Europa', *La Stampa*, 20 June 2010, http://www.lastampa.it/2010/06/20/italia/politica/berlusconi-siamo-il-paese-pi-ricco-deuropa-ZTVomyiWg4z4hvxyy2jgoM/pagina.html.

7 For background on the 2011 crisis see Alan Friedman, *Ammazziamo il gattopardo* (Rome: Rizzoli, 2014).

8 'European Union on the Rocks', Pew Research Global Attitudes Project, 29 May 2012, http://www.pewglobal.org/2012/05/29/chapter-2-views-of-european-unity.

9 International Monetary Fund, 'World Economic Outlook (April 2014)', Table A8, p. 192.

10 It is interesting to read Renzi's comments on European integration in his statement of his new government's programme (see 'Comunicazioni del Presidente del Consiglio dei Ministri Matteo Renzi', 24 February 2014, http://www.governo.it/GovernoInforma/Dossier/legge_province/RENZI_senato_20140224.pdf). On the one hand, he argues that Europeanism brings out 'that which is the best of Italy', but also that Italy needs to overcome its 'cultural cringe' in the face of the European 'stepmother'.

11 See, for example, 'Renzi: "L'Ue non può essere la patria di burocrazia e banche, sia la casa dei cittadini"', *Il Libro Dei Fatti*, 5 July 2014, http://www.adnkronos.com/fatti/politica/2014/07/05/renzi-non-puo-essere-patria-burocrazia-banche-sia-casa-dei-cittadini_Y6F9DATUDtsjet3iwZ5xgO.html.

Climate, Scarcity and Conflict

Shiloh Fetzek and Jeffrey Mazo

Soon after he took office in 2007, United Nations Secretary-General Ban Ki-moon declared that there was an urgent need to reframe the debate on climate change from an environmental to a development and security issue, and that it would be one of his top priorities as UN leader. Environmental factors, including land use, water availability, biodiversity loss, soil degradation and acute weather events, have been implicated in at least 73 conflicts since 1980, and at least 40% of intra-state conflicts since the end of the Second World War can be associated with natural resources. A rapidly growing body of research on climate change, resource scarcity and conflict has ensured that the issue is rising on the international agenda. Yet, although such concerns cut across the security, development and humanitarian sectors, there is little dialogue, let alone coordination, between and among government departments and international and non-governmental organisations responsible for these domains.

Since 2007, evidence that climate change poses a risk to international peace and security has strengthened and deepened. Climate change will act as a conflict multiplier by amplifying existing environmental stresses, creating new ones, exacerbating water and food insecurity, and adding to the pressures on weak, corrupt or repressive governments (which by their nature will find it harder to respond to such situations) but also threatening more stable and effective ones. In most cases, the role of environmental stress

---

Shiloh Fetzek is Consulting Research Associate for Climate Change and Security, and **Jeffrey Mazo** is Consulting Senior Fellow for Environmental Security and Science Policy and Consulting Editor, *Survival*, at the IISS.

Survival | vol. 56 no. 5 | October–November 2014 | pp. 143–170 DOI 10.1080/00396338.2014.962803

and resource availability is indirect, as they aggravate or amplify the effects of drivers such as poverty, inequality, ethnic tensions, corruption, weak or bad governance or institutions, regime type, high population growth, rising expectations, economic shocks (including degree of exposure to globalised hazards) and history of past conflict. The United Nations Intergovernmental Panel on Climate Change (IPCC)'s 5th Assessment Report in 2014 concluded that, although the influence of climate change and resource scarcity on conflict risk cannot yet be quantified and the precise mechanisms have not yet been established, 'climate change can indirectly increase risks of violent conflicts in the form of civil war and inter-group violence by amplifying well-documented drivers of these conflicts such as poverty and economic shocks ... Multiple lines of evidence relate climate variability to these forms of conflict.'

The attribution of importance to individual factors in such complex systems is difficult. But it is becoming increasingly evident that interactions among environmental, social, political and economic factors can continually reinforce negative trends, disproportionately increasing the risk of internal conflict and humanitarian crises, and reducing social or governmental ability to cope with repeated or multi-year crises and to further adapt to long-term climate change. Extreme weather consistent with climate-change projections has already contributed to internal conflict, civil war and humanitarian crises, notably in the Middle East and North Africa, as well as parts of sub-Saharan Africa.[1] These regions are both particularly exposed to future climate-change impacts and particularly vulnerable to multiple social, political and economic stressors that limit resilience. Looking at the Syrian conflict through the lens of climate change can provide insight into other regions of high risk and lessons for organisations involved in conflict prevention, development and humanitarian relief.

Syria and the Arab Spring

The Syrian uprising had many causes. Frustration with the political repression, brutality and corruption of the Assad regime played an underlying role. Sectarian favouritism for the largely urban, coastal Alawite minority negatively affected social cohesion among Syria's rural, eastern Sunni majority and the other ethnic groups that make up the Syrian population. Economic problems stemming from the global financial crisis as well as long-term declines in oil production and agriculture, coupled with demographic pressure from rapid population growth, amplified poverty and political discontent, contributing to a sense of grievance and desire for better governance and civil liberties.

Although the regime's response to popular unrest was a key dynamic, environmental changes and their economic consequences, and the regime's mishandling of both, were an important part of the mixture.[2] Syria has been experiencing water stress since the 1980s, and as the result of population growth, economic development and poor water-management practices reached a condition of water scarcity around the turn of the millennium.[3] Total freshwater withdrawal increased by nearly 31% between 1993 and 2003, and amounted to more than 86% of available resources in 2005.[4] More than 70% of the country's freshwater resources come from transborder flows, the bulk from Turkey via the Euphrates River.

Figures for freshwater resources are long-term averages, and mask significant variation from year to year. Given Syria's overall water scarcity and high level of withdrawal, the impact of this variation can be severe. The country suffered four consecutive years of severe drought from 2006–10, drastically reducing water availability, which halved between 2002 and 2008.[5] Although the region has regularly experienced short-term, seasonal droughts, the recent event was longer and saw lower levels of rainfall than any drought in the last century.[6] At the peak of the drought in winter 2007–08, precipitation in the impoverished northeast of the country was less than half the average, with some areas registering no precipitation at all.[7] Although the northeast is both the country's breadbasket and main oil-producing region, it is nevertheless economically underdeveloped and thus vulnerable, in absolute terms and relative to other regions. In 2008–09 the northeast again experienced severe drought, although rainfall recovered to normal levels in other areas of the country. The drought affected neighbouring countries as well, and the cross-border flow via the Euphrates reached its lowest level on record in 2009. The average annual flow has been declining for several decades, however, due both to long-term declines in precipitation and to upstream water-management practices which smooth out inter-annual variation.[8]

The effects of the drought on rural livelihoods were amplified by the government's economic and resource-management policies, which favoured large-scale infrastructure projects to increase food production and national self-sufficiency, agricultural subsidies for water-intensive wheat and cotton crops, and inefficient irrigation systems and unsustainable groundwater extraction to convert arid pastoral land into cropped fields. Overgrazing of Syria's steppes to meet national demand for animal protein amplified desertification and sandstorms. A shift away from large-scale, state-owned water and agriculture projects that characterised Ba'ath policies in the 1960s and 1970s toward a deregulated market economy impacted rural communities whose livelihoods depended on state support of the agricultural sector. These policies had serious detrimental impacts on rural livelihoods even before the drought struck. The cancellation of subsidies on diesel fuel in 2008 and chemical fertiliser in 2009 had a major impact, as farmers could no longer afford to run diesel pumps to extract groundwater to compensate for lack of rainfall, or to transport their crops to market. A 2005 law requiring licenses for wells to be renewed annually led to the extortion of bribes from farmers, amplifying resentment of the regime.[9]

Prior to the drought, Syria's agricultural sector employed up to 40–50% of its workforce (including the informal economy) and accounted for 25% of GDP.[10] In 2006, lured by high market prices, the Syrian government sold off most of its reserve wheat stock.[11] When the drought struck in 2008, Syria became a net wheat importer and more vulnerable to price fluctuations in global markets. Between 2007 and 2010, in the northeast where the majority of agriculture is rain fed rather than irrigated,[12] nearly 75% of households suffered a total crop failure.[13] During the same period, wheat and barley yields dropped 47% and 67% respectively.[14] Faced with a lack of rainfall and surface water, Syrian farmers dug unlicensed wells to extract groundwater from already depleted aquifers, dropping the water table below a level that could be accessed by their pumps. Without pasture vegetation or feed reserves, in some areas of the north 85% of livestock died; in other areas herders sold animals at well below cost, reducing national stocks by a quarter.[15] Agriculture-dependent families were left without assets or income to meet daily food requirements, and two to three million people were pushed into extreme poverty.[16]

This effect of drought and government policies on rural livelihoods pushed around 1.5 million people from the agricultural northeast to urban areas in the south, where impoverished farmers and herders congregated in tent camps around Damascus, Aleppo, Daraa and other cities. As a result, the poverty rate in Syria's urban southern region doubled between 2007 and 2011.[17] These cities were already stressed by the presence of a quarter of a million Palestinian refugees and around 200,000 Iraqis, as well as by Syria's own rapid population growth.[18] Tensions arose over competition for scarce employment opportunities. While the government offered modest cash and aid incentives for migrants to return to their drought-affected lands in the northeast (which few chose to do), no aid was provided to the tent camps themselves.[19] International awareness of the humanitarian crisis was limited by restrictions on media coverage and the Syrian government's portrayal of the country as competent and self-sufficient; this in turn may have contributed to insufficient donor response for the UN Drought Response Plan.

External factors

The drought and resulting humanitarian crisis were not proximate causes or primary drivers of the civil unrest and open conflict in Syria, but they highlighted contrasts between the political power of the Alawite elite and the impoverished rural Sunni majority, and the unwillingness and incapacity of the Assad regime to meet the needs of a majority of the people. Underlying discontent was sparked into active protest, uprising and civil war by developments elsewhere in the region. In March 2011, inspired by demands for change elsewhere in the Arab world, beginning in Tunisia in December 2010, 15 schoolchildren painted a protest chant on a wall in Daraa. Anger at the regime's heavy-handed response (the children were arrested, imprisoned and tortured, and one died in custody) sparked further demonstrations, which spread to Homs, Hama and other provincial towns, and provided an outlet for frustration with corruption and a lack of political freedom. The regime's violent attempts to suppress these protests, targeting both protesters and those not involved in the demonstrations, increased opposition to Assad's rule and the divisions within Syrian society.

The protesters may not themselves have been directly affected by the drought, but environmental stress was part of the background that led to both frustrations and protests in some areas. Specific grievances varied from locality to locality, encompassing the rising cost of living, unemployment, the depletion of water resources and the resulting devastation of the agriculture sector.[20] Daraa is a city in which agriculture was a key sector of the economy, and where livelihoods plummeted as employment opportunities in this sector, along with migrant work in Lebanon, became untenable.[21] The anti-corruption demonstrations in Daraa that followed the protests over the arrests of the children focused in part on corruption around well-licensing and groundwater use, along with a range of other grievances.[22]

The Arab Spring was, like the Syrian civil war, caused by the complex interaction of political, social, personal, ideological and environmental factors. Many of these were closely tied to economic insecurity. With 60% of the population in the region under the age of 30, and unemployment rates in this group of between 15–30%, the frustrations of the region's educated, under-employed youth at the mismatch of expectations and reality provided an engine for the uprisings. Inflation, record-high food prices, high fuel prices and dissatisfaction with corrupt and autocratic regimes that were no longer able to meet the needs of the people fuelled the unravelling of the social contract between government and society.

Extreme weather around the globe in 2010 caused crop failures in China, Russia and Canada that contributed to a global food-price spike, including a doubling of wheat prices, in 2011. This particularly affected the Middle East, which contains nine of the world's ten top wheat importers (seven of which experienced civilian deaths during political protests in 2011), and where up to 40% of family income is spent on food.[23] At the time of the uprisings at the beginning of 2011, food prices had increased 20% on the previous year, and around half of the Egyptian population relied on the corruption-plagued bread-subsidy system.[24] Rioting in Algeria in early January 2011 was a direct response to high unemployment and higher prices for staple foods.[25] Demonstrators waved baguettes on the streets of Tunisia, Jordan and Yemen.

Despite broadly similar climate stressors across the Middle East and North Africa, however, the experience of countries in the region during the Arab Spring varied widely. These differences (and similarities) can in part be explained by differences and similarities with regard to other conflict risk factors such as regime type, level of economic development, economic shocks (including degree of exposure to globalised climate hazards), income and land distribution, demographic factors and past experience of conflict and other historical contingencies. Variables such as food-price increases played a role in the unrest in both Egypt and Syria, but with very different outcomes in each country. Food-price increases themselves do not necessarily engender unrest, but they highlight state capacities to ensure that the basic needs of their citizens can be met. The same drought that affected Syria also impacted Iraq, Jordan, Lebanon and other countries in the region, but it was the economic policies and political context in Syria that created a humanitarian crisis that contributed to civil unrest.

Predictability

The Arab Spring took most analysts, institutions and even the protestors themselves by surprise.[26] Particular indicators alerted some observers to the heightening risk of instability; the United Nations Development Programme (UNDP), for example, identified many of the long-standing underlying factors, such as the youth bulge, dependence on agricultural imports and stagnating economic sectors, in successive Arab Human Development reports.[27] But analysts did not predict the timing of the Arab Spring because they missed an accelerating interaction between underlying causes and short-term catalysts, and because of the inherent unpredictability of some of the human factors involved.[28]

Before 2011, most observers attributed the political stability of the Arab world to the close relationship between undemocratic regimes and the military, which put down any unrest, and to state control over the economy, which allowed governments to placate their citizens, especially in countries with oil revenues. There was little interest in studying military–regime relationships because they had remained unchanged and were considered a fixed feature of the region.[29] Overlooked indicators for the Arab Spring include nuanced changes in these relationships, and the effect that economic liberalisation had on the electorate's expectations. Most analysts and intelligence agencies were focused on counter-terrorism and military and political power, and overlooked the political strength of the populace.

Nevertheless, some analysis of the vulnerability of the Middle East and North Africa, and Syria in particular, to climate change and environmental insecurity before 2010 proved remarkably prescient. An International Institute for Sustainable Development report in 2009 argued that

> A severe drought across the region in 2007/2008 provided a taste of what could happen in [the] future. In Syria, the wheat harvest was less than half that of previous years, and the production of chickpeas and barley fell by a third on average and more than 75 per cent in rain-fed areas ... Over the long term, climate change could fundamentally alter the distribution of world agricultural output and exacerbate volatility in prices ... Domestic food shortages could elevate existing tensions and feelings of historical injustice.[30]

By 2008 the UN Food and Agriculture Organization (FAO) had identified potential consequences of the drought, and requested funds from the US Agency for International Development (USAID) to support the UN's Syria Drought Response Plan relief efforts. The FAO representative in Syria called the situation 'a perfect storm' and predicted mass migration from the northeast, 'which could act as a multiplier on social and economic pressures already at play and undermine stability'.[31] He reported that the Syrian minister of agriculture had stated to UN officials that 'the economic and social fallout from the drought was "beyond our capacity as a country to deal with"', and that through this relief bid the UN was trying to combat 'the potential for "social destruction" that would accompany erosion of the agricultural industry in rural Syria. This social destruction would lead to political instability.' He also noted that

> the migration of 15,000[32] unskilled laborers would add to the social and economic pressures presently at play in major Syrian cities. A system

> already burdened by a large Iraqi refugee population may not be able to absorb another influx of displaced persons, particularly at this time of rising costs, growing dissatisfaction of the middle class, and a perceived weakening of the social fabric and security structures that Syrians have come to expect and – in some cases – rely on.

USAID declined to contribute, citing its existing funding for Iraqi refugees in Syria. Donor response to this appeal was low globally, with 14% of funds raised by the end of 2009.[33]

Despite awareness of certain risk factors, these were not considered significant enough to outweigh the perceived stability of the Syrian regime and the strength of its security apparatus in suppressing popular unrest. Information that the regime considered sensitive was difficult to acquire, from statistics on water quality and availability to expanding internal migrant settlements to the political dynamics within the Syrian government. That demonstrations to demand political reforms would escalate into a nationwide uprising was unforeseen by regional experts and by Syrians themselves.

Analysis of the Arab Spring, and Syria in particular, illustrates the difficulty of making specific predictions about when and where instability, conflict and violence might erupt and what the implications might be. The dynamic interaction of multiple factors can be extremely difficult (if not impossible) to forecast, and any expectation that social scientists can accurately predict future trends based on existing information is problematic. The lack of a consensus prediction of the Arab Spring and the uprising in Syria was not a 'failure' per se; rather, the difficulty of making accurate predictions is inherent to the nature of security analysis. Those observers who got it right were making generalised and heavily conditional statements, not specific predictions of events. Analysing some of the dynamics after the fact, including which indicators were overlooked or not acted upon (and why), and where assumptions about stability dynamics turned out to be incorrect, can nevertheless inform future assessments of regions with limited resilience to climate impacts, in order to minimise risks of similar instabilities.

The Horn of Africa

The large majority of studies on connections between climate change and violent conflict focus on sub-Saharan Africa.[34] The Darfur region of Sudan has been a key case study, and other countries in the Horn of Africa (broadly defined as the eight countries – Djibouti, Eritrea, Ethiopia, Kenya, Somalia, South Sudan, Sudan and Uganda – of 'IGAD', the Intergovernmental Authority for Development) have been the subject of detailed research in this context.[35] This region is vulnerable to multiple stressors that limit its resilience to current and future climate-change impacts. These include entrenched poverty, environmental degradation, governance challenges, resource stresses, ethnic divisions and demographic pressures. Three of the eight countries in the region (Somalia, Sudan and South Sudan) are, according to one index, among the top five most fragile states in the world, with four more in the top 25 (with a rank of 50, Djibouti is still considered at risk).[36] The UN Inter-agency Standing Committee (IASC) and European Commission Joint Research Centre's global risk index for humanitarian crises, InfoRM, which includes several components related to exposure to natural hazards, shows a similar profile for the region.[37]

Non-climate risk factors

The region is characterised by conflicts of varying intensities and durations, from internal wars in Somalia, South Sudan, Sudan (Darfur) and Uganda to episodic unrest such as the 2007–08 election violence in Kenya. Lower-intensity social conflicts, including protests, riots, strikes, inter-communal conflict and government violence against civilians, also occur periodically.[38] Environmental degradation from both climatic and human activities and pressures, including rapid population growth, changes in land-use patterns and chronic conflict, has contributed to the security dynamic by amplifying resource pressure on pastoralists and others.[39]

Many important non-environmental conflict risk factors, such as regime type, level of economic development, economic shocks, income and land distribution, population size or density, geography, previous history of conflict and state or social problem-solving and conflict-management capacity, are underpinned by or inextricably linked to resource scarcity and mismanagement. The significance or relative weight of a given factor is sensitive to the choice of indicator or proxy chosen to represent it, but the values of various components of the InfoRM index illustrate the variation across the dimensions of hazard exposure, vulnerability and coping capacity for countries in the region.

For example, the composite risk score for the countries in the Horn of Africa ranges from 5.2 (Djibouti) to 9.2 (Somalia) on a 10-point scale; for comparison, the OECD country with the highest score is Turkey (5.0). Djibouti's score, however, derives from relatively high vulnerability (especially aid dependency) and coping capacity (especially in the infrastructure category) components, while Turkey's score derives from high exposure to seismic hazards and political instability. Somalia, on the other hand, is the highest-ranked country in the world for overall risk, vulnerability and low coping capacity. Sudan and South Sudan have the same high overall level of risk, but Sudan faces greater political instability, while South Sudan suffers in relative terms from lack of infrastructure.

The relative scores of all eight countries in the Horn at the functional level are shown in Table 1. The variation in overall score, and the more substantial variation at the level of individual components and indicators that make up the index, suggests that countries in the region will be affected differently by similar environmental, social or economic developments.

Table 1: **Risk Factors for Humanitarian Crises in the Horn of Africa (1 = low, 10 = high)**

	Exposure to Natural Hazards	Exposure to Human Hazards	Socioeconomic Vulnerability	Vulnerable Groups	Coping Capacity (Institutional)	Coping Capacity (Infrastructure)	Composite Risk Score
Somalia	6.2	10.0	9.3	9.5	9.3	9.8	9.2
Sudan	5.3	9.8	6.0	8.4	6.6	7.8	7.6
South Sudan	5.3	8.7	5.7	8.3	6.8	9.3	7.6
Ethiopia	5.4	6.7	6.2	6.7	4.8	9.3	6.7
Kenya	6.1	7.0	5.4	7.7	5.7	7.3	6.6
Eritrea	4.8	4.2	6.9	4.9	7.9	7.4	5.9
Uganda	4.1	4.6	6.0	6.0	6.7	7.5	5.7
Djibouti	4.8	1.9	6.3	5.6	6.2	7.3	5.2

Data from InfoRM, http://inform.jrc.ec.europa.eu/, accessed 2 May 2014. See the website for definitions of variables and categories.

Environmental and climate-related risk factors

The region faces significant environmental hazards, with Eritrea, Kenya, Somalia and South Sudan scoring the maximum on a composite indicator for exposure to drought, and all but Uganda scoring above 9 on a 10-point scale. Exposure to flooding shows more variation, with Djibouti (2.0) and Eritrea (2.7) at one end of the range, and Ethiopia (7.1) and Sudan (8.6) at the other.

In 2010–12 many parts of East Africa experienced severe drought; in places it was the worst drought in 60 years. Populations in Somalia, Ethiopia and Kenya were particularly badly affected, with crop failures and widespread loss of livestock and livelihoods. Higher food prices and lower incomes combined to create a humanitarian crisis and famine by July 2011. More than 13 million people were affected, hundreds of thousands were displaced, and 50–100,000 died.[40] With countries in the region already suffering various degrees of violent conflict, there is no compelling evidence either way with regard to whether the crisis was a driver of further conflict. However, ongoing conflicts amplified the crisis by creating displaced persons and affecting the timing and distribution of international aid. Because of a lack of reliable long-term historical climate data for the region, it is also impossible to declare whether or not the 2011 crisis can be attributed to climate change.

According to the IPCC's 5th Assessment Report, however, climate change is expected to further affect food and water security, public health and ecosystem resilience in the region. Seasonal decreases in rainfall have been linked to increased warming in the Indian Ocean, which is likely to continue. A decline in summer monsoonal precipitation is expected to affect groundwater and surface-water supplies, which will in turn amplify ecosystem degradation. There is a high likelihood of extreme heat events. Rift Valley fever is likely to increase, as will malaria in the highlands, and vulnerability to health impacts will be amplified by chronic food insecurity and malnutrition. Climate change will interact with other risks to amplify vulnerability of agricultural systems, particularly in semi-arid regions, with consequences for food security. Broadly, the IPCC finds that Africa is one of the continents most vulnerable to climate change due to its high exposure and low adaptive capacity.[41]

These climate impacts will interact with other longer-term instability multipliers, including entrenched poverty, high population growth, poor governance, limited resilience, and dependence on rain-fed agriculture, pastoralism and fisheries. Shorter-term climatic events generating resource stress and disasters could act as catalysts for outbreaks of social conflict.

Mapping vulnerability and early warning

Addressing these risk factors requires well-targeted interventions from the international community, national governments and local actors. One example of a tool to better inform projections of how climate impacts and aid interventions can affect a region's security environment is the Climate Change and African Political Stability (CCAPS) project, a detailed mapping tool designed specifically to quantify and map climate-related vulnerabilities in Africa with an explicit security focus. Funded by the United States Department of Defense's Minerva Initiative,[42] the project creates a detailed picture of vulnerabilities using geographical information systems (GIS), mapping at relatively fine resolution climate-related hazard exposure, population density, household and community resilience and governance capacities, as well as foreign-assistance projects and points of intervention to promote resilience. CCAPS identifies areas of chronic vulnerability where large numbers of people could be at risk of death from exposure to climate-related hazards, and updates its Armed Conflict Location Event Data on a weekly basis.[43]

Like other analyses, prior to the Arab Spring CCAPS indicated that North Africa was at low risk of instability due to positive indicators in health, education and other resilience factors. However, the Horn (as well as parts of the Democratic Republic of the Congo and Nigeria) shows persistent vulnerability between different iterations of the model, indicating a very high level of chronic vulnerability to climate-driven risks compared to the rest of Africa.[44] Areas of South Sudan and southern Somalia, specifically its southern coast, are particularly vulnerable across different model specifications, with smaller pockets of high vulnerability also evident in western Burundi, Eritrea, Ethiopia, Kenya, Sudan, and the Karamoja triangle area of Uganda. CCAPS' maps of chronic vulnerability suggest that, among other areas of

East Africa, the agro-pastoralist zones of southern Somalia and South Sudan are highly vulnerable to recurrent crises given the number of communities situated in areas that lack local resilience and in states that lack the capacity or willingness to assist their population when needed.[45]

For more near-term crises, applying the lessons of the Arab Spring in order to anticipate, understand and prevent climate-driven security challenges in situations of acute instability will require improving conflict early-warning systems, and incorporating this analysis into a range of risk-management and aid/development bodies. Improvements to these systems are under way to incorporate climate- and environment-sensitive indicators, and to collect and disseminate information across different sectors of society more effectively.

Systems' reliability depends on data

Of the conflict early-warning systems that cover the Horn, IGAD's Conflict Early Warning and Response Network (CEWARN) is the most sophisticated. It tracks incident reports of specific violent events, as well as situation reports that monitor a range of social indicators which could make violent incidents more or less likely.[46] It draws heavily on civil-society participation, has a technical committee on early warning and response, and plans to create a conflict early-warning response unit in each country it covers. CEWARN is an example of good inter-governmental and inter-agency coordination; through integration into the administrative apparatus of some of the regional states, it complements existing state security and delivery structures.[47]

However, there are several challenges involved in adapting conflict early-warning systems to a climate-changed future. The first is building early-response capabilities to accompany early-warning systems. Closing the gap between early warning and quick response will require capacity building among responders, including the security community. Securing a timely response from decision-makers hinges on political commitment to responding, which can be hampered by financial constraints and political cost–benefit analyses, among other issues. In an environment where state capacities and finances may be under increasing strain because of climate, resource, demographic and other stressors, response capacities could be impaired.

A second related challenge is that sensitivities to military presence and intervention by extra-regional powers can further inhibit robust reactions to emergent situations. The new United States Africa Command (AFRICOM) established in 2007 raised fears among African nations that it represented a militarisation of US policy towards the continent at the expense of long-term African interests, despite an averred focus on state-building, peacekeeping and crisis response.[48] This aversion led to establishing the new headquarters in Germany rather than an African location; two of the leading candidates had been in the Horn – Djibouti, which hosts the US's only military base on the continent, and co-location with the African Union's peace and security facility in Addis Ababa. Currently, the African Union is charged with responding to situations identified by CEWARN, but their Situation Room in Addis Ababa is in need of training and equipment.[49]

A third and significant problem concerns data and information flows, although innovative technological responses are being developed in this area. Early-warning systems' reliability depends on the data they use, and in-depth and reliable data can be difficult to collect in conflict areas,or in countries whose governance system may itself be a risk factor, as was the case with Syria.[50] By their nature, these systems incorporate data that has been gathered previously and reflects a reality that may have changed in the intervening time. Information sharing can be politicised, especially where security is concerned, and timely interventions can become complicated with tensions between regional and national interest, such as between Ethiopia and Eritrea or Sudan and South Sudan.[51] Difficulties transmitting information to troops on the ground can impede their effectiveness, and engagement at the community level with early warnings is also underdeveloped.

The use of new technologies and applications to detect and analyse impending conflict, or developments in ongoing conflicts, can help to close the gap in situational awareness and response.[52] The development of mobile crisis mapping can help to transmit information to and between parties on the ground, whether those raising the alarm or those providing the first line of response.[53] These systems operate at a micro-level within a conflict region, and could draw on crowdsourcing for both early warning and early response.[54] Other new techniques involve using social-media platforms to assist in crisis response, for example using algorithms to sift Twitter messages to provide useful information for humanitarian responders.[55] Other technologies to improve situational awareness have the potential to incorporate climate-sensitive indicators. For example, satellite imagery could be used to count livestock or track environmental degradation, which can correlate with or drive violence. Such information could be integrated with other indicators to generate multi-dimensional risk assessments.[56]

Incorporating climate impacts into conflict early-warning systems will require closer cooperation between disaster early-warning and conflict early-warning systems, in order to anticipate complex emergencies in which climate impacts are a driver.[57] CEWARN has signed a memorandum of understanding with IGAD Climate Prediction and Application Centre (ICPAC) on sharing information that would be integrated into conflict early warning and early response in areas of reporting within the IGAD region, although as of yet it is difficult to gauge the success of this integration.[58]

Enhancing early-warning systems, mapping climate security vulnerabilities and targeting aid interventions are complex undertakings, and require human and financial resources, as well as technical capacities and infrastructure. Early-warning and analysis systems that are properly resourced can be continually refined with improved methodology, technological innovations, more granular climate science and other relevant data. Such systems can provide useful tools to build the body of analysis on climate-change impacts and security interactions in order to minimise risks to human security.

Eliminating the potential for surprises like the Arab Spring uprisings is impossible, but incorporating climate-sensitive indicators will enhance the effectiveness of early-warning systems and interventions to promote stability, as climate impacts accelerate.

Adapting institutions

In the Middle East and North Africa, financial and economic support packages to underpin a democratic transition following the Arab Spring have focused on incentives for democratic reforms, building civil-society institutions and providing immediate jobs for young people.[59] Without careful attention to whether these investments support long-term resilience to the factors that have undermined stability in the region in the past, however, they will not be effective in averting instability in the future. Investing in renewable energy systems, energy efficiency, water infrastructure, desalination and irrigation systems would have value in addressing multiple issues, including economic development, livelihoods and food security.[60]

More broadly, reorienting away from a reactive posture that responds to crises as they emerge and toward conflict prevention would minimise the extent to which climate change will act as a conflict multiplier. Devoting funds to crisis prevention through conflict-sensitive adaptation and development, as opposed to crisis relief, is key to promoting stability. In the most vulnerable regions of the Horn, for example, lack of resilience to recurrent problems, including climate-related hazards, necessitates large-scale relief efforts every few years.[61] However, financing for aid initiatives in the Horn is distributed to those countries most able to manage projects well (Kenya and Ethiopia) rather than those areas with the most acute vulnerabilities (South Sudan and southern Somalia). Addressing such structural challenges will be difficult, but an important prerequisite for encouraging security. Localised and discrete events affecting food, water and energy security, such as local droughts, must also be considered in a wider, even global, context and in terms of their long-term consequences for future such events.

Breaking down barriers to institutional communication and cooperation on both the operational and strategic level is also essential. The UN Office for the Coordination of Humanitarian Affairs (UNOCHA) recommended in an April 2014 report that humanitarian and development actors should use a common analysis of risk and align their planning cycles; develop and make a long-term commitment of resources to new joint initiatives for crisis anticipation, prevention, mitigation and recovery; and strengthen links between humanitarian and development teams within organisations. Governments should establish national coordination forums to jointly analyse and assess risks.[62] These recommendations apply equally to conflict risk management, with the addition that expertise from the security community be added to the humanitarian and development components.

On a higher level, suggested institutional reforms to facilitate coordinated risk management include the establishment of a UN High-Level

Council on Global Development and Environment that could pool the competencies of existing UN bodies or, less drastically, a UN Sustainable Development Board with competence to refer environmental security issues to the Security Council.[63] Since the Security Council's responsibility includes an evolving role in conflict prevention and managing emergent risks, and given the recognition of climate risks in many countries' national-security policies, climate change falls under the council's remit. In theory, this gives the Security Council authority to take action to respond directly to pre-empt explicitly climate-related threats, although in practice, given the objections and veto power of two permanent members, this authority is unlikely to be exercised. However, the council is already facing the need to take action as a result of climate-related conflict, most notably in UN Security Council Resolution 1973, which authorises intervention in Libya on humanitarian grounds.[64] As many as ten council-mandated peacekeeping operations, and half the global peacekeeping budget, have been deployed to countries where resources played a role in conflict.[65]

The study of climate change and security is a relatively new field which integrates a range of physical-science and social-science data. Climate-science data is particularly abundant, and global models are well developed and validated, although regional projections are less robust and incorporate a greater range of uncertainty. Deficiencies in monitoring capabilities on the ground in less developed parts of the world, including much of the African continent, leads to a lower level of agreement between the models there than for many other regions.[66] Yet these are precisely the areas of greatest concern for development and humanitarian organisations. Climate data from the IPCC is, however, sufficient to provide robust messages about risk and vulnerability. Extrapolating from this data to take a longer-term, pre-emptive approach to natural-resource management will require policymakers and international institutions to develop a level of scientific literacy, particularly around uncertainty, and to plan resilience measures that are robust within a range of climate projections. Changes in the reporting of degrees of consensus and uncertainty between the IPCC's 4th and 5th Assessment Reports is a step in this direction, but it will take time and focus for policymakers to integrate this information in their planning.

The current consensus on anthropogenic global warming is grounded in a consilience of method, evidence and theory.[67] Climate models may differ from one another and in different runs of the same model in their specific, detailed projections, but they agree within the limits of error on the overall trend. Conclusions are relatively insensitive to the choice of model or variables. This is not the case with quantitative conflict research, and with environmental conflict research specifically. The high sensitivity to choice of data sets, proxies, time frames, geographical scope and definitions, coupled with the complexity of interactions among multiple social, political, economic and environmental variables and a lack of scholarly agreement with regard to theoretical models of that interaction, reduces the potential for forecasting. On the one hand, there is almost too much choice with regard to the data, but too few historical cases to draw quantitatively robust conclusions. Moreover, despite the surfeit of data, it can be of variable quality. Accurate and up-to-date data on economic activity or resource availability, for example, are harder to obtain in countries with weak internal institutions or authoritarian systems, yet these states are of particular interest in terms of conflict and humanitarian risk assessment.

Climate models agree on the overall trend

UNOCHA notes that, despite calls by the Security Council and secretary-general in 2011, there is still no UN conflict-warning system. Moreover, risk assessments tend to ignore conflict, due both to the methodological difficulties and to political sensitivities.[68] The development of the InfoRM risk-assessment tool for humanitarian crises (to be launched in November 2014) is, however, a first step.[69] It combines about 50 different indicators for hazards, vulnerability and capacity, and incorporates both natural and human hazards. A product of the UN Inter-Agency Standing Committee and the European Commission Joint Research Centre, InfoRM is an example of the sort of inter-agency and inter-organisational cooperation and coordination that is required to cope with the emergent risk of climate-influenced conflict. It is intended to inform the development of shared priorities and objective allocation of resources. Since climate change acts as a risk multiplier for conflict through its effect on environmentally driven humanitarian crises such as droughts or famine, effective humanitarian early warning is a prerequisite for developing a useful conflict early-warning tool.

Tools are only as good as the hands that wield them. Despite a range of indicators and warnings, the outbreak of civil war in Syria took most observers by surprise. The human consequences of the drought in the Horn of Africa in 2011 were multiplied by delays on the part of governments and humanitarian and development organisations in reacting to the incipient crisis. Early-warning systems forecast a humanitarian emergency as early as August 2010, and yet a full-scale response was not launched for another 11 months, after the crisis was well developed.[70] Waiting to respond to certainties rather than risk multiplied the financial and human cost. Preventative humanitarian work in response to short-term warnings and forecasts could have mitigated the disaster. Failure to anticipate and address security issues contributed as well.[71]

Long-term development approaches to improve overall resilience, even in the face of uncertainty, are likewise more effective than disaster response, especially in the context of climate change. The IPCC's assessment is that increasing awareness of changing climate risks among policymakers and other actors has not sufficiently translated into adjustments of programmes or risk-management planning.[72] Adaptation planning requires an ongoing, iterative risk-management process of assessment, action, reassessment and response across multiple scales.[73] Mainstreaming (integration of adaptation into planning and decision-making) within and across sectors and levels of governance promotes synergies with development planning, improves cost-effectiveness and reduces the possibility of unintended consequences.[74]

* * *

Ban Ki-moon's ambition to reframe the debate on climate change from an environmental to a development and security issue has not been fully realised. While climate change is increasingly discussed in development and security circles, dialogue between the two domains remains limited. Yet the security risks of climate change are inextricably linked to development issues through the role of resource scarcity and environmental change as conflict risk multipliers, and by the central importance of institutional capacity to both.

Food, water and energy security are inextricably linked, and climate change directly and indirectly affects all three. Climate change will act as a conflict multiplier by amplifying existing environmental stresses, creating new ones, exacerbating water and food insecurity, undermining weak, corrupt or repressive governments and threatening more stable ones. Complex interactions among environmental, social, political and economic factors can create vicious cycles that disproportionately increase the risk of internal conflict and humanitarian crises, and reduce social or governmental ability to cope with repeated or multi-year crises and to further adapt to long-term climate change.

Without deep and early cuts in greenhouse-gas emissions beyond those to which states are already committed, the world is likely to see warming exceeding 3°C and possibly 4°C over pre-industrial levels by the end of the century. Warming on this scale and at this rate would create conditions unprecedented in human history. Under these circumstances, the relative contribution of environmental stress and resource scarcity to the risk of humanitarian crises and internal conflict will increase significantly.

As the secretary-general's 2009 report on the security implications of climate change put it, however, just as it is useful to think of climate change as a threat multiplier that can work through several channels to exacerbate existing sources of conflict and insecurity, 'conditions, policies, institutions and actions which serve to relieve and manage stresses effectively can be considered threat minimizers'.[75] These 'threat minimisers', broadly speaking, include mitigation, adaptation and related capacity-building in developing countries; economic growth and sustainable development to build resilience and adaptive capacity; effective governance mechanisms and institutions; and timely information for decision-making and risk management. But these threat minimisers, like threat multipliers, will interact in complex and unpredictable ways. Effective responses to environment-related conflict risks require continual and systematic re-examination, reassessment and adjustment.

Acknowledgements

This article is adapted from a longer report, 'Conflict Multipliers, Climate Change and Resource Scarcity', commissioned by The Prince's Charities' International Sustainability Unit (ISU) and published in June 2014. Both this article and the original report reflect the views and recommendations of the authors alone, and not necessarily those of the commissioning body or its parent organisation.

Notes

1 See, for example, Caitlin E. Werrell and Francesco Femia (eds), *The Arab Spring and Climate Change* (Washington DC: Center for American Progress, February 2013); Ban Ki-moon, 'A Climate Culprit in Darfur', *Washington Post*, 16 June 2007, p. A15; Jeffrey Mazo, *Climate Conflict: How Global Warming Threatens Security and What to Do About It*, Adelphi 409 (Abingdon: Routledge for the IISS, 2010), pp. 34–5, 73–86; *Climate Change 2014: Impacts, Adaptation, and Vulnerability*, Box 12-5.

2 Francesco Femia and Caitlin Werrell, 'Climate Change Before and After the Arab Awakening: The Cases of Syria and Libya', in Werrell and Femia (eds), *The Arab Spring and Climate Change*, pp. 23–32.

3 Most international organisations and NGOs use the Falkenmark Water Stress Index, which classifies a country with less than 1,700m^3 per capita annual runoff as water stressed; one with less than 1,000m^3 as experiencing scarcity; and one with less than 500m^3 as in a state of absolute water scarcity. The index is easy to calculate from readily available data and is straightforward to apply, but it does not take into account regional differences within countries, the quality and accessibility of resources, and variations in demand within and between countries due to levels of development, efficiency and governance. Data from AQUASTAT database, UN Food and Agriculture Organization, http://www.fao.org/nr/water/aquastat/main/index.stm; 'Country Profile: Syrian Arab Republic', in Karen Frenken (ed.), *Irrigation in the Middle East Region in Figures: AQUASTAT Survey – 2008*, UN FAO Water Reports 34 (Rome: UN Food and Agriculture Organization, 2009), pp. 339–54; US Census Bureau International Database, http://www.census.gov/population/international/data/idb/informationGateway.php.

4 'Country Profile: Syrian Arab Republic', p. 344. Using this metric, which avoids some of the limitations of the Falkenmark Index, a country is considered water scarce if the 'criticality ratio' of withdrawals to resources falls between 0.20–0.40, and severely water scarce if it exceeds 0.40 (in other words, if withdrawals exceed 40% of supply).

5 Robert F. Worth, 'Earth is Parched

where Syrian Farms Thrived', *New York Times*, 13 October 2010, http://www.nytimes.com/2010/10/14/world/middleeast/14syria.html.

6 Shahrzad Mohtadi, 'Climate Change and the Syrian Uprising', *Bulletin of the Atomic Scientists*, 16 August 2012, http://thebulletin.org/climate-change-and-syrian-uprising.

7 UN Office for the Coordination of Humanitarian Affairs, 'Syria Drought Response Plan 2009–2010, Mid-Term Review', February 2010, p. 4.

8 *Inventory of Shared Water Resources in Western Asia* (Beirut: UN Economic and Social Commission for Western Asia and Bundesanstalt für Geowissenschaften und Rohstoffe, 2013), pp. 58–61.

9 Francesca de Châtel, 'The Role of Drought and Climate Change in the Syrian Uprising: Untangling the Triggers of the Revolution', *Middle Eastern Studies*, online publication, 27 January 2014. DOI: 10.1080/00263206.2013.850076.

10 H. Harding, 'Working in the Grey Zone', *Syria Today*, no. 61, May 2010.

11 *Syria Grain and Feed Annual Report 2007*, Global Agriculture Information Report SY7001 (Washington DC: USDA Foreign Agriculture Service, 6 February 2007).

12 In 2000, 28.5% of agricultural land was irrigated, while 71.5% was rain fed. Yields from irrigated agriculture are many times higher than from rain-fed agriculture, however, so irrigation accounts for a much higher percentage of total agricultural production. 'Country Profile: Syrian Arab Republic', p. 348.

13 Wadid Erian, Bassem Katlan and Ouldbdey Babah, *Drought Vulnerability in the Arab Region: Special Case Study: Syria* (Damascus: Global Assessment Report on Disaster Risk Reduction, United Nations Office for Disaster Risk Reduction, 2010).

14 Wadid Erian, *Drought Vulnerability in the Arab Region: Case Study: Syria. Ten Years of Scarce Water (2000–2010)* (Damascus and Cairo: Arab Center for the Study of Arid Zones and Dry Lands and Secretariat of the UN International Strategy for Disaster Reduction, 2011), http://www.unisdr.org/files/23905_droughtsyriasmall.pdf.

15 Erian et al., *Drought Vulnerability in the Arab Region*.

16 Olivier De Schutter, 'Report of the Special Rapporteur on the Right to Food, Mission to the Syrian Arab Republic', United Nations General Assembly, 27 January 2011, http://www.srfood.org/images/stories/pdf/officialreports/20110121_a-hrc-16-49-add2_country_mission_syria_en.pdf.

17 Lahcen Achy, 'Syria: Economic Hardship Feeds Social Unrest', Carnegie Middle East Center, 31 March 2011, http://carnegie-mec.org/2011/03/31/syria-economic-hardship-feeds-social-unrest/axs1.

18 *Statistical Report on Registered Iraqis in Syria, Jordan, Lebanon, Turkey and Egypt* (Geneva: UN High Commissioner for Refugees, 25 September 2008).

19 de Châtel, 'The Role of Drought and Climate Change in the Syrian Uprising'.

20 International Crisis Group, 'Conflict Risk Alert: Syria', 25 March 2011, http://www.crisisgroup.org/en/publication-type/media-releases/2011/

conflict-risk-alert-syria.aspx.

21 International Crisis Group, 'Popular Protest in North Africa and the Middle East (VI): The Syrian People's Slow Motion Revolution', Middle East/North Africa Report no. 108, 6 July 2011.

22 de Châtel, 'The Role of Drought and Climate Change in the Syrian Uprising'.

23 Troy Sternberg, 'Chinese Drought, Wheat, and the Egyptian Uprising: How a Localized Hazard Became Globalized', in Werrell and Femia (eds), *The Arab Spring and Climate Change*, pp. 7–14.

24 'Food Price Index', UN Food and Agriculture Organization, http://www.fao.org/worldfoodsituation/FoodPricesIndex/en/; Annie Lowrey, 'Protesting on an Empty Stomach', Slate, 31 January 2011, http://www.slate.com/articles/business/moneybox/2011/01/protesting_on_an_empty_stomach.html; Mary Curtis, Richard Kersley and Mujtaba Rana, *Emerging Consumer Survey 2011* (Zurich: Credit Suisse Research Institute, 2011); Sarah Johnstone and Jeffrey Mazo, 'Global Warming and the Arab Spring', in Werrell and Femia (eds), *The Arab Spring and Climate Change*, pp. 15–22.

25 'Two Dead and 400 Injured in Algeria Riots: Minister', Al-Arabiya, 8 January 2011.

26 UK Parliament, Foreign Affairs Committee Report, 'British Foreign Policy and the "Arab Spring"', July 2012, http://www.publications.parliament.uk/pa/cm201213/cmselect/cmfaff/80/8002.htm.

27 See Arab Human Development Reports (AHDR), UN Development Programme, http://www.arab-hdr.org/.

28 Florence Gaub, *Understanding Instability: Lessons from the Arab Spring*, AHRC Public Policy Series 9 (Swindon: Arts and Humanities Research Council, December 2012).

29 F. Gregory Gause III, 'Why Middle East Studies Missed the Arab Spring', *Foreign Affairs*, vol. 90, no. 4, July–August 2007, pp. 81–90.

30 Oli Brown and Alec Crawford, *Rising Temperatures, Rising Tensions: Climate Change and the Risk of Violent Conflict in the Middle East* (Winnipeg: International Institute for Sustainable Development, 2009).

31 Confidential cable, US Embassy Damascus, 26 November 2008, available at https://www.wikileaks.org/plusd/cables/08DAMASCUS847_a.html.

32 The 15,000 figure reflects the situation in 2008; the number of migrants increased as the drought continued.

33 'Syria Drought Response Plan 2009–2010, Mid-Term Review'.

34 *Climate Change 2014: Impacts, Adaptation, and Vulnerability*, section 12.5.1.

35 See, for example, Kidane Mengisteab, *Critical Factors in the Horn of Africa's Raging Conflicts*, Discussion Paper no. 67 (Uppsala: Nordiska Afrikainstitutet, 2011); and five papers from the *Journal of Peace Research*, vol. 49, no. 1, January 2012: Christopher K. Butler and Scott Gates, 'African Range Wars: Climate, Conflict and Property Rights', pp. 23–34; Clionadh Raleigh and Dominic Kniveton, 'Come Rain or Shine: An Analysis of Conflict and Climate Variability in East Africa', pp.

51–64; Wario R. Adano et al., 'Climate Change, Violent Conflict and Local Institutions in Kenya's Drylands', pp. 65–80; Ole Magnus Theisen, 'Climate Clashes? Weather Variability, Land Pressure and Organised Violence in Kenya, 1989–2004', pp. 81–96; and Tor A. Benjaminsen et al., 'Does Climate Change Drive Land-use Conflicts in the Sahel?', pp. 97–112.

36 Fund for Peace, Failed State Index 2013, http://ffp.statesindex.org/. For a discussion of the FSI methodology and comparison to other metrics of state stability, see Mazo, *Climate Conflict*, pp. 88–90. In 2008–09, by average rank across three indices (including the FSI), five of the eight states were in the top 20 (South Sudan only gained independence in 2011).

37 See http://inform.jrc.ec.europa.eu/. The index will be published in November 2014, but has been available in beta release since January 2014.

38 Cullen S. Hendrix and Idean Salehyan, 'Social Conflict in Africa Database (SCAD)', Program on Climate Change and African Political Stability, Robert S. Strauss Center for International Security and Law, The University of Texas at Austin, http://www.scaddata.org.

39 Mengisteab, *Critical Factors in the Horn of Africa's Raging Conflicts*.

40 *A Dangerous Delay: The Costs of Late Response to Early Warnings in the 2011 Drought in the Horn of Africa*, Joint Agency Research Paper (Oxford: Oxfam International and Save the Children UK, 2012), p. 5.

41 *Climate Change 2014: Impacts, Adaptation, and Vulnerability*, sections 22.2.2, 22.2.1, 22.3.5.

42 Initiated by then-US Secretary of Defense Robert Gates in 2008, the Minerva Initiative seeks to build deeper understanding of the social, cultural and political dynamics that shape regions of strategic interest to the United States in order to support more effective strategic and operational policy decisions. Further information is available at http://minerva.dtic.mil/.

43 'Advances in Mapping Climate Security Vulnerability in Africa', Research Brief no. 13, Program on Climate Change and African Political Stability, Robert S. Strauss Center for International Security and Law, The University of Texas at Austin.

44 CCAPS Climate Security Vulnerability Model, Program on Climate Change and African Political Stability, Robert S. Strauss Center for International Security and Law, The University of Texas at Austin, http://ccaps.aiddata.org/climate.

45 Josh Busby, Todd Smity and Kaiba White, 'Climate Security and East Africa: A GIS-Based Analysis of Vulnerability', University of Texas at Austin, 2011.

46 Patrick Meier, 'Networking Disaster and Conflict Early Warning in Response to Climate Change', in Hans Gunter Brauch et al. (eds), *Coping with Global Environmental Change, Disasters and Security*, Hexagon Series on Human Environmental Security and Peace no. 5 (Berlin: Springer, 2011), pp. 1,429–40.

47 Jakkie Cilliers, *Towards a Continental Early Warning System for Africa*, ISS paper 102 (Pretoria: Institute for Security Studies, 2005), pp. 1–25.

48 Jonathan Stevenson, 'African

American', *Survival*, vol. 51, no. 1, February–March 2009, pp. 249–56.

49 Rick Barton et al., *A Review of Conflict Prediction Models and Systems* (Washington DC: Center for Strategic and International Studies, 2008).

50 *Ibid.*

51 Dorcas Ettang, 'Early Warning and Early Response Mechanisms in Africa: Gaps and Prospects', Consultancy Africa Intelligence Discussion Paper, 16 February 2011, http://www.consultancyafrica.com/index.php?option=com_content&view=article&id=679.

52 Andrew Robertson and Steve Olson, *Sensing and Shaping Emerging Conflicts* (Washington DC: National Academies Press, 2013).

53 *Preventing Violence, War and State Collapse: The Future of Conflict Early Warning and Response* (Paris: OECD Publishing, 2009).

54 Kumar Rupesinghe, *FCE Citizen-based Early Warning and Response System: A New Tool for Civil Society to Prevent Violent Conflict* (Colombo: Foundation for Co-existence, 2009), http://early-warning.files.wordpress.com/2009/03/fce-citizen-based-early-warning-and-early-response-system.pdf.

55 Patrick Meier, 'Towards a Twitter Dashboard for the Humanitarian Cluster System', 30 July 2012, http://irevolution.net/2012/07/30/twitter-for-humanitarian-cluster/.

56 Robertson and Olson, *Sensing and Shaping Emerging Conflicts*.

57 Meier, 'Networking Disaster and Conflict Early Warning'.

58 'Policy Organs Meet in Kampala', *CEWARN Monthly*, no. 13, November 2008.

59 Nick Mabey et al., *Underpinning the MENA Democratic Transition: Delivering Climate, Energy and Resource Security* (London: E3G, February 2013).

60 *Ibid.*

61 Busby et al., 'Climate Security and East Africa'.

62 *Saving Lives Today and Tomorrow: Managing the Risks of Humanitarian Crises*, OCHA Policy and Studies Series (New York: UN Office for the Coordination of Humanitarian Affairs, 2014), pp. 59, 76–7.

63 Schubert et al., *Climate Change as a Security Risk*, p. 97; *Delivering As One: Report of the High-Level Panel on System-side Coherence*, A/61/583 (New York: UN General Assembly, 20 November 2006).

64 UN Security Council Resolution 1973 (2011), 17 March 2011.

65 UN Security Council, press release, 20 July 2011, http://www.un.org/News/Press/docs/2011/sc10332.doc.htm.

66 This has led CCAPS to design their own regional climate model to provide more granular projections on variables relevant to their project.

67 Naomi Oreskes, 'The Scientific Consensus on Climate Change: How Do We Know We're Not Wrong?', in Joseph F.C. DiMento and Pamela M. Doughman (eds), *Climate Change: What it Means for Us, Our Children, and Our Grandchildren* (Cambridge, MA: MIT Press, 2007), pp. 65–99.

68 *Saving Lives Today and Tomorrow*, pp. 55–6.

69 See http://inform.jrc.ec.europa.eu/.

70 *A Dangerous Delay*, p. 8.

71 Hugo Slim, 'IASC Real-Time Evaluation of the Humanitarian Response to the Horn of Africa

Drought Crisis in Somalia, Ethiopia and Kenya', UN Inter-Agency Standing Committee, June 2012, available at reliefweb.int/sites/reliefweb.int/files/resources/RTE_HoA_SynthesisReport_FINAL.pdf.

72 *Climate Change 2014: Impacts, Adaptation, and Vulnerability*, 'Summary for Policymakers', p. 5.

73 *Ibid.*, pp. 5–6.

74 *Ibid.*, p. 7.

75 *Climate Change and its Possible Security Implications: Report of the Secretary-General*, A/64/350 (New York: UN General Assembly, 11 September 2009), p. 6.

Review Essay

Wealth and the Good Society

David P. Calleo

Capital in the Twenty-First Century
Thomas Piketty. Arthur Goldhammer, trans. Cambridge, MA: The Belknap Press of Harvard University Press, 2014. £29.95/$39.95. 696 pp.

Thomas Piketty's *Capital in the Twenty-First Century* has attracted a great deal of attention, and deservedly so. It is a seductive book that soars above the myopia of ordinary economic analysis. It summons rich visions of the past and future and explores their myriad linkages. The result is a complex chain of arguments, inevitably with disruptive disconnections. In the end, perhaps the author suggests more redistribution than his proposals would deliver.

Like Karl Marx, Piketty believes that in capitalist economies the supply of capital regularly grows faster than the economy itself. Piketty admits this is 'a historical fact, not a logical necessity' (p. 353). He nevertheless finds ample historical evidence for it.[1] Piketty's research shows considerable variation in the ratio over recent centuries. In 1870, for example, the national capital stock of Britain, France and Germany was in each case at a level roughly equal to seven years of the country's national income. Starting in around 1910, however, the accumulated supply of capital in the three countries had started to fall sharply. By the 1950s, it had fallen to the equivalent of around two-and-a-half years of national income.[2]

David P. Calleo is University Professor at Johns Hopkins University, Dean Acheson Professor at its Paul H. Nitze School of Advanced International Studies (SAIS), and a *Survival* Contributing Editor.

 DOI 10.1080/00396338.2014.962804

Not only did the supply of capital fall in relative terms, but its ownership also began to spread. In 1910, the richest 10% of capital holders in Britain and France owned around 90% of the capital stock. By the 1960s, their share had dropped to around 60%. Similarly, the share of national capital held by the top 1% of the rich had fallen from around 60% in 1914 to around 30% in 1960.[3]

This broader ownership of capital, typical of much of the twentieth century, seems closely linked to political trends and government policies. The whole era was shaped by the rise of social democracy, two world wars, a deep depression, Keynesian economics, left-wing and fascist politics, vigorous labour unions and expanding state power, fed from both left and right. In this environment, students of the economy possibly have as much to learn from history, literature, politics and international relations as from conventional economics.

Throughout much of the twentieth century, as the relative growth of private capital lessened, overall economic growth, boosted by much bigger government spending, grew faster than before, although never enough to outpace the growth of private capital.[4] The principal benefits of this higher overall growth were not being exclusively accumulated by the top 10%, but by what Piketty sees as a prosperous new class – a 'patrimonial middle class' – formed from the middle 40% of the population. By the 1970s, the share of the old-rich inheriting class had fallen by half, while the middle 40% had garnered one-third of the accumulated national capital in Europe and one-quarter in the US.[5] Piketty sees the rise of this new patrimonial middle class as 'a major transformation, which deeply altered the social landscape and the political structure of the society and helped to redefine the terms of distributive conflict'.[6]

Return of the super-rich

Piketty's view of current trends suggests, however, that traditional capitalism is resuming its old habits. Once again, rapid growth of capital and extreme concentration of its ownership are being combined with slower growth of the economy as a whole. Piketty's research shows how the top 10% is regaining its old share of national capital.[7] Today, it owns 70% of capital in the US, and 65% in Europe.[8]

As Piketty also notes, the trend toward renewed concentration of capital wealth is accompanied by a parallel concentration of income paid to labour, meaning those who work for wages and including high salaries.[9] By 2008, Piketty saw the top 10% of income earners in America claiming roughly 50% of national income. The earnings of the top 1%, the high achievers with 'supersalaries', rose from 9% of national income in the 1970s to about 20% in 2000–10.[10] More than half of this rise has gone to the population's top 0.1% (p. 296).

The same combination of concentrated income and capital holdings appears to be continuing after the crash of 2008. It is these trends that provoke Piketty's deepest fear: a 'hypermeritocratic' society, dominated by supersalaries, merging with a 'hyperpatrimonial' society characterised by giant inheritances. The huge new salaries of the super-achievers are being transformed into giant new holdings of capital. Both salaries and capital holdings are approaching the relative levels of inequality of 1910. This was the belle époque, whose extreme inequalities and slow growth pointed to the violent revolutionary consequences that Marx anticipated. It is worth noting, moreover, that today's return to the old inequalities favouring the very rich is gradually being accompanied by a return to the slow economic growth experienced in the decades before the Second World War.[11] Historically, the rejuvenation of the rentier class that Piketty foresees (and fears) does not promise a renewed pursuit of rapid growth. The future, as Piketty sees it, promises instead a high return to capital, a high concentration of earned income at the top levels and slow overall growth – not a pattern that the population is likely to accept indefinitely.

Piketty's challenge is to define a state policy that encourages higher growth without further concentrating income or the ownership of capital. His solution is redistributive taxation: an annual international tax on capital holdings. In one of his formulations, he proposes a 1% annual tax on assets of €1 million to €5 million and a 2% tax for capital wealth above €5 million.[12] Elsewhere, Piketty calls for rates ranging from 0.1% for holdings of up to €200,000 to 2% for holdings beyond €5 million. Either way, an estate of €5 million would pay an annual tax of roughly €100,000. Anyone with assets worth €50 million would pay €1 million; those with a fortune of €100 million would pay €2 million.

Balancing act

Whether Piketty's rates are appropriate depends on what he is aiming to accomplish. Behind a serious wealth tax should be a coherent vision of a good society accepted by public opinion, fostered by tax policy and protected by constitutional balances. But while Piketty's writings present a heroically voluminous assemblage of data, the model he is pursuing is not always clear. His enthusiasm for a 'patrimonial middle class' suggests a strong instinct for constitutional balance. So too does his driving fear of a political fusion of hyperpatrimonial and hypermeritocratic elites. To provide a national constitution that can balance and contain the burgeoning combined financial power of the super-rich and the super-achievers will presumably require a new political and social balance – a patrimonial balancing class able to limit the excesses of runaway capitalism and effect a distribution of wealth less favourable to the super-rich and more favourable to the poor, the middle class and the well-to-do. Presumably, this new class alignment will draw from the lower strata of the top 10%, as well as from Piketty's middle 40%.

Piketty's actual proposals, however, do little to advance or protect the economic interests of a serious patrimonial balancing class. On the contrary, the proposals are a major threat to upper-middle-class wealth in general. Oddly, they seem much less of a threat to the super-rich. An annual tax of €1 million seems likely to be felt less heavily on a capital of €50 million than a tax of €100,000 on a capital of €5 million, let alone a tax of €10 million on a capital of €500 million. In short, instead of taxing heavily the excess earnings of the super-rich, Piketty proposes levelling off his wealth-tax rates at fortunes of €5 million. In other words, if Piketty's goal is to foster a patrimonial middle class, he is aiming at the wrong targets. This is likely to prove a great lost opportunity.

The distributional deformations revealed by Piketty are so large, however, that they appear to offer a golden opportunity to improve greatly the lot of a significant portion of Western citizenry without anything like a confiscatory assault on the super-rich. In the US, for example, the poorest 50% absorb only 25% of national income and own only 2% of national capital (p. 257). If more capital were shifted, for example, to the working class through subsidised mortgages, life would be richer and more agreeable for a large part of the population. What would be the harm? Would it not be better to subsidise the ambitious poor directly rather than their incompetent banks? Is there an economic law that requires 1% of the population to possess 33% of the country's wealth, or the top 0.1% to have 14%? Would the economy collapse if the top 0.1% owned only 10% of the nation's capital instead of 14%? Would capitalism disappear if America's wretched infrastructure were repaired? Would the suffering for the rich be unbearable if taxes on estates valued at over €30 million were very high, even as they remained low or non-existent for estates up to €10–20 million? Would it be impossible to achieve widespread acceptance for such a distribution? If reform is to succeed, it must be radical enough to provide the elements needed for real change. If Piketty's aim is to provide a public-spirited patrimonial balancing class, secure and confident enough to balance and contain the super-rich, then it is essential that this patrimonial class be adequately endowed.

To be effective over the long-term, Piketty's balancing class will require enough income and inherited wealth to enjoy a reasonably cultivated life, sustain independent and principled politics and have the possibility to provide its children with a serious education. In a well-ordered state, sustaining such an upper or upper-middle class should be considered a political end in itself. Ideally, it should constitute an educated political power in reserve, ready and able to check hyperactive political and economic groups running out of control. In a society that lacks such a balancing class, liberty is almost always at risk. This kind of middle class will almost certainly be closely tied to the professions, education and the arts. It should be reasonably efficient economically. Certainly it should be honest and open to rising new elites and ideas. But it is unlikely to remain effective as a balancing class without a cushion of modest inherited wealth. As it is, the failure to look realistically at the role of wealthy elites in achieving and preserving constitutional balance weakens any serious effort at reform.

It seems unwise to embark on so radical a project as a new wealth tax without a clear idea of the end in view. Of course, many economists may not be well equipped professionally to imagine social reconstruction. Not the least of Piketty's own virtues, however, is his familiarity with the nineteenth century's rich Anglo-French tradition of novels and social history. He invokes the insights of literature not merely as an elegant decoration but as an essential part of his own methodology as an economist. Jane Austen and Honoré de Balzac are invoked to suggest the complex ways in which the economic relations of a society are linked to its moral, aesthetic and political culture. Piketty is openly scornful of analysts who encase their views within mathematical formulas that hide social and political realities, often to justify a manifestly unbalanced status quo. Leading economists, he admits, may not always be particularly well equipped to blaze the trail to reform. Many are themselves major gainers from today's mounting inequality. They find it all too easy to take refuge behind the 'chaste veil' provided by their digitalised profession.

Piketty's research suggests how much economists might benefit from a broader sociological study of the groups that play a role in their economic analysis. Categories like 'top 10%' and 'middle 40%' are statistical constructions with uncertain connections to social and economic realities (see pp. 250–2). They are not necessarily the real demarcation points of society's social and economic groupings. As Piketty himself points out, large and sharp inequalities of fortune exist within his top 10%, and even more within his top 1%. Today, the sharpest disparity of wealth actually lies between the top 1%, which in the US owns 33% of the nation's capital, and the top 0.1%, which in the US owns 14% of the nation's capital.[13] Roughly speaking, the average fortune is €4 million for the bottom of the top 1%, whereas it is, on average, €30 million for the top 0.1%. In the face of these numbers, Piketty's proposed taxes seem both too high and too low. They are too high because they would fall heavily on fortunes of €5 million. They are too low because they propose the same rate for a fortune of €10 million as for a fortune of €50 million. In other words, Piketty's taxes penalise harshly the moderately wealthy upon whom his patrimonial balancing class will depend. At the same time, his taxes appear surprisingly forgiving to the super-rich.

* * *

Piketty clearly means well. Indeed, his observations and prescriptions form a major contribution to a better future. But the provisions he suggests for his tax would serve to weaken the very people most likely to check the runaway power of the super-rich. Meanwhile, he seems unaware of how much his patrimonial balancing class is already at serious risk of extinction. Far from fostering the strength of this balancing class, Western governments seem to be working to destroy it. The reckless creation of official credit with negative interest rates robs capital of its ability to produce income for savers – a prime necessity for an independent middle class. Meanwhile, old capital itself is being systematically destroyed as governments assume huge new debt and cover it by the uncontrolled creation of new money. As Piketty admits, in this sort of incipient inflationary environment it is ultimately the holders of big wealth who are greatly advantaged.

Countering the forces of giant capital, heroically greedy management or non-productive labour requires, as Piketty seems to acknowledge, a well-educated and patriotic upper-middle class, a patrimonial elite with the wealth and confidence needed to avoid domination and endow independence. This is the constitutionalist model that evolved in the happier moments of American and European history. It has made us rich and kept us free. In reminding us that unbounded wealth is dangerous both to liberty and to capitalism itself, Piketty does us a great favour. But the timidity of his provisions for balancing excessive wealth prevents him from offering a truly credible solution.

Acknowledgements

The author would like to thank Giacomo Tagiuri for invaluable research assistance in preparing this article.

Notes

1 Piketty affirms: 'throughout most of human history, the inescapable fact is that the rate of return on capital was always 10 to 20 times greater than the rate of growth of output (and income)' (p. 353). This was primarily

because 'economic growth was virtually nil throughout much of human history: combining demographic growth with economic growth, we can say that the annual growth rate from antiquity to the seventeenth century never exceeded 0.1–0.2 percent for long' (p. 353). In most agrarian societies, the return on land was instead 4–5%, which coincides with Piketty's estimated average return on capital. This condition remained true in the European societies of the nineteenth century. In France, for example, from 1820 to 1913, the average return on capital was around 5%, compared with an average growth rate of 1% (p. 351).

2 For a more detailed description of this capital destruction see pp. 146–150. Piketty notes that 'the budgetary and political shocks of two wars proved far more destructive to capital than combat itself'. Two further causes were the collapse of foreign portfolios and the very low saving rates characteristic of the time. Furthermore, in the 1950s and 1960s, asset prices stood at historic lows.

3 See the additional table available on Piketty's website: 'Concentration of Wealth in Europe and in the USA, 1810–2010 (series used for figures 10.1 and 10.6, pp. 340-349)', http://piketty.pse.ens.fr/files/capital21c/en/pdf/supp/TS10.1.pdf.

4 In other words, capital formation was declining and growth was rising, but never enough for economic growth to catch up with private capital growth.

5 See pp. 260–2 and 346–7. Piketty presents a more complex picture of wealth inequality in America, where a white patrimonial middle class had existed before, during the nineteenth century. This group 'suffered a setback during the Gilded Age, regained its health in the middle of the twentieth century and then suffered another setback after 1980' (p. 350).

6 Piketty also notes, however, that the rise of this new middle class did little for the relative position of the bottom 50% of the population, which continued to own less than 5% of the nation's capital (p. 262).

7 In France, the annual flow of inheritance as a proportion of national income reached 20–25% in the nineteenth century until 1914, then fell to less than 5% in the 1950s and returned to about 15% in 2010 (p. 380).

8 From the 1980s, Piketty records a new increase in the share of the American top 10% from 64.2% in the 1970s to 71.5% in the early 2010s. This increase, however, was almost totally absorbed by the top 1%, whose share rose from 28.2% to 33.8%. In Europe, the increase of wealth inequality was smaller and started in the 1990s. The share of the top 10% went from 59.3% in the 1980s to 64% in 2010. Again, most of this increase benefitted the top 1%: from 20.4% to 24.4%.

9 In the US, the share of national income claimed by the top 10% rose from 30–35% in the 1970s to 45–50% in the decade starting in 2000 (see http://piketty.pse.ens.fr/files/capital21c/en/pdf/F0.I.1.pdf). This increase was mostly owed to the rise of the top 1% of income earners (making above $352,000 in 2010). Their share of national income was just below 10% in the 1970s. At the end of that decade, it started rising steadily and

was at 20% in 2010 (see http://piketty.pse.ens.fr/files/capital21c/en/pdf/F8.6.pdf). The share earned by the European top 10% experienced a similar trend. It rose from just below 30% in 1980 to 35% in 2010.

10 See pp. 294–6. Again, Piketty shows that 'the increase in wage inequality in the United States is mainly owed to increased pay at the very top end of the distribution: the top 1 percent and even more the top 0.1 percent'. Members of the bottom 9% of the top 10% of the income distribution have increased their shares only slightly. In other words, people making 'between $100,000 to $200,000 have seen their pay increase only slightly more rapidly than average, whereas those making more than $500,000 have seen their remuneration literally explode' (p. 314).

11 The so-called *Trente Glorieuses,* the 30 years between the late 1940s and the late 1970s during which economic growth was unusually high (especially in Europe, with an average growth rate of 4%) were, in historical perspective, an exceptional period. In fact, most of this rapid growth can be explained by the fact that Europe had fallen behind the US, technologically, during the wars. Most of this growth was catch-up. 'Once this catch-up was complete, Europe and the United States both stood at the global technological frontier and began to grow at the same relatively slow pace' (pp. 96–7).

12 In Chapter 15, Piketty explores various proposals for a global annual levy on wealth. The base would include all financial assets (bank deposits, stocks, bonds, partnerships and other forms of participations) and non-financial assets (real estate). Piketty offers two proposals for the tax rates: one features a tax rate of 0% for net assets below €1 million, 1% between €1 and 5 million and 2% above €5 million. Such a tax, if implemented at the European level, would produce revenues equal to 2% of Europe's GDP. The alternative imagines minimal rates on modest wealth: 0.1% on capital below €200,000, 0.5% between €200,000 and €1 million, 1% between €1 and €5 million and 2% beyond €5 million. In a somewhat obscure footnote, Piketty admits he sees no very strong reason why the top rate should be limited to 2%, and sees serious reasons for taxing fortunes above €100 million at higher rates. A tax rate of 5% on the largest fortunes is, he admits, probably necessary to maintain the current level of inequality. An even higher rate would be needed if the goal is to reduce that current level. Piketty notes, however, that he is thinking of a permanent annual tax, and therefore prefers moderate rates that can be accepted permanently (pp. 517, 529, 530). This appears to be the general bias of his proposal.

13 See the supplemental data presented on Piketty's website at http://piketty.pse.ens.fr/files/capital21c/en/pdf/supp/TS10.1.pdf.

Review Essay

Within the Sacred Walls

Massimo Franco

The Vatican Diaries: A Behind-the-Scenes Look at the Power, Personalities and Politics at the Heart of the Catholic Church
John Thavis. New York: Viking, 2013. $27.95. 336 pp.

This volume is a warning to Pope Francis: an engaging, ironic report of 300 pages or so, whose implicit message is that a change of pontiff alone is not enough to change the Vatican. From this perspective, *The Vatican Diaries* by John Thavis, a respected reporter and Rome bureau chief for the Catholic News Service of 30 years' standing, packs a metaphorical punch. The diaries describe an enduring self-referential mentality – a conviction that nothing can actually change inside the Vatican walls and in the Catholic Church, and that in this universe of secrecy and mystery the truth is something to be manipulated and from time to time even fabricated for a 'superior interest', no matter what the faithful believe or what the media write and broadcast.

What emerges is a world of nobility and misery, humour and sadness – not at all a 'holy' environment, and not at all the 'perfect society' the Catholic Church tries to present itself as being. This world may well contain great personalities, but in the book they seem overwhelmed by the 'Vatican *popolino*', the anonymous humanity of papal Rome: characters who might have been plucked from the grim age of the Borgias, or from a movie about serial

Massimo Franco is a political columnist for the leading Italian daily *Corriere della Sera*. He is the author of *The Crisis in the Vatican Empire* (Mondadori, 2013) and *The Vatican According to Francis: From Buenos Aires to Santa Marta* (Mondadori, 2014), a Spanish edition of which will be published in Argentina by Penguin Random House (Latin America) later this year.

 DOI 10.1080/00396338.2014.962805

sex abusers. That is the value of a book dominated by day-to-day problems and concerns, power struggles, miserable competition and the bureaucratic mentality – both its value, and its limitation.

Everything is viewed through the eyes of an American journalist confronting, over time, the stubbornness of the Vatican bureaucracy. Thavis has developed a love–hate relationship with the world he has studied and reported on for many years, years filled with the difficulties and frustrations inherent in dealing with a power structure. And he has found a zoo of humans from which to draw inspiration.

The titles of the *Diaries'* ten chapters can be misleading. Telling episodes are often left hidden, and anecdotes and side-shows tend to get the upper hand. These are intriguing, and useful in conveying an impression of how things work (or fail to work) inside the rooms and corridors of the Holy See, but they rarely reveal any of the bigger picture.

Probably this is because the book is the result of years mostly chronicling a declining Vatican. The *Diaries* cover the papacies of John Paul I (pope for just 33 days before his death, in September 1978), John Paul II (1978–2005) and Benedict XVI (2005–13). They indeed offer a 'behind-the-scenes look' at key developments, as the subtitle suggests; and they shrewdly mix major and minor events: on the one hand, the building of a parking lot near the Vatican, sacrificing archaeological treasures, on the other, meetings between popes and heads of state. Throughout, Thavis maintains his disenchanted approach and light touch.

Particularly detailed, disturbing and telling is the chapter on Marcial Maciel Degollado (commonly referred to as Father Maciel), the head of the Legion of Christ religious order. What is striking is not just his disgusting and criminal behaviour, but the way in which the Vatican, under John Paul II, handled it for years without the cultural capability or will to understand what was happening in the Legion. The tormented developments of the broader paedophilia scandal are recorded, as are the differing views inside the Curia on how to deal with it.

Also presented are the conflicts between Benedict XVI's controversial secretary of state, Tarcisio Bertone, and Italian bishops; the sacking of the president of the Vatican Bank (IOR), Ettore Gotti Tedeschi, over a murky internal fight about financial transparency; and the author's own guided visit to the Vatican Secret Archives, a bunker with almost 100km of shelf space, waterproof and climate-controlled, which 'could even withstand a nuclear attack – or so I was told' (p. 209).

And there is the surreal conversation between George W. Bush and Pope Benedict XVI in the gardens of Vatican City, during Bush's 2008 visit to Rome. The president asked how much land the Vatican owned, to which the Pope let Monsignor Harvey, an American prelate, reply: '109 acres. Not quite as big as Texas'. 'But more important', Bush retorted (p. 249). Here was a sideshow of banalities and mutual embarrassment in the shadow of what was supposed to be a historic meeting.

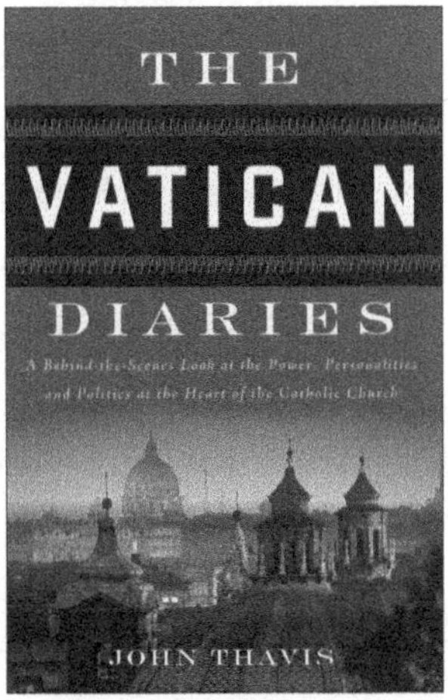

Sacred mysteries

This book is a fresco, so to speak, of a long period, ending with the resignation of Benedict XVI in February 2013, a man whose legacy is the misunderstandings, the scandals, and the mess left by disreputable (if not criminal) priests and lay Vatican officers: quite an inheritance. Yet all these facts are somewhat dwarfed by the epochal enormity of the first resignation of a pontiff for almost 700 years, a Ground Zero for the Catholic Church, and the starting point of a new era.

The book is certainly an amusing and interesting description of the past. It enumerates all the daily contradictions, limitations and occasional gaffes of great popes like Karol Wojtyla and of more controversial ones like Joseph Ratzinger. But it lacks any in-depth analysis to explain the major changes of the last year and a half within the Sacred Walls, which are to some extent a reflection, inside the Vatican, of what has happened worldwide in the last 15 years or so.

Reading the Diaries, one might get the impression that the Vatican is and will always stay the same, no matter what happens around it; that its people, its culture, and its Roman–Italian style and approach to problems will never change. That may be so. The possible objection, however, is that in the meantime a papacy has collapsed, marking the failure of a model of governance. A conclave decided to elect Francis: not just an Argentine, but an outsider to the Curia, and even a geopolitical outsider. Why? What does this mean? In the book there is much to tell us *what* happened, but there is less to tell us *why*.

Why did these scandals arrive all at once? Why did paedophilia all of a sudden became such a destructive issue, just at the end of the last millennium? Why did the IOR's wrongdoings force the Holy See to act as never before? Why was John Paul II declared a saint in spite of his failings on the issue of Father Maciel? And, furthermore, why did Benedict XVI give up the papacy after seven centuries of pontificates that had ended only with the death of their popes? If the Vatican were simply as it is pictured in the *Diaries*, things should have carried on as usual. On the contrary, they are dramatically changing. A subtle, gripping fight is under way.

In this sense, the choice to write the book in diary form turns out to be double-edged. Historical context is ignored or undervalued – in fact, it seldom appears. Thavis describes, but apparently does not fully grasp, the crisis in the most important religious institution of the West, and the coincidence between this moral crisis and a more general loss of identity by the West on the international stage. He relates a lot of anecdotes, but it is difficult to infer from them what is at stake, and what the potential consequences might be. The *Diaries* thus become a long chronicle of what the Vatican has been during the last 25 years or so, and probably partially still is; but they do not explain the root of the collapse or its outcome, the arrival of an Argentine pope.

This, one should add, was not Thavis's intention. As he explains in the Introduction:

> I wanted to depict the culture behind the headlines and explain how things really work at the Vatican ... not through political analysis of Vatican policy but from the inside, where the business of governing the universal church churns and sputters ... I am convinced that the backstage reality at the Vatican is infinitely more interesting than the caricature of power and authority that dominates mainstream media (p. 6).

Quite true. The risk, however, is that in destroying this caricature of papal Rome he may have created a different one, probably more interesting but equally misleading. Today's 'backstage reality' appears heavily challenged; more importantly, it is overshadowed by the terrific novelties of Francis's pontificate.

Review Essay

Maxed Out?

Russell Crandall

Maximalist: America in the World from Truman to Obama
Stephen Sestanovich. New York: Knopf, 2014. $28.95. 416 pp.

Hard Choices
Hillary Rodham Clinton. London and New York: Simon & Schuster, 2014. £20.00/$35.00. 656 pp.

Looking back on how decisively the Cold War ended in America's favour, it is easy to forget how much doubt there was at the start, among Americans and Soviets alike, that the United States was up to the task of defending its vision of the post-war world order. George Kennan, the storied American diplomat responsible for the 1946 'Long Telegram' from Moscow, recalled in his memoirs that the Soviets 'thought it probable that ... Americans, in particular, would not be able to muster, as a nation, the leadership, the imagination, the political skill, the material resources, and above all the national self-discipline necessary' to prevail in the emerging global contest. Certain members of President Harry Truman's administration apparently harboured doubts of their own: Secretary of State Dean Acheson, for one, thought it necessary to 'shock the country' into the realisation that supplying large amounts of economic and military aid to a devastated Europe was vital to America's interests at a time when American–Soviet nego-

Russell Crandall is Associate Professor of International Politics and American Foreign Policy, Davidson College, and a Contributing Editor of *Survival*. His latest book is *America's Dirty Wars: Irregular Warfare from 1776 to the War on Terror* (Cambridge University Press, 2014).

 DOI 10.1080/00396338.2014.962810

tiations over the continent's future were going badly.[1] Truman himself would outline what became known as the 'Truman Doctrine' in a speech before a joint session of Congress on 12 March 1947 requesting aid for Greece and Turkey. In that speech, he made clear his own view that a global struggle was under way and that 'the free peoples of the world look to us for support in maintaining their freedoms'.[2] At this opening stage of the Cold War, the president's hawkish stance was a controversial one. Asked to comment on an early draft of Truman's speech, George Marshall, America's military chief of staff during the Second World War and Acheson's predecessor as secretary of state, commented that it contained 'too much flamboyant anti-Communism'.[3]

Within a month, however, Marshall would take an even harder line than his boss had. In April 1947, after futile marathon meetings with his Soviet counterparts, Marshall gave a national radio address in which he explained that Moscow's plans for Europe, and for Germany in particular, would not only involve 'an indefinite American subsidy, but could result only in a deteriorating economic life for Germany and Europe and the inevitable emergence of dictatorship and strife'.[4] Later that year, he would deliver an address at Harvard University unveiling the massive economic rebuilding programme for Europe that would come to bear his name.[5] Several months would pass between Marshall's speech and Congress's approval of the $17 billion programme (the Europeans had asked for $28 billion; $13 billion was ultimately paid out), but it was better late than never for the war-ravaged continent, which had been struggling to raise the export revenue needed to feed its people and keep its industries going. With the infusion of American dollars, Europe's dire conditions improved almost overnight. In only three years, German exports, for example, grew six-fold. Europe's trade deficit with Washington – $8.5 billion in 1947 – dropped to $1 billion in 1950.[6] Perhaps a bit self-servingly, Marshall called the plan 'a historic step in the foreign policy of this country'.[7] Winston Churchill labelled it 'a turning point in the history of the world'.[8] Certainly, together with the Truman Doctrine, the Marshall Plan signalled that the United States would henceforth be taking a more aggressive stance toward the perceived threat of communist expansion in Europe.

Passing the test?

America's resolve to resist communism was soon to be tested on the battlefield – not in Europe, as it turns out, but in Asia. When North Korea launched its invasion of South Korea on 25 June 1950, it was immediately clear that this was not some garden-variety communist subversion but, as one American author put it, 'raw, naked aggression … with blazing tanks and artillery'.[9] In Truman's view, the challenge faced by the United States in Korea was as great as the challenge faced by the democracies in opposing fascism in the 1930s. The invasion, he said, was 'the test of all [our] talk … The Reds were probing for weakness in our armor'.[10] The first US troops to reach the Korean Peninsula landed in July 1950, under a United Nations banner.

By October, the US-led forces had succeeded in expelling the North Koreans from the South, following General Douglas MacArthur's amphibious landing at Inchon in September. Yet Truman and MacArthur wanted more. As George Kennan put it, their aim was nothing less than 'total enemy defeat, total destruction of the enemy's armed forces, his unconditional surrender, the complete occupation of his territory, and the removal of the existing government and its replacement by a regime that would respond to our concepts of "democratization"'.[11] As North Korean troops retreated across the 38th parallel, UN forces followed them.

At first, it appeared as though the United States and its allies might succeed in forcibly reunifying the Korean peninsula – that is, until American forces encountered a massive Chinese invading force at the North Korean border with China. As allied troops were forced to give up the territory they had gained, American public opinion, until then overwhelmingly supportive of the war, turned against it. When US Deputy Secretary of Defense Robert Lovett appeared before the House Armed Services Committee in early December 1950, at least one committee member put to him the view that 'our entire entry into Korea had been a mistake and that we ought to pull out as rapidly as possible.'[12] Yet Truman was determined to fight on. During a press conference in late 1950, he pledged that the United States would take 'whatever steps are necessary' to deal with the deteriorating military situation, including the use of nuclear weapons.[13] In April 1951, he dismissed MacArthur, who was replaced by General Matthew Ridgway.

Under Ridgway's leadership, American forces managed to fight their way back to the 38th parallel without using nuclear weapons, bombing China, or even receiving any reinforcements. The Korean War would ultimately end in a stalemate memorialised in an armistice signed on 27 July 1953. The existential danger had passed, yet the United States' approach to the emerging Cold War had changed dramatically. In 1950, the Pentagon's budget was only 5% of GDP; with the outbreak of the Korean War this would surge into the teens, where it would remain for decades. By the 1960s, the United States had upwards of 450 military bases in 36 countries, up from just a small network a decade earlier.[14] As senior diplomat Charles Bohlen observed, 'it was the Korean War and not World War II that made us a world power'.[15]

One step forward, one step back

In his wise and well-written book *Maximalist: America in the World from Truman to Obama*, Columbia University professor and former US government official Stephen Sestanovich contends that, in the lead-up to the Korean War, Truman and his advisers had come to believe that no adversary was strong enough to withstand the totality of American 'power and energy' when applied to the shaping of global events (p. 38). For Sestanovich, this belief typifies what he calls the maximalist approach to American grand strategy. According to him, maximalists hold that aggressive American responses are required to meet global threats and challenges. The author considers not just Truman but also John F. Kennedy, Ronald Reagan and George W. Bush to have been maximalist presidents.

Yet Sestanovich warns against the view that maximalism is the only approach to have left its mark on American foreign policy. On the contrary, he believes that US policy has been characterised by periodic swings between maximalism and retrenchment at least since the beginning of the Cold War. While he stresses that maximalism does not automatically mean reckless or mindless action, he argues that its proponents have at times been blind, self-deluding and even 'simply deceptive' about the costs involved in this all-out approach (p. 333). Retrenchment, by contrast, has usually resulted when these costs have become clear, typically in the aftermath of strategic failures, such as Korea following the Chinese invasion, Vietnam and, more recently, Iraq and Afghanistan. Sestanovich adds that these two approaches are inescapably linked: 'When the maximalist overreaches, the retrencher comes in to pick up the pieces. Then when the retrenchment fails to build American power, meet new challenges, or compete effectively, the maximalist reappears, ready with ambitious formulas for doing so' (p. 9).

Sestanovich identifies Dwight Eisenhower as the first retrenchment president of the Cold War era. (Richard Nixon, Gerald Ford, Jimmy Carter and Barack Obama are also labelled retrenchers, with George H.W. Bush and Bill Clinton considered hybrid cases.) In April 1958, the former war hero told a meeting of the National Security Council that while some believed the best military strategy was to have 'the most and best of everything', his own view was that 'enough is enough', and that the United States 'should not attempt to be the greatest military power in the world' (p. 6). America, he felt, could get its way without risking becoming an 'armed camp' by exerting the right kind of leadership. 'I'll tell you what leadership is,' he continued. 'It's persuasion – and conciliation – and education – and patience. It's long, slow, tough work. That's the only kind of leadership I know – or believe in – or will practice' (p. 66). This view was informed in part by Eisenhower's belief that, after the bloodshed of the Second World War and then Korea, the American people wanted peace – or, as Sestanovich would have it, retrenchment. Eisenhower was prepared to go from 'Timbuktu to the North Pole' to give it to them (p. 72).

Yet Eisenhower would also champion policies that would seem to call his status as a retrencher into doubt. In September 1954, for example, the tiny islands of Quemoy and Matsu (then under the control of Chiang Kai-shek's Kuomintang government) were shelled from the Chinese mainland. Churchill advised his former wartime collaborator to simply ignore the incident, believing it was not worth sparking a war with China's patron, the Soviet Union. Eisenhower, however, felt otherwise, concluding a mutual-defence treaty with Chiang that promised direct military assistance in case of an invasion. Indeed, Eisenhower told reporters that nuclear weapons were available to repel an attack by the Chinese Communists, declaring, 'I see no reasons why they shouldn't be used just exactly as you would use a bullet or anything else' (p. 76). This hawkish and seemingly flippant stance on the use of nuclear weapons in a tactical setting was also evident in the Korean theatre and in Indochina after the French loss at Dien Bien Phu in 1954. Eisenhower would also preside over the decidedly maximalist operations that overthrew leftist democrats Jacobo Arbenz in Guatemala and Mohammad Mossadegh in Iran, and over the planning for the Bay of Pigs fiasco in early 1961. In fact, soon after the Cuban Revolution in 1959, Eisenhower's team considered ways of 'restraining Castro if he should develop into a menace' (p. 88). All of this suggests that while Sestanovich's notions of maximalism and retrenchment are enormously useful in making sense of presidents' motivations and actions at various moments during the past six decades, there is likely more overlap between the two approaches in every presidential administration than he acknowledges.

Overlap

The Barack Obama administration is a case in point. Given that he inherited the twilight of two immensely costly, politically unpopular and strategically nebulous wars, one would assume, following Sestanovich's analysis, that Obama is a retrenchment president. Yet if Obama had any thought of pursuing a more modest approach to foreign relations, his senior civilian and military advisers seemed to have adopted more maximalist positions (at least with respect to Afghanistan), even if these fell far short of the ambitions of their predecessors in the George W. Bush administration. Influenced by the apparent success of the last-minute military surge into Iraq a few years earlier (a conflict that is on track to cost the US Treasury $4 trillion, to say nothing of the human cost[16]), the president's advisers dismissed the minimalist option of solely pursuing al-Qaeda and other terrorist groups in favour of a long term counter-insurgency and nation-building campaign. Concluding in summer 2009 that a large gap existed between the Afghan state's capacities and what it needed to build a stable, successful country, these advisers 'agreed [the United States] would have to fill it' (pp. 305–6). Then-Secretary of Defense Robert Gates, for example, told Obama that the right goal in Afghanistan was 'victory' (p. 306). Secretary of State Hillary Clinton cautioned Obama not to whittle down the request for additional troops that had come from commanding officer General Stanley McChrystal in Kabul. Doing so, she contended, would waste 'time, lives, and money ... If we go half-hearted, we'll achieve nothing' (p. 306). Meanwhile, General David Petraeus, then head of US Central Command and still fresh from his public success as one of the key architects of the Iraq surge, told the president that he should not try to get by with fewer than the 40,000 troops requested by McChrystal, asserting, 'You've got one bite at this apple. It ought to be a decisive one' (p. 306).

Obama himself, however, was deeply reluctant to sign off on the maximalist approach, instead initiating a three-month policy review to consider the options. At the end of this process, he agreed to send a sizable portion of the requested troops to Afghanistan. Yet this apparently maximalist strategy included one critical caveat that had apparently not come up in all the months of meetings and deliberations, a caveat that caught his advisers by surprise. To the traditional mantra of counter-insurgency – clear, hold and build – Obama had added a fourth phase: transfer. In a December 2009 speech at the US Military Academy at West Point announcing the troop surge in Afghanistan, he stressed that 'the nation that I'm most interested in building is our own'.[17] A retrenchment president telling the nation that he wishes to do more at home may be par for the course, but this one was doing so at the same time that he was sending tens of thousands of additional troops to war.

Several years later, Obama would be criticised for his defence of a foreign policy that many felt was excessively cautious. Such an approach 'may not always be sexy', he said, 'but it avoids errors. You hit singles; you hit doubles. Every once in a while, we may be able to hit a home run.'[18] American conservatives in particular took umbrage at what they saw as Obama's conceding American's vital role in the world.[19] It was a moment that might have seemed peculiar to the Obama administration were it not for Sestanovich's book. For better or worse, America's foreign-policy instincts and self-identity are decidedly maximalist. Yet, as Sestanovich makes clear, eras of retrenchment are also a well-established, even inescapable, American tradition. His excellent book reminds us that the Obama administration's apparently ambivalent approach to Afghanistan (among other conflicts) is perfectly in keeping with persistent trends in modern American foreign policy.

Choosing restraint

Obama himself might have the instincts of a retrencher, but his Afghanistan policy demonstrated the influence of the maximalists in his administration. It is perhaps unsurprising that Robert Gates, whom Obama had retained from the George W. Bush administration, was an advocate for a more aggressive approach. The president might not have fully anticipated the hawkish tendencies of his pick for secretary of state, however. Hillary Rodham Clinton's domestic liberalism might be in keeping with Obama's own views, but on a range of foreign-policy issues she has often appeared to advocate the more forward-leaning of the available policy options. In 2011, for example, she was said to have recommended that American troops remain in Iraq (the troops withdrew as planned).[20] She is also said to have pushed for the raid that killed Osama Bin Laden.[21] The question is whether policies like these mean that Clinton – and, by extension, the Obama administration – can be fairly described as maximalist.

We are fortunate to now have Clinton's engaging and valuable memoir of her State Department years (entitled *Hard Choices*), in which she writes of visiting 112 countries and travelling nearly one million miles over a period beginning with the 'painful end' of her 2008 campaign to become the Democratic Party's presidential nominee and spanning her years working in 'unexpected partnership' with her former rival, Barack Obama (p. xi). Some reviewers have charged that *Hard Choices* is a decidedly 'political' memoir, implying that, given the likelihood that she will make another bid for the presidency, Clinton's account is a guarded one lest she create fodder for critics or alienate potential allies for future political campaigns.[22] To be sure, Clinton makes clear from the get-go that her book is not for followers of 'Washington's long running soap operas', but instead for ordinary Americans who might want to understand how, say, a 'collapsing economy in Athens, Greece affects businesses in Athens, Georgia' (p. xi). Yet while undeniably a book written by an active politician, *Hard Choices* is not vapid – indeed, it offers a lively and at times quite gripping read. Clinton's emotional account of her role in the Benghazi attacks in Libya in 2012 might be the book's best chapter.

There is much in *Hard Choices* that, at least at first glance, suggests that Clinton was a maximalist secretary of state, or at least tried to be. She supported the Petraeus/McChrystal proposal to 'bring COIN [counter-insurgency] to Afghanistan', for instance, contending: 'I believed more military forces were crucial to create space for a transition process to Afghanistan and the region, to bring the conflict to the end.' This certainly appears to be a maximalist perspective, even if she shared her boss's concerns about a troop surge leading to an 'open-ended commitment without any conditions or expectations' (p. 147). She also dismisses 'talk of America's decline', countering that 'everything I have done and seen has convinced me that America remains the "indispensible nation"' (p. xii). In her view, the Obama administration inherited many global lemons from its predecessor, but has worked hard to turn them into policy lemonade, pursuing goals that have included bolstering America's standing in the world.

How might these maximalist impulses be squared with Obama's own desire to focus on domestic policy? Perhaps the answer resides in the fact that there have been instances of both retrenchment and maximalism in every presidential administration since the start of the Cold War, the Obama administration being no exception. This suggests that a more helpful term to use in connection with Obama's grand strategy is 'restraint'.[23] If we define this as dispassionate and moderate behaviour stemming from the sober realisation that American resources are finite, acting forcefully does not ensure success, and domestic challenges are acute, we might better capture the goals and possibilities of the Obama administration than by applying a strict maximalist-versus-retrenchment perspective. Obama is still committed, at least notionally, to the kind of universal maxims that often precipitate maximalist actions, but has prioritised getting soldiers home and reducing foreign entanglements. To be sure, this restraint could in fact be 'just isolationism that dares not speak its name', a possibility explored by Michael Ignatieff in his excellent overview of Obama's foreign-policy choices.[24] In Obama's case, and as his administration's escalated drone-strike campaigns have demonstrated, restraint does not have to be dovish – a point his critics often miss. After reading these two books, this reviewer is inclined to view Obama as a kind of liberal realist or Niebuhrian, a president who has faced up to domestic fiscal realities and global complexities that require caution lest America end up yet again biting off more than it can chew.

Notes

1 James Chace, *Acheson: The Secretary of State Who Created the American World* (New York: Simon & Schuster, 1998), p. 170.

2 'President Harry S. Truman's Address Before a Joint Session of Congress, March 12, 1947', available from Yale Law School Lillian Goldman Law Library, http://avalon.law.yale.edu/20th_century/trudoc.asp.

3 As quoted in Dennis W. Johnson, *The Laws That Shaped America: Fifteen Acts of Congress and Their Lasting Impact* (New York: Routledge, 2009), p. 240.

4 As quoted in Stephen Sestanovich, *Maximalist: America in the World from Truman to Obama* (New York: Knopf, 2014), p. 23. See also 'Soviet Stand Blamed' *Sydney Morning Herald*, 29 April 1947, http://trove.nla.gov.au/ndp/del/article/18024087.

5 George C. Marshall, 'The Marshall Plan Speech', 5 June 1947, available from the George C. Marshall Foundation, http://marshallfoundation.org/.

6 Sestanovich, *Maximalist*, pp. 26–7.

7 As quoted in *ibid.*

8 As quoted in Martin Gilbert, *Churchill and America* (New York: Free Press, 2005), p. 389.

9 Sestanovich, *Maximalist*, p. 50.

10 As quoted in *ibid.*

11 As quoted in Sestanovich, *Maximalist*, p. 63.

12 As quoted in Steven Casey, *Selling the Korean War: Propaganda, Politics, and Public Opinion, 1950–1953* (New York: Oxford University Press, 2008), p. 139.

13 Harry S. Truman, 'The President's News Conference', 30 November 1950, http://www.presidency.ucsb.edu/ws/?pid=13673.

14 Sestanovich, *Maximalist*, p. 62.

15 As quoted in *ibid.*

16 Nicholas Kristof, 'On Iraq, Echoes of 2003', *New York Times*, 18 June 2014, http://www.nytimes.com/2014/06/19/opinion/nicholas-kristof-on-iraq-echoes-of-2003.html?ref=opinion&_r=0. See also Linda

J. Bilmes, 'The Financial Legacy of Iraq and Afghanistan: How Wartime Spending Decisions Will Constrain Future National Security Budgets', Faculty Research Working Paper Series, Harvard Kennedy School, John F. Kennedy School of Government, March 2013, available at http://web.hks.harvard.edu/publications.

17 Barack Obama, 'Remarks by the President in Address to the Nation on the Way Forward in Afghanistan and Pakistan', West Point, NY, 1 December 2009, http://www.whitehouse.gov/the-press-office/remarks-president-address-nation-way-forward-afghanistan-and-pakistan.

18 Barack Obama, 'Remarks by President Obama and President Benigno Aquino III of the Philippines in Joint Press Conference', Manila, Philippines, 28 April 2014, http://www.whitehouse.gov/the-press-office/2014/04/28/remarks-president-obama-and-president-benigno-aquino-iii-philippines-joi.

19 See, for example, Peggy Noonan, 'Apathy in the Executive', *Wall Street Journal*, 2 May 2014, http://online.wsj.com/news/articles/SB10001424052702304677904579536170749456890.

20 Josh Rogin, 'Hillary Clinton Pushed Obama to Keep Troops in Iraq', The Daily Beast, 18 June 2014, http://www.thedailybeast.com/articles/2014/06/18/hillary-clinton-pushed-obama-to-keep-troops-in-iraq.html. More recently, she has criticised the decision not to become more involved in Syria. See Jeffrey Goldberg, 'Hillary Clinton: "Failure" to Help Syrian Rebels Led to the Rise of ISIS', *Atlantic*, 10 August 2014, http://www.theatlantic.com/international/archive/2014/08/hillary-clinton-failure-to-help-syrian-rebels-led-to-the-rise-of-isis/375832/.

21 See, for example, John A. Gans, Jr, '"This is 50–50": Behind Obama's Decision to Kill Bin Laden', *The Atlantic*, 10 October 2012, http://www.theatlantic.com/international/archive/2012/10/this-is-50-50-behind-obamas-decision-to-kill-bin-laden/263449/; and Greg Bluestein and Jim Galloway, 'Hearsay from Hillary Clinton: On Joe Biden and the Osama bin Laden Raid', ajc.com, 15 October 2013, http://www.ajc.com/weblogs/political-insider/2013/oct/15/hearsay-hillary-clinton-theres-more-life-slim-jims/.

22 See, for example, Noam Scheiber, 'The Unsentimental Strategy Behind Obama and Hillary's Marriage of Convenience', *New Republic*, 9 June 2014, http://www.newrepublic.com/article/118052/hillary-clintons-book-suggests-marriage-convenience-obama.

23 See Barry R. Posen, *Restraint: A New Foundation* (Ithaca, NY: Cornell University Press, 2014).

24 Michael Ignatieff, 'Are the Authoritarians Winning?', *New York Review of Books*, 19 July 2014; http://www.nybooks.com/articles/archives/2014/jul/10/are-authoritarians-winning/?insrc=toc.

Book Reviews

Middle East

Ray Takeyh

The Limits of Détente: The United States, the Soviet Union and the Arab–Israeli Conflict, 1969–1973
Craig Daigle. New Haven, CT: Yale University Press, 2014.
£40.00/$60.00. 448 pp.

The recent release of documents from the American archives makes the 1973 Arab–Israeli War a subject of increased historical curiosity. Although long overshadowed by the more spectacular Six-Day War with its conquests and occupations, the Yom Kippur War is emerging from the shadows. Indeed, the war had all the elements of a thrilling international crisis: Arab armies, whose daring and skill surprised a complacent Israeli military and intelligence establishment; an embattled American president facing impeachment, who was often too mentally drained to manage the war; and a superpower stand-off that led to a nuclear alert.

In his engaging and impressively researched book, Craig Daigle tries to situate the war in its indispensable regional setting. Too often, orthodox historians have erred in suggesting that during the Cold War the superpowers imposed their priorities and preferences on the local actors, portraying regional states as mere pawns in the hands of diabolically clever Russians and Americans as they pursued their global competition. No episode has lent itself to such historical misdirection more than the 1973 war. In order to fend off the Soviet challenge, Richard Nixon and Henry Kissinger unwisely escalated the crisis to the point of putting American forces on a high alert. Thus, a regional conflict that could have been soberly resolved was transformed into a global crisis.

 DOI 10.1080/00396338.2014.962811

Daigle punctures through all this by stressing that Anwar Sadat came to view both Israeli indifference to his peace pleas and superpower amity during the era of détente as obstructing his recovery of Sinai. The status quo was too appealing to the Israelis and too stable for the Americans to contemplate a realistic peace process. A war, limited in its duration and circumspect in its objectives, could shake up the prevailing mood and compel Israel to contemplate territorial concessions and Washington to re-engage in regional diplomacy. For this to work, the Arab armies had to perform better than they did in the 1967 debacle. By crossing the canal and overrunning Israel's defences, Sadat regained Egypt's pride and made it possible for Cairo to leave the Arab–Israeli morass.

To be sure, the Israelis rebounded, as Ariel Sharon with his unusual mixture of brilliance and insubordination managed to press the Egyptians back across the canal. But that came too late – the crossing had achieved its objectives. The stench of defeat that had permeated Arab capitals yielded to a spirit of triumph and defiance. Only then could peacemaking be possible.

Daigle belongs to a new generation of historians who are reconsidering the Cold War from the perspective of the regional actors. Such reconceptualisation is coming a bit late to the study of the Middle East, as historians of Asia and Latin America have been at the forefront of this effort for a long time. Still, *The Limits of Détente* is an important and thoughtful contribution to the study of the Cold War and its impact on the Middle East.

The October 1973 War: Politics, Diplomacy, Legacy
Asaf Siniver, ed. London: C. Hurst & Co., 2013. £30.00. 320 pp.

The collection of essays in this edited volume is meant to elucidate the October War from the perspective of all the actors. Although uneven in quality, the essays do succeed in reconstructing the conflict. Read as a whole, the book offers a comprehensive account of events leading up to the war and the actual course of the conflict.

The October 1973 War is at its strongest when assessing Israeli calculations. By autumn 1973 it was evident that the Arab states of Egypt and Syria were preparing for an invasion of Israel. In spring that year King Hussein of Jordan even secretly met with Israeli Prime Minister Golda Meir to inform her of the impending attack. (It is one of the peculiarities of the Middle East that an Arab monarch would inform the Israelis of an invasion that he would eventually participate in, albeit modestly.) All these signs were ignored as Israeli officialdom was attached to the so-called 'concept' – the notion that Egypt would not undertake an invasion until its air force was capable of hitting targets deep within

Israel. Israeli intelligence assured itself that such a capability would not be at hand until 1975. From then on, all the mounting evidence was either discounted or dismissed altogether. The Israelis, as with the Americans, simply could not comprehend a country going to war not to destroy its nemesis, nor even to retrieve its territory, but simply to shake up an unappealing status quo.

To the extent that the conflict had an indisputable loser, it was Hafez Assad of Syria. Assad was lied to by Sadat about Egypt's war plan. Cairo never intended the comprehensive war of annihilation that was promised to Damascus. Once Egypt achieved its limited aims, Assad was left alone to face the Israeli armour. In due time, Israeli forces would come within mere miles of Damascus. Assad would slouch out of the war with his enmities intact, his army in shambles and his territory occupied by Israel. While Sadat won back the Sinai and was eventually acclaimed worldwide as a great peacemaker, Assad was left in Damascus to nurture his grievances and plot his revenge. With war out of his reach, terrorism became his instrument of statecraft, bringing with it more Israeli retaliation and further global opprobrium.

If Assad was the loser of the war, Henry Kissinger was one of its winners. During the war, he sought to ensure Israeli victory without Egyptian humiliation. At the same time, he sought to sustain the momentum of détente while further diminishing Soviet influence in Arab affairs. In the end, he managed to achieve all of these objectives at a time when the domestic underpinnings of the Nixon administration were collapsing all around him.

The 1973 war would be the last time that the Arab world united against Israel in the field of battle. Egypt used its triumph to leave behind the rest of the Arab world and its militant rejection of Israel. Peace between Egypt and Israel ended the possibility of Arab states once more conspiring to invade Israel. The problem for Israel from then on was the Arabs that it ruled within the occupied territories.

Origins of the Suez Crisis: Postwar Development Diplomacy and the Struggle over Third World Industrialization, 1945–1956
Guy Laron. Baltimore, MD: Johns Hopkins University Press, 2013. £28.50/$55.00. 260 pp.

The Suez Crisis is among the most-explored episodes of the Cold War. The fading British Empire attempted to rid itself of the troublesome Gamal Abdul Nasser by mounting an invasion of Egypt. It did so, in conspiracy with France and Israel, on the false grounds that the operation of the Suez Canal was being hindered. The United States was left in the dark as its allies plotted their revenge against Nasser for nationalising the canal. The Soviet Union took full advantage of this Western imperial folly by invading its rebellious Hungarian satellite and establishing a measure of moral equivalency between the two contending Cold War blocs. An irate Dwight Eisenhower imposed economic sanctions against Britain, provoking a financial crisis that compelled its withdrawal and ended the premiership of Anthony Eden.

Is there anything new to add to this well-known historical episode? Laron brings to the crisis a deft hand and a careful eye for detail. The author has explored the mountains of secondary literature, as well as the available primary sources. In the end, however, the depiction of the Suez Crisis offered here does not add much to what we already know – the historical lines are too well-delineated for the author to make a substantial contribution to the conventional narrative. Moreover, Laron's attempt to tie Nasser's Egypt to the rise of twenty-first-century powers such as Brazil and China is maladroit and without much value. To be sure, Laron may have thought that he had stumbled on a novel way of looking at Suez; the notion that there is a clear linkage between the Suez war and the developing bloc of nations may have been too tantalising to resist. But resist, Laron should have done.

One of the ironies of the Suez Crisis is that if Anthony Eden had retired from public life in 1955 he would be remembered as one of the great leaders of his generation. As an emerging politician he had stood against the trend of appeasement so common to the British aristocracy in the 1930s. And during the war and its immediate aftermath, he distinguished himself as a superb practitioner of great-power diplomacy. Instead, he stands today as a discredited figure whose impetuous behaviour brought down what was left of the British Empire.

In the end, Laron has crafted a nicely written book that, stripped of its attempt to tie Suez to today's emerging powers, can still enrich and enliven those interested in this most peculiar of episodes.

Iran and the United States: An Insider's View on the Failed Past and the Road to Peace
Seyed Hossein Mousavian and Shahir Shahidsaless. London: Bloomsbury, 2014. £24.00. 368 pp.

Anyone looking for a book that absolves Iran of all accusations of terrorism, presents the nuclear crisis as a manufactured event, and suggests that Iran's theocrats are reasonable men whose pragmatism is persistently abjured by the Americans, will find it in Mousavian's tome. Yet, despite the author's intentions, his book does offer some useful, even important, insights.

Firstly, we must dispense with the absurdities that lace Mousavian's account. He casually dismisses the assassination of the Kurdish dissidents in Berlin that marred relations between Iran and Europe in the 1990s as the work of Iranian oppositionists, in direct contradiction with the findings of the German courts that identified Iran's leadership as the culprits. Likewise, he attributes the 1996 Khobar Towers bombing that killed 19 US servicemen in Saudi Arabia to al-Qaeda, and describes the 2002 shipment of Iranian arms to the Palestinians that put Tehran in the Bush administration's cross-hairs as (naturally) the work of the Israelis themselves. In short, he repeatedly insists that Iran has not been involved in terrorism, despite massive documentary evidence to the contrary.

A similar set of explanations is offered regarding Iran's nuclear programme. For Mousavian, Iran's intentions are always benign and its many nuclear infractions are mere misunderstandings. If its nuclear programme appears in an unfavourable light, that is only because of Western double standards and unfounded Israeli suspicions. The solution for Mousavian is obvious: Iran should build an industrial-size nuclear programme in exchange for greater transparency. After all, the Supreme Leader Ali Khamenei has issued a religious verdict prohibiting the construction of nuclear weapons. Any demands beyond that are further indications of American obstinacy.

Mousavian's account manages to escape the realm of useless polemic by shedding light on a number of important episodes. In 2003, for example, it was alleged that Iran had offered the United States a grand bargain. All points of contention were to be discussed and resolved on terms that Washington would find acceptable. And yet the bellicose Bush administration, seduced by the mirage of regime change, rejected the altogether reasonable Iranian offer. Mousavian suggests that Khamenei was not aware of the offer and had not endorsed it. This will come as bad news to the legion of American analysts who have long claimed that the United States, having missed this important opportunity to reconcile with its perennial Iranian nemesis, is to blame for the impasse in US–Iranian relations.

Mousavian is at his best when dissecting Mahmoud Ahmadinejad's presidency. His claim that Ahmadinejad was not really an ideologue but an opportunist who was simply dedicated to his personal aggrandisement rings true. Ahmadinejad attempted to reach out to the United States with a string of letters to American presidents while simultaneously appealing to the Arab street with his crass denials of the Holocaust. He never saw the contradictions between these two acts. A toxic Iranian president could never have served as a useful interlocutor with the West, even though he may have been prepared to offer more exacting nuclear concessions than the pragmatist Hassan Rouhani.

All in all, Mousavian's account is a useful reminder that even the more reasonable voices in Iran still harbour delusions and ambitions that make the Islamic Republic a most unusual adversary for the United States.

The Struggle for Mastery in the Fertile Crescent
Fouad Ajami. Stanford, CA: Hoover Institution Press, 2014.
$9.95. 75 pp.

Fouad Ajami, a long-time observer of the Middle East, passed away in June 2014. This slim essay thus constitutes his last major published work. Ajami spent much of his life defying the conventions of his field. He attributed the maladies of the Arab world to its ruling class rather than to lingering colonial influences and American interventions. This gained him much opprobrium among the professoriate. He remained unabashedly and at times too uncritically supportive of the American enterprise in the Middle East. And he became a vocal proponent of the invasion of Iraq, the reverberations of which will now outlive him.

Ajami's elegant essay is yet another lament on the ways of the Arab world. The new Middle East is no longer tormented by the machinations of the Cold Warriors, but by revived sectarian identities. Arab nationalism has yielded to religious wars, with Iran and Saudi Arabia taking each other on throughout the region. True, the Middle East has always insisted on dividing against itself, but these new fragmentations are likely to be more enduring, as they are based on primordial identities. Meanwhile, the American sentry that often mediated such disputes seems indifferent and distant.

Ajami is particularly pointed when discussing how Shia Islam is being hijacked by Iranian mullahs and members of the Revolutionary Guard. A sect of Islam that has struggled to emancipate itself from the weight of Sunni repression is now suddenly an instrument of Persian expansionism. This was not the way things were supposed to unfold. Iraq, cleansed of Saddam Hussein and Sunni presumptions, was to offer the region a new model of sectarian accommodation. A democratic, inclusive Iraq tied to the United States was to humble the Iranians and the rejectionists. Instead, civil wars, rebellions and uprisings have left the region in flames. The promise of Iraq has all but vanished, as the ruling Shi'ites are proving no more tolerant that the Sunnis they displaced.

The story it tells may be a tragic one, but this important and subtle essay stands as a suitable capstone to the career of a brilliant and sensitive scholar of the Middle East.

Politics and International Relations
Pierre Hassner

Global Governance at Risk
David Held and Charles Roger, eds. Cambridge: Polity Press, 2013. £17.99/$24.95. 272 pp.

David Held is certainly the most imaginative and eloquent defender of global governance, multilateral institutions and cosmopolitan democracy today. One cannot but admire his creativity in imagining and proposing new democratic, multilateral institutions at every level of international relations. But one also cannot help wondering whether his creativity can overcome the various obstacles posed by the multiplicity of states and of non-state actors, by their varying power, and by their sometimes diverging interests.

This doubt seems to have inspired this very interesting and original collection of essays, edited by Held with Charles Roger. In the introduction they write: 'While the demand for governance has been sharply rising as global interdependence has intensified, our ability to support it appears to be declining. Perhaps the most important variable underpinning this fact has been the emergence of new powers, such as Brazil, China, India, Indonesia and Turkey' (p. 41). Elsewhere they declare: 'In area after area international cooperation has been faltering. To some extent, the current international environment is worryingly reminiscent of the interwar period, which was marked by the failure of the concert of great powers to contain competitive interests' (p. 8).

Most of the chapters, all by distinguished specialists, emphasise two aspects of this situation: the general disorder in international relations and the incomplete shift in power away from the West to the East and the South. Martin Wolf, for example, considers this shift in terms of the shock of the post-2008 crisis, concluding that the prospects for the world economy are not without danger. Similarly, Benjamin Cohen announces a 'coming global monetary disorder'. In a particularly rich and subtle chapter, George Magnus analyses the difficulties affecting China in spite (and partly because of) its rise, and finds the country more vulnerable than the United States. Michael Cox's chapter is well summed up by its title ('Why the West Rules for Now – And is Likely to for a Long Time to Come'), while Robert Wade shows how Western states cling to their privileges in international organisations. Ha-Joon Chang deplores the paradoxical disappearance of development as a theme in today's 'development discourse', which seems reduced to the diminution of poverty. Robert Skidelsky, in a brilliant and original chapter, argues that a combination of John A. Hobson's, Karl Marx's and John M. Keynes's insights offers the best approach to understanding the present crisis.

In their conclusion, Held and Roger point out both the parallels and the links between the financial crisis and the crisis of world governance in the area of security. In both cases, they conclude that we face 'a choice between a rule-based multilateral system and the continued fragmentation of an ineffective global order that simply lurches from crisis to crisis' (p. 294). And yet, in this book at least, they do not present any particular strategy to achieve this rule-based world, nor to fight the present trends which they describe and denounce.

Armed State Building: Confronting State Failure, 1898–2012
Paul D. Miller. Ithaca, NY: Cornell University Press, 2013.
$35.00. 264 pp.

This is a serious and interesting book, but also a very frustrating one, both in terms of its content and its gaps. The author is a particularly experienced student of and practitioner in South Asia, especially Afghanistan, where he served in the US Army before holding important positions in government related to that region. Yet this book could not be further from a memoir. The author does not make a single allusion to his own experience, nor does he offer any thoughts about the ambiguities and possible misunderstandings between external state-builders and the populations of the states they are trying to build.

His central idea is that different types of state failure call for different types of armed state-building. He adopts the methods of an objective social scientist, 'coding' every case he studies according to the functional areas in which the respective states have failed (legitimacy, capacity, productivity) and the various roles of the armed external state-builders (administrator, trainer, organiser and so on). He defines state-building as 'the attempt by liberal states to use military, political and economic power to compel weak, failed or collapsed states to govern more effectively and accountably, as understood by Westphalian and liberal norms' (p. 205), a definition which explicitly excludes imperialism and annexation. According to him, the distinction between state-building and imperialism is based on the intentions of the intervener and the duration of the intervention. But surely, at least for the recipient, the distinction is primarily in the eye of the beholder: the perceptions of the locals can be influenced by the nature or the past of the intervening power, potentially provoking a nationalist reaction against the alien invader.

Another surprising gap concerns the way in which the intervening military force should be organised and the strategy and tactics it should apply to its state-building task, a much-discussed subject in the context of the Vietnam and Afghanistan experiences. The central question – whether one can build a state while waging a war on its territory – is addressed in only two, unrelated paragraphs. Miller seems to conclude that such an enterprise is extremely difficult, and that the intervening power had better win the war first and build the state afterwards. He gives the example of Iraq, which does not seem a very edifying one as far as state-building is concerned.

The most convincing contribution of the book lies in its very rigorous critique of earlier theorists of state-building. The author shows that past theories relied on a partial definition of the state (as the holder of a monopoly on legitimate violence), whereas it also embodies a conception of justice, and is a producer and distributor of goods. He is particularly effective against 'sequentialist' theories (according to which the various reforms necessary to state-building, such as repairs to the economy or legal system, must follow a fixed and universally valid order) usually linked to 'transitology' (the general study of transitions from one type of regime to another, insofar as it claims to be a rigorous and universal science).

Miller is not immune, however, from making mistakes (or proposing doubtful approximations) of his own. This is particularly true when he ventures outside his special subject, as where he falls into monumental errors about Hegel's theory of the state or about the origins of the notion of 'totalitarianism'. He also makes at least one mistake linked to his main theme: when analysing the Afghanistan war, he constantly attributes political, strategic and even tactical decisions to 'the International Community'. Attributing legitimate and probably justified military moves to a mysterious, ambiguous and perhaps mythical 'International Community' will raise some eyebrows not only among traditional state actors but also among readers who applaud Miller's general efforts towards precision and objectivity.

Recognition
Cillian McBride. Cambridge: Polity Press, 2013. £14.99/$22.95.
224 pp.

Few concepts have as many dimensions or are covered by as many disciplines as 'recognition': the concept has implications for psychology, anthropology, philosophy and ethics, as well as for politics, sociology and law. This book succeeds in touching on all these areas and approaches; in critically reviewing the relevant – and highly diverse – literature; and in making an original contribution, not only by synthesising the work of several important authors but also by offering original observations and by clarifying (without simplifying) some very complex issues.

The book starts with a critique of the two authors who have initiated the contemporary discussion on recognition. The first, the Canadian philosopher

Charles Taylor, is above all a critic of liberal universalism and a defender of cultural particularism, inspired by the case of the French Canadians, among other minorities. The second, the German philosopher Axel Honneth, has criticised Taylor for insisting too much on particularism and for overemphasising the cultural dimension rather than the social one. For Honneth, the development of the human personality is based upon a combination of three types of relations: love, esteem and respect. McBride accepts Honneth's criticism of Taylor, but argues that Honneth's own 'developmental' theory is too harmonious and minimises the tensions between his three dimensions and between the individual and his social and political environments.

McBride's own theory is essentially interactive. He shows how being part of a group (such as a cultural or sexual minority) that gains recognition as such may mean that one's unique individuality is overlooked. He stresses the tension between respect, which is due to all human beings, and esteem, which is not equally deserved by all. He also shows that one's self-appraisal and appraisal by others can either reinforce each other or enter into conflict.

McBride also examines the role of collective structures and institutions. Some appraisals can be legislated from above, others not. He usefully introduces the notion of justice: a society in which each individual does not enjoy respect and dignity is unjust, but no society can provide all its members with the degree of recognition to which each of them personally aspires or feels entitled. He ends by pointing out that each person's search for recognition by others can often be frustrating and disappointing, but that this is an unavoidable part of the human experience.

While McBride gives ample consideration to the problems of different types of minorities, one might regret that his excellent book does not also consider relations among nations. After all, the craving of some states or nations for recognition as great powers, or of others for affirmation of their dignity and identity despite any inferiorities in terms of size or power, is an essential part of international politics.

Sovereignty: Moral and Historical Perspectives
James Turner Johnson. Washington DC: Georgetown University Press, 2014. £24.00/$29.95. 181 pp.

James Turner Johnson is one of the most learned and productive thinkers and historians on the subject of the just war and, more generally, on the role of morality in international relations. The present short volume addresses the same problems through the concept of sovereignty, offering a concise but rich history of sovereignty's evolution, and of doctrines on the use of force, from Augustine to the recent 'responsibility to protect', via Thomas Aquinas, Francisco de Vitoria and Martin Luther, the Westphalian settlement and the UN Charter, and many other authors, documents and institutions.

The guiding thread, repeated in every chapter, is the opposition between the old conception of sovereignty, based on the responsibility of the ruler for justice and the common good (a responsibility that extended beyond the borders of his realm), and the modern one, which has been reduced to territorial integrity and non-interference in internal affairs. The first is based on morality and, ultimately, on religion, the second on the balance of power and self-interest.

One hesitates to argue with an author whose knowledge on these issues is infinitely superior to one's own, but this reviewer cannot help feeling that Johnson's presentation seems biased in favour of the classical version and unfair, or at least reductionist, concerning the modern one. It is possible to share Johnson's preoccupation with reintroducing morality in international politics (not to mention debates surrounding the justifications for war) and yet be surprised at his failure to consider the concrete experience of his favoured model. There has always been a temptation for rulers to postulate that the road to justice and the common good lies through their own power, glory and conquests. Johnson is surely familiar with Charles V's dictum, 'I see eye to eye with my brother Francis of France: each of us wants Milan', or with that of the celebrated seventeenth-century Christian thinker Blaise Pascal: 'Funny justice which is bound by a river: truth on one side of the Pyrenees, error on the other!'.

The key question, of course, is who will be the judge or arbiter. The original answer was God, or his representative on Earth (that is, the Church), which returns us to the old struggle between the pope and the emperor. If God's commandments are to be interpreted by rulers themselves, slogans such as 'Gesta Dei per Francos' (God's work through the French) and self-appointed 'chosen peoples' will abound. The 'just war' will become a 'holy war' fought in the name of God (as has happened in the case of present-day Islamic jihad, which is analysed by Johnson in an interesting chapter).

After the European religious wars of the sixteenth and seventeenth centuries, and the revolutions of the eighteenth, the secular state on the one hand, and the sovereignty of the people on the other (not just in terms of territorial integrity, as Johnson seems to claim, but as an ultimate source of legitimacy), became the norm, along with interdependence and mutual recognition. Of course, there was still a need to stabilise the internal rule of law and for independent external arbitration, leading to the founding of institutions such as the nineteenth-century Concert of Europe, the League of Nations and the United Nations (though it was far from universally accepted that these institutions enjoyed any monopoly on the use of force). New initiatives continue to appear, including international criminal courts and conventions permitting or ordering international interventions in certain exceptional cases such as genocide. Great powers can still get away with murder, of course, but new criteria for intervention, along with ongoing attempts to regulate or legitimise it (including the 'responsibility to protect' mentioned by the author) make, in spite of all their failings, for a more diverse and ambiguous situation than Johnson's dualistic model would suggest.

Belonging: Solidarity and Division in Modern Societies
Montserrat Guiberneau. Cambridge: Polity Press, 2013.
£17.99/$24.95. 240 pp.

While Guiberneau is not the only author currently preoccupied with the disappearance of friendly, cohesive neighbourhoods, leaving the lonely individual to himself, or to the influence of the mass media, her book goes a step further than others. It describes how an increasing number of individuals are seeking new identities by joining groups, an act of freedom that can, paradoxically, lead to the abandonment of one's own identity (and hence one's freedom) in favour of a collective one.

Guiberneau finds that 'the novel context defined by the consequences of globalisation, which include economic insecurity, cultural anxiety and political alienation' (p. 6) has produced a reaction comparable to that described by the great psychologist Erich Fromm in his 1941 book *The Fear of Freedom*, which analyses the escape from freedom into totalitarian movements. Guiberneau's own analysis is replete with valuable observations and interpretations on the forms, instruments and consequences of 'belonging by choice'. This abundance is sometimes a little confusing. The author helpfully provides an outline at the beginning of the book and a summary after each chapter, but the order of the chapters themselves is rather bizarre. The only developed case study is to be found, in the midst of more general material, in Chapter 4 ('The New Radical Right and the Resurgence of Authoritarian Politics'). The analysis here is excellent and precise, but it is preceded, in Chapter 3, by a very abstract discourse on freedom, containing a rather odd comparison between Immanuel Kant, Michel Foucault and Fromm. Chapter 5 addresses the 'rituals of belonging', and is followed by an important chapter on 'loyalty, citizenship and the nation'. The brilliant final chapter discusses the role of emotions.

Other dimensions or examples of 'belonging by choice' are merely alluded to, here and there: religion, for example, is discussed in a section on Francisco Franco's Spain and in the conclusion; violence is essentially relegated to the brief discussion of war. The Arab world is mentioned, but only with reference to the Arab Spring. Might not a discussion of how terrorist jihadism has been prevailing over Arab nationalism(s), and how thousands of young men (not all of them Arabs) have been rushing to distant lands to carry out jihad, have been relevant to the subject? Moreover, would it not have been more satisfactory, with the same material, to briefly present and compare the varieties of 'belonging by choice', from football supporters through street gangs, mafias, sects and fundamentalist communities, not to mention national and regionalist movements?

One should never criticise the author of a remarkable book for not having written a different one. But a broader and more comparative approach would have made this book's message even more convincing and, perhaps, would have led Guiberneau to slightly qualify her conclusion that the nation is still the main identity-creating institution.

South Asia
Teresita C. Schaffer

The Blood Telegram: Nixon, Kissinger, and a Forgotten Genocide
Gary J. Bass. New York: Knopf, 2014. $30.00. 528 pp.

In April 1971, horrified by the Pakistani authorities' mass killing of Bengalis calling for an independent Bangladesh and by the strongly pro-Pakistan policies the Nixon administration adopted in dealing with this conflict, the staff of the American Consulate General in East Pakistan used the State Department's 'dissent channel' to send a cable that castigated the administration's position and called for policies that reflected US support for self-determination and human rights. Archer K. Blood, a veteran Foreign Service officer who was in charge of the Consulate General, sent the cable on to Washington with his own endorsement. To the consternation and embarrassment of the Nixon administration, the cable – soon to be called by the double entendre 'The Blood Telegram' – was widely leaked. Blood's promising diplomatic career was badly damaged.

Gary J. Bass, a professor at Princeton University, has adopted 'The Blood Telegram' as the title of his study of this brutally suppressed Bengali uprising and the genocidal way it played out before Indian military intervention brought independence to Bangladesh in December 1971. His admirable account accurately and sympathetically describes and analyses chiefly how the United States appraised and tried to shape it.

Bass tells a good story that will be especially useful to those interested in US foreign policy during this time. It complements Srinath Raghavan's broader history of the same events (see below). It does not, however, break much new ground in reporting and interpreting policymaking. A good deal of what he has written, especially about the characters, motives and policies of President Richard Nixon and his national security adviser, Henry A. Kissinger, has been told before, if not so vividly and ardently. He is much stronger in providing a worm's-eye view of the terrible scene unfolding on the ground in East Bengal and how Americans involved there dealt with it.

The Blood Telegram focuses, as its subtitle suggests, on the way Nixon and Kissinger misinterpreted developments in East Bengal to avoid impairing their useful relationship with Pakistan's military ruler, General Yahya Khan. Yahya facilitated the opening to China that was probably the Nixon administration's greatest diplomatic achievement. Bass is not the first analyst to dwell on the pro-Pakistan and anti-Indian prejudices of Nixon and Kissinger and their unrealistic appraisals of Soviet and Chinese South Asia policies. He illustrates these by long passages taken from the White House tapes, an invaluable source for appraising the antics of the president and his assistant for national security. These tapes also give us some useful – and often frightening – insights into how the two men interacted: Nixon, rash, violent, foul-mouthed; Kissinger, always the faithful courtier, saying what he thought his boss wanted to hear.

Bass's account highlights the importance to policy and diplomacy of a sound understanding of regional dynamics. Nixon and Kissinger knew little about South Asia and, relying on their highly personal views of the leaders involved, saw little reason to learn. They sought to construct a grand, new global order that would accommodate Beijing and discomfit Moscow. Bass demonstrates that India, Pakistan and, most poignantly, the people of East Bengal seemed to them little more than pawns in their great game. US interests in South Asia suffered in consequence both then and later.

1971: A Global History of the Creation of Bangladesh
Srinath Raghavan. Cambridge, MA: Harvard University Press, 2013. £22.95/$29.95. 358 pp.

Indian scholar Srinath Raghavan's admirable study of the events surrounding Bangladesh's bloody birth adds a great deal to our understanding of that major milestone in post-imperialist South Asian history. Admirably researched, remarkably dispassionate, and both wide- and deep-ranging in its coverage, it is diplomatic history at its best.

Raghavan is adept both at analysing the big picture and at digging up all the small but important details that give weight to his arguments. He seems to enjoy challenging long-accepted historical verities. A good example is his dismissal of the contention that the break-up of united Pakistan was inevitable – a state comprising two wings that had nothing in common but Islam and that were separated by 1,000 miles of hostile territory simply could not survive. But it did, for 24 years. Raghavan concludes that only once the politicians of East Bengal finally recognised that they would not be allowed to enjoy the spoils of national office did they decide to withdraw. Even then, they could have been lured back had the Pakistan Army and the West Pakistani politicians been a little more accommodating.

Raghavan calls his book a 'global history'. This is not just because he takes into careful account the diplomacy of the main non-South Asian players (the United States, the Soviet Union and China), as well as the sub-continental actors. He also tries to place the uprising in East Bengal in the context of broader movements that roiled the late 1960s and early 1970s: these include the rise of the Third World, which not only altered world politics but also put the spotlight on North–South economic disparities, and the onset of globalisation. This caused a wider diffusion of standards in various spheres, including language and political action.

In discussing the diplomacy of the main local and national players in the Bangladesh conflict, Raghavan successfully tries to relate them to other factors in each country's recent political experience, for example, Mao's foiling of his domestic rivals and the impact of the Cultural Revolution. He is especially strong on the politics and bureaucratic nature of Indira Gandhi's India and has made good use of the private papers of senior officials and other hard-to-obtain documents. He sheds new and useful light on the relations between the Indian government and the Bangladeshis-in-exile. The material on China and the Soviet Union has also been well researched; in writing of these two countries the author shows excellent understanding of the dilemmas they faced. The material on the United States covers the waterfront, but American historians and others have peered so deeply into the strange antics of President Nixon and Henry Kissinger that Raghavan has little to add to earlier accounts.

I agree with Raghavan's contention that his story is relevant to contemporary history. Bangladesh in 1971 was indeed the harbinger of a post-Cold War world characterised by tensions between the principles of sovereignty and human rights, and the virtues of unilateralism vs multilateralism; and by the rising importance of international media, non-governmental organisations, ethnic diasporas and transnational public opinion. As Raghavan rightly puts it, his study is 'not merely a narrative of the past but a tract for our times' (p. 273).

The Taliban Revival: Violence and Extremism on the Pakistan–Afghanistan Frontier
Hassan Abbas. New Haven, CT: Yale University Press, 2014.
£18.99/$30.00. 280 pp.

Hassan Abbas is a former Pakistan police officer who teaches at the US National Defense University, and has also held positions at Columbia and Harvard universities. His analysis draws on extensive interviews in Pakistan and Afghanistan, and is informed by his police background. There are many books on the Taliban, but this one stands out for the way it weaves together the tribal, governmental and national aspects of this movement, and its Pakistani and Afghan wings.

The heart of the book starts with the return of the Taliban from its near-death experience after the fall of its government in Afghanistan in 2001. Abbas recounts unsparingly how the ambivalent views of the Musharraf government and the Pakistani army created the space that permitted the movement to revive, with a more militant presence in Pakistan than it had ever had before. He recounts the 2004–07 negotiations with the Pakistani Taliban, in which Islamabad repeatedly sought a kind of non-aggression pact, only to discover that the Taliban had no intention of being hemmed in by such agreements. The parties to these negotiations had no common ground. Pakistan sought to preserve peace and governmental control, at least outside a recognised geographic area; the Taliban did not accept the 'idea of Pakistan' outside the framework of their goal of an Islamic emirate.

This problem has plagued efforts to arrive at reconciliation – or even a truce – for decades. The Pakistan government has repeatedly expressed confidence in its ability to fine-tune relations with the Taliban and related insurgents operating in its territory. In fact, as Abbas recounts with skill and in detail, Pakistani governments – civilian and military alike – have systematically deluded themselves (as well as their outside friends), hoping to retain the services of the 'good Taliban' to ward off the threat they most fear, from India.

The most valuable part of Abbas's account deals with contemporary Pakistan. As he notes, the Pakistani Taliban directed the bulk of its 2013 election violence against the more secular parties, going relatively easy on Nawaz Sharif's Muslim League and Imran Khan's Pakistan Tehreek-e-Insaf. Once in power, Sharif pushed for negotiations with the Taliban, and eventually discovered that it was not interested in returning the favour. Once again, the Pakistani authorities failed to recognise that the Taliban was not interested in a modus vivendi: it was fundamentally challenging the state of Pakistan. The same kind of blind spot, Abbas argues, affects Pakistan's analysis of Afghanistan. Members of the Afghan Taliban are not only divided: they are also, like other Afghans, deeply suspicious of Pakistan, and their approach to dealing with more powerful forces is to play them off against one another.

This last point should not surprise anyone with even a cursory knowledge of Afghan history, and yet the newspapers are filled with example after example of outsiders – Americans, Pakistanis and others – expecting linear logic to govern their dealings with Afghans. What makes Abbas's message so powerful is the spotlight he shines on the illusions that, tragically, keep Pakistan's leaders engaged in a conspiracy game that threatens the country itself.

Vying for Allah's Vote: Understanding Islamic Parties, Political Violence, and Extremism in Pakistan
Haroon K. Ullah. Washington DC: Georgetown University Press, 2014. £21.00/$26.95. 272 pp.

Haroon K. Ullah sets out to situate Pakistan's Islamic political parties in a new theoretical context and to demolish the most prevalent assumptions about what makes them tick. The author, who works in the US State Department's Policy Planning Council (the book carries the obligatory disclaimer that it does not represent the US government's views), comes from a Pakistani family, was reared in a farming community in the United States, and has written extensively on the dynamics of Pakistani politics.

The author divides Pakistan's Islamic political parties into three broad groups. The first are Muslim democratic parties, represented chiefly by the Muslim League, which provided the political base for Pakistan's founder, Muhammad Ali Jinnah, who famously envisaged Pakistan as a secular state. Most observers would not put this party in the 'Islamic party' pigeonhole. It started out, as the author recounts, as the party of powerful elites in the parts of India that did not become Pakistan, but who wanted to create a separate state; its descendants and namesakes dominated Pakistan's politics for several decades. The author's decision to put the party into the 'Islamic' framework makes sense when considering the last three or four decades, by which time its core constituency also shifted: it is now primarily a party of Punjabi feudals and their rural 'vote banks'.

The author's other two categories consist of Islamist parties: 'Hierarchical Islamist parties', illustrated by the Jamaat-e-Islami (JI), built on a small core of intellectual elites, with a significant urban presence, a highly structured leadership and the most systematic ideology of the group; and 'Network Islamist parties', illustrated by the Jamiat Ulema-e-Islam (JUI), led by local religious leaders with a network of madrassas, far more, rural, diffuse and decentralised than the JI, and seeking a broad popular following.

The author successfully discredits facile assumptions about how economic deprivation fosters Islamic extremism and modernisation leads to 'moderation'. Perhaps the most thought-provoking observation in his analysis of what drives party behaviour is that participation in the political process does indeed encourage pragmatism – but not in the way many of his readers expect. Both the Muslim League and the two Islamist parties have been driven to positions far more doctrinaire and tolerant of violence than their stated beliefs would support, because they believed that this position would gain them votes. In other words, they have displayed pragmatism that tilted toward extremism.

The author also describes in fascinating detail the different motivations and economic benefits that encourage some parties to focus chiefly on national politics (where the Muslim League is powerful), and others to focus almost entirely on local politics (the prime arena for JUI).

The author's focus on articulating a theoretical framework for understanding Islamic politics may have led him to ignore the regional identification of the parties. The Muslim League has little presence outside Punjab, and this profoundly colours its approach to politics. The JI too is chiefly Punjabi, but the JUI has a stronger presence in the northwestern province of Khyber Pakhtunkhwa. In a country as regionally fragmented as Pakistan, this is a fundamental aspect of the parties' identities. Thinking about them strictly in terms of their position on the secular-to-sharia continuum is woefully incomplete.

Still, this is an important book because so little serious analysis of Islamic politics is available to Western students of Pakistan. The author's closing plea is right on target: that US diplomats, and presumably others as well, spend more time listening to this constituency and seeking common ground on such key issues as education and reducing poverty. In practice this may turn out to be more difficult than he suggests.

Forged in Crisis: India and the United States Since 1947
Rudra Chaudhuri. London: C. Hurst & Co., 2014. £30.00/$29.95.
368 pp.

Rudra Chaudhuri sets out to explain US–India relations through eight brief case studies of US–India negotiations, starting with the implicit negotiation over India's decision to base its foreign policy on Jawaharlal Nehru's signature concept of non-alignment, and ending with the epic, multi-layered negotiations over the 2008 India–US agreement enabling civil nuclear trade. Chaudhuri's research on written sources is prodigious, his list of interviews impressive, and his command of Indian foreign policy masterful.

Chaudhuri argues that non-alignment was not simply an expression of

Nehru's idealistic view of the world and India's place in it. Non-alignment was also intended to serve India's needs in a more tangible way, by preserving India's 'non-dependence' as it set about obtaining the material benefits it needed, whether armaments or economic aid. '[Non-alignment] made allowances for ensuring non-dependence while carving a distinct persona for a nation unimpressed by the somewhat dogmatic ideological policies underpinning containment during the Cold War' (p. 257).

This theme has remained central to Indian foreign policy, despite changes in the meaning of non-alignment over time. The issues India negotiated with the United States, explicitly or implicitly, changed too. Indian diplomacy, as Chaudhuri reminds us, made a real contribution toward solving the vexing problem of Korean War prisoners – and made the United States uncomfortable from beginning to end. After the mid-1960s, India became less willing to invest the same level of diplomatic resources in global peacemaking, and the United States less interested in India's input. Chaudhuri's discussion of India's appeal for US arms when China invaded in 1962, one of the very few times that India actually requested assistance, accurately reflects President John F. Kennedy's sensitivity to Indian fears of being sucked into a deeper relationship with Washington than it wanted. (By then, the US was also cautious about drawing India into anything like an alliance.) Americans recall this as the one time the US responded quickly and effectively to Indian security needs, and were puzzled that their response had so little hold on Indian memories.

The book's only case that deals with India's South Asian regional relationships was the ill-fated US effort to encourage India–Pakistan talks over Kashmir after India's war with China. Chaudhuri is rather kinder to US diplomacy than other Indian (and Pakistani) accounts have been. John Kenneth Galbraith, US Ambassador in Delhi at the time, commented that the only thing India and Pakistan agreed on was their dislike for US proposals.

Chaudhuri's chapter on the American effort to persuade India to contribute a division to the occupation of post-Gulf War Iraq is probably his most original contribution, and it captures the remarkable hopes on both sides from that time. His account of the nuclear negotiations is strong, though I would have put more stress on the way this negotiation exposed both sides to the inner workings of the other country's political institutions, a lesson both of them found uncomfortable.

This is an important book about India's foreign policy. I believe that the hold of non-alignment on India's view of its global role is both stronger and more isolationist than Chaudhuri suggests. The one element I find somewhat lacking is India's consistent commitment to maintaining primacy in the immediate Indian Ocean/South Asia region, and with it, the neuralgia that US–Pakistan relations regularly inserted into ties between Washington and Delhi.

War, Conflict and the Military
H.R. McMaster

Out of the Mountains: The Coming Age of the Urban Guerrilla
David Kilcullen. London: C. Hurst & Co, 2013. £20.00. 368 pp.

In *Out of the Mountains,* Dave Kilcullen, author of *The Accidental Guerrilla* and CEO of a Washington-based strategy and design firm, introduces a set of ideas intended to better explain 'the conflict ecosystem – the non-linear, many-sided, wild, and messy world of real conflict' (p. 17). He uses case studies to illuminate 'megatrends' that he believes will shape not just armed conflict but everyday life in the next three decades, and introduces a 'theory of competitive control' to explain the complex interactions between people, government, and state and non-state groups in urban environments, especially littoral megacities. This is an important book because, as the author makes clear, such cities, and the security threats they contain, are not just expanding, but also exhibiting increased local and transnational connectivity.

While acknowledging the continued likelihood of conflict between nation states and in remote areas, Kilkullen argues that trends such as increased urbanisation, littoralisation (population growth in littoral areas) and connectedness at both the local and transnational levels suggest that conflict is more likely in coastal cities in underdeveloped regions of the Middle East, Africa, Latin America and Asia. He draws this conclusion with reference to case studies of conflict in urban environments (including Syria, which Kilcullen sees as a harbinger of future conflicts) that reveal how non-state armed groups compete for control over populations and territory at the local level, and how increased connectivity allows local actors to draw on international networks, as they did during the Arab Spring. He predicts that future conflicts in urban areas will exhibit 'operational continuity' as state and non-state actors alike employ both conventional and unconventional tactics (p. 238). But, he argues, the environments in which future armed conflicts will take place will exhibit discontinuity: in contrast to recent and ongoing conflicts in Mali, the Sinai and Afghanistan, for example, future conflicts will take place mainly in areas that are 'crowded, coastal, urban, and connected' (p. 238).

Kilcullen argues that any given city should be conceived of as an organism that 'both reflects and perpetuates the conflicts that created it' (pp. 240–1). Recent events in Iraq and Syria highlight the need for military forces and civil-military teams to be ready to operate in urban areas if they are to make a lasting impact. The advantages of Western armed forces, such as long-range surveillance and strike capabilities, are limited in urban areas by the complexity of the environment and the need to avoid unnecessary civilian casualties. Kilcullen's analysis militates in favour of developing a range of adaptable military and civilian capabilities, especially among land forces, that are suited to 'the widest possible variety of environments, perform the widest possible range of missions, and transition rapidly and smoothly between terrain and mission types' (p. 239). At a time when many Western militaries are slashing defence budgets while increasing investments in high-tech weapons, Kilcullen's book provides an argument for reassessing defence priorities, or at least acknowledging that while technological advantage remains important, it may be insufficient to address current and future threats to international security.

The Outpost: An Untold Story of American Valor
Jake Tapper. London: Back Bay Books, 2013. £13.99. 681 pp.

As debates continue over the future of the international security assistance effort in Afghanistan, few in the West appreciate the character of combat in that country at the tactical level, especially in the rugged terrain of the eastern provinces. This is in part because only a small proportion of Western populations undertake military service, and because media coverage of combat in Afghanistan has been paltry compared to previous wars. The few reporters who have actually ventured into the most difficult and contested areas, however, have been particularly courageous and effective at telling the stories of the soldiers who have fought there during the past 13 years. Marcus Luttrell's memoir, *Lone Survivor*, and the Hollywood movie of the same title, recount a particularly harrowing and costly special-operations mission in the Kunar Mountains in June 2005. The setting for *The Outpost* is nearby, in the remote Korengal Valley of Nuristan province. Jake Tapper, a CNN anchor and chief Washington correspondent, chronicles the experiences of the soldiers, platoons and companies that operated there for five years, between 2006 and 2011. He has produced one of the seminal accounts of the American military experience in Afghanistan.

The story is important not only because it captures the human experience of combat, but also because it highlights the need to connect tactical military operations to political strategies and sustainable outcomes worthy of the risks that soldiers take and the sacrifices they make in battle. The Afghan War, like any number of conflicts both before and after it, demonstrates that isolated tactical victories do not equate to progress unless they are linked to a larger effort. In Afghanistan, soldiers and leaders struggled with the country's demanding geographical setting and with its tribal, social, economic and historical dynamics, which made it difficult to consolidate military gains. US forces based in different areas were unable to connect tactical successes either to each other or to the overall mission in Afghanistan.

Combat actions in the Korengal Valley highlighted the importance of junior leaders and fundamental tactical principles. Decentralised operations against a determined enemy demanded sergeants, lieutenants and captains able to understand complex local dynamics, think ahead, fight and consolidate gains politically. The operations also required cohesive, confident teams that remained resilient in the face of austere conditions, casualties, combat trauma and persistent danger across long periods of time.

Tapper's description of the resource limitations under which American forces often operated in Afghanistan – especially the shortage of air support – may surprise some readers. In several cases, forces in isolated outposts were not only outnumbered, but also outgunned. American technological capabilities were important in every battle, but battles also highlighted the limitations of technology. The enemy, while technologically inferior, often initiated battles under favourable conditions to gain temporary physical, temporal and psychological advantages. Thus, the story of *The Outpost* serves as a caution against assuming that technology can substitute for manpower. Indeed, battles in the Korengal Valley revealed that numerical strength and mutual support between ground forces still matter when fighting elusive enemies in complex terrain.

Tapper's narrative engenders admiration and empathy for the soldiers who fought these battles, as well as for their families at home. He illuminates the lives and actions of the young men who were killed and severely wounded, along with the effects of these traumas on their wives, children, parents and siblings. He includes other relevant perspectives and experiences too, such as those of higher-level commanders, the Afghan security forces, the enemy and the civilian population. This is a book not only for soldiers, but also for anyone who wishes to understand the character of contemporary infantry combat in difficult terrain. *The Outpost* may be particularly important for those charged with ensuring that military forces are prepared to overmatch the enemy and accomplish the mission in future armed conflict.

Thank You For Your Service
David Finkel. New York: Sarah Crichton Books, 2013. $26.00.
256 pp.

In *Thank You for Your Service*, David Finkel, writer for the *Washington Post* and author of *The Good Soldiers*, observes that most of the more than two million Americans who fought in Iraq and Afghanistan 'describe themselves as physically and mentally healthy' (p. 11). His book, however, is about the estimated 500,000 mentally wounded American veterans, their families, and the US Army's efforts to care for them. Following soldiers whom he met and wrote about during the 2007 'surge' of US troops into Baghdad, Finkel delivers a powerful story that goes beyond statistics and illuminates the difficulties some soldiers have reintegrating into normal life after experiencing combat trauma and serving in environments of persistent danger for extended periods.

The soldiers' experiences and reactions reveal the principal causes of post-traumatic stress, including survivor's guilt (associated either with feeling that one should have done more to prevent a comrade's death, or with difficulties in understanding why one was spared while others were lost). Other causes include difficult memories linked to combat trauma or soldiers' doubts about whether they conducted themselves honourably and ethically. Some soldiers may have had pre-existing frailties that were aggravated by wartime experience. The distinctiveness of each case and the associated requirements for bespoke treatment make the management of post-traumatic stress disorder particularly challenging.

Families also play a critical role. Family circumstances and relationships are often complicated and can generate, rather than alleviate, stress for the soldier and other family members. Some of the most powerful chapters of the book are those in which Finkel gives a voice to the wives of physically or mentally wounded soldiers, as well as to a widow whose husband was killed in action.

Finkel describes the US Army's efforts to de-stigmatise the seeking of help, to understand the problem, and to treat those who are afflicted. He also covers the Army's Vice Chief of Staff's effort to understand the causes of military suicides and to implement effective suicide prevention. Finkel relates stories of how, despite the best of intentions, soldiers found themselves required to navigate cumbersome bureaucratic procedures, retell their stories multiple times, and cope with treatments chosen more on than basis of availability than on what might be best for them as individuals.

Finkel's empathetic and compelling accounts raise questions more than they provide answers. How might military authorities de-stigmatise seeking help without eroding the mild form of stoicism that helps soldiers cope with combat stress and combat trauma? How might caregivers involve families in a way that reinforces treatment and strengthens relationships critical to the soldier's recovery? How might treatments be matched to a particular soldier's circumstances, and how might the effectiveness of those treatments be evaluated? How might citizens in Western societies stay connected to the ever-diminishing percentage of the population that fights in their name in conflicts that are underreported and little understood? How might those citizens support soldiers (and thank them for their service) without regarding them as victims (rather than warriors) or objects of pity (rather than fellow citizens who answered the call to service and did their duty)?

Thank You for Your Service holds valuable insights for military leaders and caregivers. The former must recognise that mental preparation for combat, control of stress, and care for those affected by combat trauma are military-command responsibilities. The latter, meanwhile, may find in these stories opportunities to streamline bureaucratic practices and improve the quality and continuity of care. This book will also be of interest to citizens who wish to better understand how some of their soldiers, along with their families, are struggling to cope with the aftermath of war.

International Security: A Very Short Introduction
Christopher S. Browning. Oxford: Oxford University Press, 2013. £7.99. 131 pp.

Christopher Browning, reader in international security at the University of Warwick, has produced a useful summary of a topic that demands public knowledge if democratic societies are to remain attentive to current and emerging threats to their security. The book is accessible and well suited to courses in security studies; it would also serve as a useful introduction for citizens who would like to know more about the risks they face and the ways in which their governments might respond to those risks.

The topics covered include both what Browning labels 'traditional' concerns, such as geopolitical competition, nuclear proliferation, terrorism and rogue states, and more unconventional security issues such as 'the rights and wrongs of humanitarian intervention, the spread of infectious diseases, food supplies, migration patterns, transnational organized crime, terrorism, environmental change, and poverty' (p. 2). The author argues persuasively that an inclusive approach to the study of international security is important because of 'complex dynamics and multiple factors that frequently underlie narrower concerns with war and peace' (p. 2). He contends that a wide range of risks to international security are connected in terms of three main analytical points: the centrality of power and politics; considerations of justice, morality, and responsibility; and inherent limitations in the structure of the international system for coping with security issues. These points are both appropriate and important in that they might help protect new students of international security against common pitfalls such as neglecting the political nature of threats, attaching a false nobility to neutrality when confronting criminal or terrorist organisations, and believing than an amorphous international community possesses the will or capacity to provide security or respond to crises.

Precisely because this book will be used to help orient students as they begin to grapple with the complexities of international security, the author's chapter on the threat of terrorism, entitled 'The Politics of Fear and Control', may disappoint. In it, Browning characterises the US response to the mass murders of 11 September 2001 as the 'flexing of American military muscle'. He also presents a moral equivalency between Western forces, whom he blames for the 'killing of thousands of civilians in Afghanistan and Iraq in the name of fighting terrorism', and al-Qaeda, the Taliban and other groups which regularly carry out the premeditated mass murder of civilians as their principal tactic in an effort to impose mediaeval societal norms (p. 110). This unfortunate interpretation of transnational terrorism, and the Western response to it, is regrettable in an otherwise useful introductory text.

Treasury's War: The Unleashing of a New Era of Financial Warfare
Juan Zarate. London and New York: PublicAffairs, 2013.
£12.99/$18.99. 488 pp.

Juan Zarate, former US Deputy National Security Advisor for Combating Terrorism and the first Assistant Secretary of the Treasury for terrorist financing and financial crime, has written a timely and important book. As transnational terrorist organisations gain strength across Africa and the greater Middle East, the connections between such organisations and transnational organised-crime networks are becoming increasingly apparent. As such, it is clear that success against terrorist organisations depends on much more than military operations. Zarate observes that while 'money is the lifeblood for terrorist organizations, criminal syndicates, and rogue regimes', it is also a critical vulnerability (p. 1). As he points out, the US government was the first to apply financial power against threats to national security, but he warns that 'the domain of financial warfare will no longer remain the sole province of American power'. He concludes that the US must work with allies and partners to minimise vulnerabilities in the financial system and to prepare for the 'financial wars' of the future (p. 421).

Zarate tells the story of how a small team in the US government developed the capability to wage financial warfare, directing campaigns against al-Qaeda, North Korea, Iran and others. Part I recounts efforts to map al-Qaeda's operational and financial networks; to follow financial trails; and to develop tools to disrupt the group's operations. Particularly important was the effort to condition the international financial system to reject capital tainted by connections to terrorism and transnational organised crime. Part II describes the reorganisation of US intelligence and law enforcement following the 9/11 terrorist attacks, an account which highlights the importance of unity of effort in policy implementation. Zarate and his colleagues overcame bureaucratic impediments through sheer tenacity while targeting the finances of al-Qaeda, the government of Saddam Hussein, and the A.Q. Khan nuclear-proliferation network. Part III describes US efforts to target the illicit activities of the Iranian and North Korean regimes. Part IV covers the transition to the Barack Obama administration and the Treasury's efforts to continue with its work exerting financial pressure on terrorist, proliferation, and other illicit networks. Zarate provides examples of how 'financial rogue' regimes work together to evade sanctions and provide financial outlets to terrorist and criminal organisations, highlighting the need for continuous adaptation and innovation in what must be a long-term struggle to constrain the finances of organisations that threaten international security.

The book's final chapter will be of particular value to those working in intelligence, law enforcement, defence, banking and foreign relations. It describes both vulnerabilities within the US financial system and external dangers to that system, including the threat from cyber espionage. Zarate calls for a redefinition of national economic security (in the American case) as 'the ability of the United States to project its power and influence through economic, financial, and commercial means and defend against systemic and specific risks and threats derived from America's economic vulnerabilities.' (pp. 413–14). While the book focuses on the US experience, its findings are applicable to other nations and international institutions. And Zarate is clear that the successful use of financial power and influence to advance national and international security demands a coordinated, sustained, multinational effort.

Erratum: In the August–September 2014 issue of *Survival* (vol. 56, no. 4), the publisher of *Military Politics and Democracy in the Andes* by Maiah Jaskoski was incorrectly identified. The book is published by Johns Hopkins University Press.

Closing Argument

The Ukraine Impasse

Samuel Charap

I

On 7 December 1991, the leaders of the Soviet republics of Belarus, Ukraine and Russia met at a hunting lodge in Europe's last primeval forest, *Belavezhskaya Pushcha* (Belavezha Woods), near what is today the Belarus–Poland border. In August, the failed coup attempt against Soviet President Mikhail Gorbachev had significantly strengthened the hand of the republics in their push for greater autonomy. Stanislav Shushkevich, the Belarusian leader, had invited Boris Yeltsin and Ukrainian President Leonid Kravchuk to Belavezha both to find a mutually acceptable formula for the Soviet Union's dissolution and to agree on a structure to govern relations among the republics in their newfound independence.

The role of Ukraine, second in importance only to Russia among the Soviet republics, was key in determining the viability of the union. On 1 December, 90% of the Ukrainian electorate, including a majority of ethnic Russians living there (about one-fifth of the population), had voted for independent statehood. Yeltsin understood the implications of this. 'What kind of union would there be without Ukraine? I cannot imagine it,' he said.[1] Gorbachev had held a summit of the republics' leaders during the previous month, in a last-ditch attempt to cobble together a new Union Treaty, but Kravchuk had not attended. It was the last nail in the Soviet Union's coffin.

At Belavezha, Yeltsin sought some kind of supranational umbrella struc-

Samuel Charap is IISS Senior Fellow for Russia and Eurasia.

Survival | vol. 56 no. 5 | October–November 2014 | pp. 225–232 DOI 10.1080/00396338.2014.962813

ture for the newly independent states. According to a participant in the meeting, Kravchuk bargained hard:

> Smiling and calm, he parried Yeltsin's arguments and proposals. Kravchuk did not want to sign anything! His argumentation was as simple as could be. He said that Ukraine had already determined its path in the referendum, and that path was independence. The Soviet Union no longer existed, and parliament would not allow him to create new unions of any kind. And Ukraine needed no such unions: the Ukrainians did not want to exchange one yoke for another.[2]

In the end, both Kravchuk and Yeltsin were willing to compromise. The need to preserve economic cooperation among the republics compelled Kravchuk to consider a new supranational structure.[3] And Yeltsin did not insist on maintaining a union, because he both sought independence for Russia and recognised that a union that excluded Ukraine would be meaningless.

The three leaders eventually agreed to the Belavezha Accords. In addition to noting that the Soviet Union 'is ceasing to exist as a subject of international law and a geopolitical reality', the agreement created the Commonwealth of Independent States (CIS), headquartered in Minsk, which had limited powers over issues such as trade, finance and migration. All three countries' shared interest in breaking away from the Soviet Union's centre overrode their disagreements about the terms of the divorce. And both the Russian and Ukrainian presidents were willing to engage in genuine give and take. Moreover, their publics were largely behind them: shortly after the accords were signed, a poll conducted in Moscow and Kiev indicated 84% and 50% support respectively.[4]

Nearly 23 years later, on 26 August 2014, the Belarusian president invited his Russian and Ukrainian counterparts to a seemingly similar gathering in Minsk. Both the issue – the nature of the relationship between Russia and its neighbours, particularly Ukraine – and the participants were essentially the same, although Kazakhstan and the EU were also represented at the meeting. Unlike the summit at Belavezha, however, the Minsk gathering produced no agreements of any consequence.

II

Since the end of February, the arc of the Ukraine crisis has followed a peculiar trajectory. The situation in the country has been steadily deteriorating, and international tensions progressively escalating. This steady downward trend has been punctuated by a series of false denouements. Examples include the election of a new Ukrainian president in May; June meetings at the Normandy commemorations; the downing of Malaysia Airlines flight MH17 and the death of its 300 passengers in July; breaking headlines about new Russian interventions; and the Minsk meeting between Russian President Vladimir Putin and Ukrainian President Petro Poroshenko.

The media – and some Western policymakers – have seized on these events as signs of a definitive turning point in the crisis. However, each event has proven immaterial to the steadily worsening realities both on the ground and in the international system.

Of course, journalists cannot be blamed for the natural human cognitive bias towards narratives with discrete beginning and end points, be they happy or otherwise. But an analysis of the fundamental drivers of the conflict suggest that we are moving further away from a genuine resolution. We can expect the Ukraine crisis to continue until the root causes are at least ameliorated, if not fully addressed.

These causes exist on two interrelated, but analytically distinct, levels: internal Ukrainian and international. While the latter now rightly receives the most attention, it is important to recall that the crisis began as a domestic Ukrainian one. Since gaining independence, Ukraine has featured strong regional divides as a fact of its political life. The events that led to the change of power in February this year, and the civil conflict that began thereafter, exacerbated these divisions. An inclusive political process will be needed to return to a semblance of normal politics.

While the protests centred on Maidan Square were largely a broad-based civic movement, the revolutionary vanguard – without which the change of power would not have occurred when it did – was an amalgam of armed, far-right groups. That (extra-constitutional) change dramatically shifted the balance of power in Kiev from the south and east of Ukraine to the country's west. Former President Victor Yanukovich's government, made up of southerners and easterners like him, was replaced with a new cabinet in which around 60% of top officials (ministers and above) come from the four former Hapsburg provinces in the west. These regions are home to only 12% of Ukraine's population. The Yanukovich government drew 75% of its ministerial-level leadership from the south and east of the country, with 42% from Donetsk, Yanukovich's home province. While that government was equally regionally unbalanced, the south and east are home to nearly 50% of the country's total population. New appointments in the interim have slightly righted the balance in Kiev, but the war in Donetsk and Luhansk (together referred to as the Donets Basin or Donbas) broke the scales.

Donbas accounts for 15% of Ukraine's population, 16% of its GDP, 25% of its industrial output and 27% of its total exports.[5] Losing it is not an option. But the population there was hostile to the post-Maidan government even before the shelling of the regional capitals began. The promise of greater regional autonomy, which might have reduced this hostility and transformed Ukraine's diversity from a weakness into a strength, remains unfulfilled. Poroshenko's proposed decentralisation plan was a half measure at best, and was devised in secret without input even from members of the governing coalition. Unsurprisingly, it has stalled in parliament and will now likely be delayed until after the early parliamentary elections scheduled for 26 October.

Early parliamentary elections might have proven an effective glue for the polity if they had been conducted before the war intensified. Now, they might have the opposite effect. Just as attitudes have hardened in the conflict zone, so too have those in Kiev and the rest of the country. Civil conflict tends to empower radicals at the expense of moderates. Ukraine has been no exception. Public-opinion surveys conducted in July put the Radical Party of Oleh Lyashko at the top of the polls.[6] Lyashko, often likened to Russia's Vladimir Zhirinovsky for his public antics and extreme views, gained prominence after he joined the paramilitary groups fighting in the east and posted recordings of his interrogations of alleged separatists. Those paramilitary groups – one of which openly embraces Nazi symbolism, while another is led by a violent convict – will be a potent radicalising political force once they return from the front-lines.[7]

The July survey showed all the parties that traditionally represented the south and east – particularly the Party of Regions and the Communists – polling below the minimum threshold to enter parliament. Efforts to create a new party to fill the void have only just gotten off the ground. Meanwhile, it remains unclear how Donbas will vote in the current security environment, particularly given the exodus of hundreds of thousands of its residents to Russia and other parts of Ukraine. In short, Ukrainian domestic politics is more divisive and polarised than ever. And there is no process to reverse the slide under way; instead, events such as the war and the election campaign are making it worse.

Although this crisis became international when Russia invaded Crimea following the late-February change of power, its root cause at the strategic level was the failure of the post-Cold War European and Euro-Atlantic institutional architecture to achieve its stated aim of creating a Europe that was whole, free and at peace. Instead, Russia has seen the eastward enlargement of the European Union and NATO as an economic and security threat, while most of the country's neighbours see membership of these organisations as not only the key to prosperity and security but also as the only means of keeping Moscow's imperial ambitions at bay.

A counterfactual exercise reinforces this point: imagine that Russia was a member of NATO and the EU. It would not have invaded Crimea in February, nor would it have destabilised the east. It would not have sought guarantees that Ukraine would stay out of the Alliance, nor would it have taken steps to undermine Ukraine's EU Association Agreement.

Counterfactuals aside, Russia wants a say on matters that the US and Europe consider to be none of its business. In the narrow sense, those matters include Ukraine's geopolitical and geo-economic future, and its constitutional structure. But, even if compromise can be made on those issues, the broader conflict between Russia and the West will not come to an end until some agreement is reached on the broader European-integration agenda.

Russia's brazen actions in Ukraine, and the US and EU sanctions in response, have made even a discussion of these issues, let alone a new agreement on the underlying principles, seem like a distant fantasy. Meanwhile, Russian and Western leaders are preparing their publics for confrontation, not compromise.

Moreover, Western leaders do not suggest that the root causes of the crisis have been anything other than Putin's aggression since February. The outcome they demand – and that the Ukrainian authorities pursue on the ground – entails an immediate halt to Russian intervention and assistance to the insurgents that would allow government forces to crush the insurgency, establishing full control over Ukraine's sovereign territory. As US President Barack Obama said on 29 July,

> the sooner the Russians recognize that the best chance for them to have influence inside of Ukraine is by being good neighbors and maintaining trade and commerce, rather than trying to dictate what the Ukrainian people can aspire to, rendering Ukraine a vassal state to Russia … the sooner we can resolve this crisis.[8]

But, for President Putin, this scenario represents total strategic defeat and public humiliation. He will therefore keep the insurgency in Ukraine alive until he gets a deal on his terms. If the rebels are crushed, he will lose his leverage, and then Russia, he seems to believe, will have 'lost' Ukraine to the West, an outcome that he cannot accept under any circumstances.

For Western policymakers, it is Russia's determination that ultimately makes this crisis so different to others in the post-Cold War period. Never before have they faced a major nuclear power as an adversary in a regional dispute occurring in that power's backyard. In Kosovo, Russia was an opponent, but Kosovo barely registered in the hierarchy of Russian national-security imperatives. Ukraine, by contrast, ranks just short of national survival. And eastern Ukraine is one of a few places beyond Russia's borders in which Moscow can deliver the assets required to sustain an insurgency.

Moscow took the decision to do everything it takes to avoid losing Ukraine several months ago. It will not be reversed. The Russian leadership is willing to pay a price for this decision. At least in the medium term, so too are the Russian people, whose support for Putin is at record levels: 85%, according to one recent poll.[9]

In other words, without a negotiation process involving genuine give and take, Western sanctions will fail to change Russian behaviour. And there is no serious crisis diplomacy under way at the moment, either overtly or through back channels. Talking to Moscow is a policy of necessity; it is not one that any Western leader would want to embrace publicly. If they want Ukraine to survive, however, they might not have a choice. Time is not on Ukraine's side. Its economy is already teetering on the brink of collapse, sustained only by a massive IMF loan. An insurgency that continues into 2015 might well send the economy over the edge.

III

The Minsk meeting began with televised speeches by the heads of state, all of whom were sitting around the same table. In his remarks, Poroshenko said, 'we do not impose, and do not want anyone to impose on us, a constitutional structure or international integration course. Ukraine has made its choice for a unitary, democratic, European state.' He added, '[the Association Agreement] can in no way negatively impact our traditional trading partners in the CIS.'[10]

Putin kept his public remarks focused on precisely this point, alleging that the Association Agreement would have serious consequences for economic relations between the two countries:

> Russia has stated on numerous occasions that full acceptance by our Ukrainian friends of all the tariff liberalisation requirements and the adoption of the European Union technical, sanitary and veterinary norms will have a negative impact on the scope and dynamics of trade and investment cooperation in Eurasia ... By very conservative estimates, the total loss for the economy of Russia alone may amount to 100 billion rubles on the first stage, that is $3 billion. This will affect entire sectors of our economy and agriculture, with all the consequences for economic growth and employment rates.[11]

He went on to explain that Moscow would take steps to protect its economy should its concerns go unaddressed.

After the meeting, Pavlo Klimkin, Poroshenko's foreign minister, explained that Ukraine was unwilling to compromise on this or other matters of principle. He stated, 'I hope that we can, and should, find a solution. This is peace, de-escalation, but the price of this solution is not compromises.'[12] He later wrote on Twitter, 'about the Association [Agreement]: don't confuse the wishes of our Russian colleagues with reality. We will not change the text of the Agreement. We will ratify and implement it.'[13]

In other words, the factors that allowed Yelstin and Kravchuk to come to an agreement at Belavezha – a degree of flexibility in negotiating positions, an overriding shared interest in getting a deal and domestic support for compromise – were notable for their absence in Minsk. Unless these conditions are created, summits might make for good headlines, but they will not make history.

Acknowledgements

The author is grateful to John Drennan for his research assistance.

Notes

1 Timothy J. Colton, *Yeltsin: A Life* (New York: Basic Books, 2008), pp. 204–5.

2 Serhii Plokhy, *The Last Empire: The Final Days of the Soviet Union* (New York: Basic Books, 2014), p. 304.

3 *Ibid.*, p. 305.

4 *Ibid.*, p. 359.

5 Robert Kirchner and Ricardo Giucci, 'The Economy of the Donbas in Figures', Institute for Economic Research and Policy Consulting, June 2014.

6 Kyiv International Institute of Sociology, 'Elektoral'ni nastroi naselennya Ukrainy: Vybory do Verhovnoi rady Ukrainy', 4 July 2014.

7 Tom Parfitt, 'Ukraine Crisis: The Neo-Nazi Brigade Fighting Pro-Russian Separatists', *Telegraph*, 11 Aug 2014; Philip Shishkin, 'Ukraine Taps Volunteers Fueled by Anger, Bravado', *Wall Street Journal*, 15 August 2014.

8 Barack Obama, 'Statement by the President on Ukraine', Washington DC, 29 July 2014.

9 Levada Center, 'Iul'skie reitingi odobreniya i doveriya', 24 July 2014.

10 Channel 5, 'Rech' Poroshenko v Minske. Vstrecha Ukraina–ES–Evraziiskaya troika', 26 August 2014.

11 Kremlin, 'Speech at the Meeting of the Customs Union Heads of State with President of Ukraine and European Union Representatives', 26 August 2014.

12 Presidential Administration of Ukraine, 'Ya gorzhus' tem, kak Prezident vel peregovory – Ministr Klimkin', 28 August 2014.

13 Pavlo Klimkin, Twitter, 27 August 2014.